Maths Progress

Purposeful Practice Book

Series Editors:

Dr Naomi Norman and Katherine Pate

◆ Skills practice ◆ Problem-solving practice

3

Pearson

Published by Pearson Education Limited, 80 Strand, London, WC2R 0RL.

www.pearsonschoolsandcolleges.co.uk

Text © Pearson Education Limited 2019
Edited by Haremi Ltd.
Typeset by York Publishing Solutions Pvt. Ltd.
Cover design by Pearson Education Limited 2018
Cover illustration by Robert Samuel Hanson
Index compiled by LNS Indexing

The rights of Dr Naomi Norman, Diane Oliver and Katherine Pate to be identified as authors of this work have been asserted by them in accordance with the Copyright, Designs and Patents Act 1988.

First published 2019

22 21 20 19
10 9 8 7 6 5 4 3 2 1

British Library Cataloguing in Publication Data
A catalogue record for this book is available from the British Library

ISBN 978 1 292 27997 8

Note from the publisher
Pearson has robust editorial processes, including answer and fact checks, to ensure the accuracy of the content in this publication, and every effort is made to ensure this publication is free of errors. We are, however, only human, and occasionally errors do occur. Pearson is not liable for any misunderstandings that arise as a result of errors in this publication, but it is our priority to ensure that the content is accurate. If you spot an error, please do contact us at resourcescorrections@pearson.com so we can make sure it is corrected.

Contents

Maths Progress
Purposeful Practice Book 3

8 key messages from Series Editors
Dr Naomi Norman and Katherine Pate

These Maths Progress Purposeful Practice books offer:

1 Lots of practice – you can never have too much!

2 Practice that develops mathematical confidence.

3 Purposeful practice questions that lead students on a path to understanding.
These questions:

- cannot be answered mechanically, by rote
- make connections to prior knowledge
- develop thinking skills
- target specific concepts

4 Reflect and reason questions to:

- make students aware of their understanding
- show teachers what students do (or don't yet!) understand
- encourage students to think about the underlying mathematical patterns

5 Problem-solving practice to:

- allow students to apply their understanding to problem-solving questions and contexts
- practise problem-solving strategies
- lay the groundwork for GCSE exams

6 Embeds the key skills and builds confidence to succeed at KS3 by supporting the new Maths Progress (Second Edition), preparing students for their GCSEs.

7 Designed with the help of UK teachers so you can use them flexibly alongside your current resources, in class or for independent study.

8 Purposeful practice and problem-solving practice all in one book – the first of its kind.

Get to know your Purposeful Practice Book

2.5 Index laws and brackets

Key points

- When multiplying powers of the same letter, you add the indices.
- When dividing powers of the same letter, you subtract the indices.
- To factorise an expression completely, take out the highest common factor (HCF) of its terms.

△ Purposeful practice 1

1 Simplify
a $x \times x$ b $x \times x^2$ c $x \times x^3$ d $x^2 \times x^2$
e $2x \times x^2$ f $x \times 2x^2$ g $3x^2 \times x^3$ h $3x \times 5x$
i $3x^2 \times 5x$ j $3x^2 \times 5x^2$ k $4x^2 \times 3x$ l $4x^2 \times 3x^2$

2 Simplify
a $n^3 \div n$ b $n^5 \div n$ c $n^8 \div n^2$ d $n^6 \div n^2$ e $\frac{2n^3}{n}$ f $\frac{2n^2}{2}$
g $\frac{2n^3}{2n}$ h $\frac{2n^3}{2n^2}$ i $\frac{6n^4}{6}$ j $\frac{6n^4}{n}$ k $\frac{6n^4}{6n}$ l $\frac{6n^4}{6n^2}$
m $\frac{6n^4}{2n^3}$ n $\frac{6n^4}{12n^2}$ o $\frac{6n^3}{3n}$ p $\frac{3n^3}{6n^4}$ q $\frac{2n^5}{6n^2}$ r $\frac{6n^4}{2n^4}$

Reflect and reason

Each student A–D has made an error. Explain the error and write the correct answer.
A: $x^2 \times x^4 = x^8$ B: $3x^2 \times 5x^4 = 8x^6$ C: $\frac{x^5}{x^2} = x^3$ D: $\frac{6x^4}{2x^3} = 4x^2$

△ Purposeful practice 2

1 Expand the brackets in each expression.
a $x(x^2 + 3)$ b $x^3(x^2 + 3)$ c $x^5(x^2 + 3x)$
d $5x^2(x^2 + 3x)$ e $5x^2(2x^3 + 3x)$ f $5x^3(2x^3 + 3x^2)$

2 Expand the brackets in each expression.
a $y^2(y - 1)$ b $y^3(2y - 1)$ c $y^3(2y - 3)$ d $4y^3(2y - 3)$
e $4y^3(2y - 3y^2)$ f $-y(y^2 - 2)$ g $-y(3y^3 - 2y)$ h $-4y^3(3y^2 - 2y)$

3 Factorise each expression completely.
a $n^3 + n$ b $n^2 + 5n$ c $n^3 + 5n^2$ d $5n^3 + 5n^2$
e $10n^3 + 5n^2$ f $5n^3 + 10n^2$ g $2n^2 + 10n^2$ h $4n^3 + 10n^2$

4 Factorise each expression completely, using only one pair of brackets.
a $m^5 - m^3$ b $-m^5 + m^3$ c $3m^5 - m^3$ d $3m^3 - 3m^3$
e $9m^3 - 3m^3$ f $8m^2 - 2m$ g $2m^6 - 8m^2$ h $6m^6 - 8m^2$

Reflect and reason

How can you tell whether or not these expressions are fully factorised?
$2(3x + x^3)$ $x^3(2x - 4)$ $2x^3(x - 1)$ $5x(4x + 2x^4)$

17

⊠ Problem-solving practice

1 Copy and complete the multiplication grid for powers of x.

×	$2x$		$4x^3$
$3x$		$3x^3$	
	$6x^3$		
		$8x^6$	

2 The term in each rectangle comes from multiplying the terms in the two circles that are linked to the rectangle. Copy and complete the diagram.

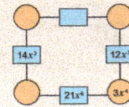

$14x^3$ $12x^2$
$21x^5$ $3x^4$

3 Copy and complete
a $4x \times \square x^\square = 12x^4$ b $\frac{8y^6}{\square y^\square} = 2y^4$ c $\frac{\square z^2}{5z} = 5z^7$

4 Write three different multiplications involving powers of x that simplify to $20x^4$.

5 Write three different divisions involving powers of x that simplify to $3x^3$.

6 Copy and complete
a $2x^2(x^2 + \square) = \square + 6x^3$ b $5y^3(4y^4 - \square) = \square - 25y^3$

7 Alesha and Ryan are asked to expand $2x^3(4x - 5)$.
Alesha writes   Ryan writes
$2x^3(4x - 5) = 6x^4 - 7x^3$ $2x^3(4x - 5) = 8x^4 - 5$
Both Alesha and Ryan are incorrect.
a Explain what Alesha has done wrong.
b Explain what Ryan has done wrong.
c Write the correct answer.

8 Match these expressions into equivalent pairs.

$24p^5 + 8p^3$ $24p^5 + 16p^3$ $8p^3(3p^2 + 1)$ $12p^3(2p^2 + 1)$
$24p^5 + 12p^3$ $24p^5 + 12p^3$ $8p^3(3p^2 + 2)$ $12p^3(2p^2 + 1)$
$24p^5 + 8p^3$ $24p^5 + 16p^3$ $8p^3(3p^2 + 2)$ $8p^3(3p^2 + 1)$

9 Sameer is asked to factorise $24x^9 - 36x^6$.
Sameer writes
$24x^9 - 36x^6 = 4x^6(6x^6 - 9x^3)$
Write two mistakes that Sameer has made.

10 Isaak says, 'Factorising $15a^3 - 25a^2$ and factorising $18a^4 - 30a^3$ both result in having the same expression in brackets.'
Is Isaak correct? Explain why.

Mixed exercises A

Mixed problem-solving practice A

1 These are the ages, in years, of 15 females at a tennis club.
17, 19, 19, 20, 24, 24, 25, 27, 30, 34, 37, 43, 44, 48, 51
The stem and leaf diagram shows the distribution of the ages of the males at the tennis club.
Compare the distributions of the ages of the females and the distributions of the ages of the males.

2 This formula is used to work out the body mass index, BMI, for a person of mass m kg and height h m.
$BMI = \frac{m}{h^2}$
A 'healthy' BMI for an adult is generally considered to be between 18.5 and 25.
Harry has a mass of 86 kg. He has a height of 1.85 m.
Is Harry's BMI considered 'healthy' by this definition? You must show your working.

3 $A = b^2 \times c$
Estimate A when $b = 412.95$, $c = 8.9 \times 10^7$.
Give your answer in standard form.

4 In the diagram, all angles are in degrees.
Angle PQR = angle QOR.
Work out the value of x.

5 The first table gives some information about the masses, in kg, of a sample of 34 calculators.

How Purposeful Practice builds the skills to succeed:

△ **Purposeful practice** has been embedded in 3 different ways:

1. **Variation**
   Carefully crafted questions that are minimally varied throughout an exercise.
   As students work out the answers, they are exposed to what stays the same and what changes, from question to question. In doing so, by the end of the exercise, students deepen their understanding of the mathematical patterns, structures and relationships that underlie concepts.

2. **Variation and progression**
   A mixture of minimally varied questions, along with small-stepped questions that get incrementally harder. These exercises are designed to both deepen understanding and move students on.

3. **Progression**
   Questions where the skills required become incrementally harder. These small-stepped questions mean there are no uncomfortable jumps, and help to build students' confidence.

Reflect and reason

Metacognition (reflection) is a powerful tool that is used to help students become aware of their own understanding. Reasoning is a key part of the GCSE (9–1), so we've included lots of opportunities for students to show what they do (or don't yet!) understand.

⊠ **Problem-solving practice** is where the skill(s) from each sub-unit can be demonstrated and applied. These problem-solving activities will be a mixture of contextualised problems, 'working backwards' problems, and synoptic problems, ensuring that the skills practised in each sub-unit are fully embedded in new and interesting ways to build confidence.

Maths Progress Second Edition

These KS3 Purposeful Practice Books are part of *Maths Progress Second Edition*.

Textbooks with tried-and-tested differentiation

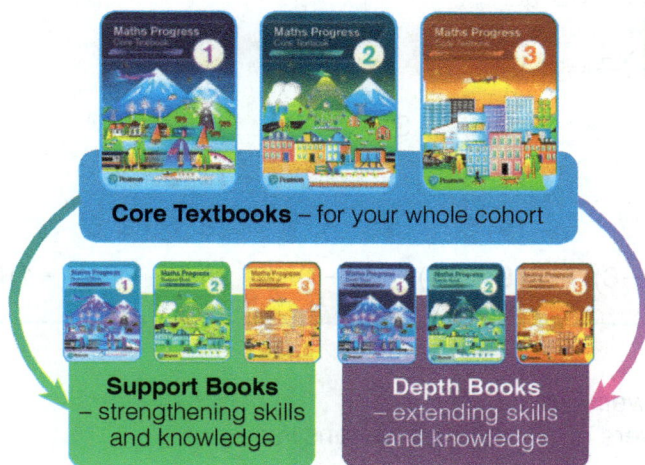

Core Textbooks – for your whole cohort

Support Books – strengthening skills and knowledge

Depth Books – extending skills and knowledge

ActiveLearn – your online toolkit

Teaching Resources

Planning

*Active*Learn

Progress & Assess

Student Resources

Purposeful Practice Books – a brand-new kind of practice book

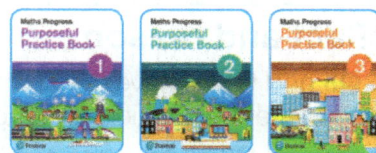

For more information go to www.pearsonschools.co.uk

1 Indices and standard form

1.1 Indices

Key points

- A small raised number is called an index or a power. Indices is the plural of index.
- When multiplying powers of the same number, add the indices.
- When dividing powers of the same number, subtract the indices.

◢ Purposeful practice 1

Write each product as a single power. Some have been started for you.

1 $4 \times 4^2 = 4 \times 4 \times 4 = 4^\square$

2 $4^2 \times 4^2 = 4 \times 4 \times 4 \times 4 = 4^\square$

3 $4^3 \times 4^2 = 4 \times 4 \times 4 \times 4 \times 4 = 4^\square$

4 $4^4 \times 4^2 = 4 \times 4 \times 4 \times 4 \times 4 \times 4 = 4^\square$

5 $4^4 \times 4^3$ **6** $4^5 \times 4^3$ **7** $4^5 \times 4^4$ **8** $4^7 \times 4^4$

9 $4^7 \times 4^6$ **10** $4^7 \times 4^{10}$ **11** $3^4 \times 3^5$ **12** $3^4 \times 3^8$

13 $3^7 \times 3^8$ **14** $3^{10} \times 3^8$ **15** $5^2 \times 5^3$ **16** $6^2 \times 6^3$

17 $(-6)^2 \times (-6)^3$ **18** $(-7)^2 \times (-7)^3$ **19** $(-7)^6 \times (-7)^3$ **20** $(-11)^6 \times (-11)^3$

Reflect and reason

Can you use the same method to write $3^5 \times 5^3$ as a single power? Explain your answer.

◢ Purposeful practice 2

Write each division as a single power. Some have been started for you.

1 $4^5 \div 4 = \dfrac{4^5}{4} = \dfrac{4 \times 4 \times 4 \times 4 \times 4}{4} = 4^\square$

2 $4^5 \div 4^2 = \dfrac{4^5}{4^2} = \dfrac{4 \times 4 \times 4 \times 4 \times 4}{4 \times 4} = 4^\square$

3 $4^6 \div 4^2 = \dfrac{4^6}{4^2} = \dfrac{4 \times 4 \times 4 \times 4 \times 4 \times 4}{4 \times 4} = 4^\square$

4 $4^6 \div 4^3 = \dfrac{4^6}{4^3} = \dfrac{4 \times 4 \times 4 \times 4 \times 4 \times 4}{4 \times 4 \times 4} = 4^\square$

5 $4^7 \div 4^3$ **6** $4^7 \div 4^4$ **7** $3^7 \div 3^4$ **8** $3^8 \div 3^4$

9 $2^8 \div 2^4$ **10** $2^{12} \div 2^4$ **11** $3^{12} \div 3^4$ **12** $3^{12} \div 3^8$

13 $3^{12} \div 3^2$ **14** $3^{10} \div 3^2$ **15** $5^{10} \div 5^5$ **16** $6^{10} \div 6^5$

17 $(-6)^{10} \div (-6)^5$ **18** $(-6)^{10} \div (-6)^3$ **19** $(-1)^{10} \div (-1)^3$ **20** $(-1)^9 \div (-1)^3$

Reflect and reason

Q1, **Q3** and **Q5** all have the same answer. Explain why.
Write another calculation dividing powers of 4 that gives this answer.

Q2, **Q4** and **Q6** all have the same answer. Explain why.
Write another calculation dividing powers of 4 that gives this answer.

Write each calculation using powers of a single number. Some have been started for you.

1 $4 \times 2^3 = 2^\square \times 2^3 = 2^\square$ 2 $4 \times 2^4 = 2^\square \times 2^4 = 2^\square$ 3 4×2^5

4 $8 \times 2^5 = 2^\square \times 2^5 = 2^\square$ 5 $16 \times 2^5 = 2^\square \times 2^5 = 2^\square$ 6 16×2^6

7 $16 \times 8 = 2^\square \times 2^\square = 2^\square$ 8 32×8 9 32×16

10 $16 \div 2^3 = 2^\square \div 2^3 = 2^\square$ 11 $32 \div 2^2 = 2^\square \div 2^2 = 2^\square$ 12 $64 \div 16$

13 $25 \times 5^4 = 5^\square \times 5^4 = 5^\square$ 14 $125 \times 5^4 = 5^\square \times 5^4 = 5^\square$ 15 625×5^4

16 625×25 17 $125 \div 5^2$ 18 $625 \div 25$

Reflect and reason

Can you write 18×9 using powers of a single number? What about $18 \div 9$? Explain your answers.

⊠ Problem-solving practice

1 Copy and complete the multiplication grid for powers of 5.

×	5^2	5^6		5^8	
5^3			5^7		
		5^8			
5^6					5^{11}
5^7					
				5^{17}	

2 Copy and complete the multiplication pyramid. Each brick is the product of the two bricks directly below.

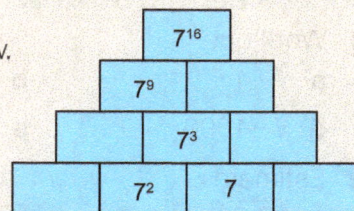

7^{16} / 7^9 / 7^3 / 7^2, 7

3 Write each of these as a power of a single number.

a $64 \div 2^3 \times 2^2$ b $32 \times 2^2 \div 2^4$

c $5^7 \div 5^2 \times 125$ d $16 \times 2^5 \div 8$

e $27 \times 3^4 \div 9$ f $5^8 \div 125 \times 25$

4 Felix is asked to write $3^3 \times 3^6 \div 3^2$ as a single power.
Felix says, '$3^3 \times 3^6 \div 3^2 = 3^9$ because $3 \times 6 = 18$ and $18 \div 2 = 9$.'
Felix is incorrect. Explain what Felix has done wrong.

5 Write three different multiplication calculations that have an answer of 10^{12}.

6 Write three different division calculations that have an answer of 7^4.

7 Write three different calculations using multiplication and division that have an answer of 13^5.

8 Work out the value of x if $2^3 \times 2^x = 2^9$.

9 Copy and complete each calculation.

a $2^7 \times 2^8 \div 2^\square = 2^6$ b $5^9 \times 5^\square \div 5^3 = 5^8$ c $10^\square \times 10^{10} \div 10^7 = 10^{11}$

10 $5^a \times 5^b = 5^{14}$
a and b are different integers. Give a possible value for each of a and b.

11 Write these calculations in order of size, starting with the smallest.

$3^4 \times 3^9$ $3^{15} \div 3^5$ $3^{20} \div 3^9$ $3^8 \div 3^5 \times 3^9$

Key points

- To estimate the square root of a number, round to the nearest square number then square root it.
- To estimate the cube root of a number, round to the nearest cube number then cube root it.
- When estimating the answer to a calculation that involves division, round the numerator and the denominator to make it an easy division.

△ Purposeful practice 1

Estimate

1 $\sqrt{8}$ **2** $\sqrt{10}$ **3** $\sqrt{15}$ **4** $\sqrt{17}$ **5** $\sqrt{48}$

6 $\sqrt{51}$ **7** $\sqrt{99}$ **8** $\sqrt{102}$ **9** $\sqrt{140}$ **10** $\sqrt{150}$

Reflect and reason

The answers to **Q1** and **Q2**, **Q3** and **Q4**, **Q5** and **Q6**, **Q7** and **Q8**, and **Q9** and **Q10** are the same. Explain why.

How would you estimate $\sqrt{12.5}$?

△ Purposeful practice 2

1 Work out

  a $\sqrt[3]{-1}$ **b** $\sqrt[3]{-8}$ **c** $\sqrt[3]{-27}$

  d $\sqrt[3]{-1000}$ **e** $\sqrt[3]{-8000}$ **f** $\sqrt[3]{-27\,000}$

2 Estimate

  a $\sqrt[3]{7.9}$ **b** $\sqrt[3]{-7.9}$ **c** $\sqrt[3]{26}$ **d** $\sqrt[3]{-26}$

  e $\sqrt[3]{63}$ **f** $\sqrt[3]{-63}$ **g** $\sqrt[3]{122}$ **h** $\sqrt[3]{-122}$

Reflect and reason

Tarek's working for **Q1e** starts like this

$$\sqrt[3]{-8000} = \sqrt[3]{-8 \times 1000} = \sqrt[3]{\Box} \times \sqrt[3]{\Box} = \Box \times \Box = \Box$$

Copy and complete Tarek's working.

Is this the method you used? If not, explain your method.

△ Purposeful practice 3

Estimate

1 $\sqrt{62.9} + 2.01$ **2** $(\sqrt{62.9} + 2.01) \times 48.1$ **3** $\dfrac{48.1}{\sqrt{62.9} + 2.01}$

4 $\dfrac{48.1}{\sqrt{62.9} + 2.01^2}$ **5** $\sqrt[3]{62.9} + 2.01$ **6** $(\sqrt[3]{62.9} + 2.01) \times 48.1$

7 $\dfrac{48.1}{\sqrt[3]{62.9} + 2.01}$

8 $\dfrac{48.1}{\sqrt[3]{62.9} + (-2.01)^2}$

Reflect and reason

Crista says, 'In calculations involving the number 48.1, I sometimes rounded to 48 and sometimes to 50.'

Which calculations do you think she rounded to 48? Explain your answer.

Which calculations do you think she rounded to 50? Explain your answer.

⊠ Problem-solving practice

1 A square has area 50 cm².
Estimate the perimeter of the square.

2 a Match each calculation A–D with its equivalent estimated calculation E–H.

A $\dfrac{26.7}{\sqrt{10} + 1.95^2}$	B $\dfrac{26.7}{\sqrt{21.5} + 2.03^2}$	C $\dfrac{26.7}{\sqrt{1.05} + 2.95^2}$	D $\dfrac{26.7}{\sqrt{1.05} + 1.95^2}$
E $\dfrac{27}{\sqrt{25} + 2^2}$	F $\dfrac{25}{\sqrt{1} + 2^2}$	G $\dfrac{28}{\sqrt{9} + 2^2}$	H $\dfrac{30}{\sqrt{1} + 3^2}$

b Work out the answer to each estimated calculation.

3 Estimate an answer for each calculation.

a $\dfrac{76.5}{\sqrt{19} + 1.88^2}$

b $\dfrac{\sqrt{75} + 5.91^2}{4.68}$

c $\dfrac{41.3}{\sqrt{105} - 2.22^2}$

d $\dfrac{61.9}{\sqrt[3]{130} + (-1.12)^2}$

e $\dfrac{32.4}{\sqrt[3]{12.5} \times 1.87^2}$

f $\dfrac{5.63 + 2.05^2}{\sqrt[3]{-980}}$

4 Daisy and Ethan are asked to work out an estimate to $\dfrac{38.5}{\sqrt[3]{100}}$.

Daisy says, '38.5 rounds to 39 and $\sqrt[3]{100}$ rounds to 5, so an estimate is 39 ÷ 5 = 7.8.'
Ethan says, '$\sqrt[3]{100}$ rounds to 5 and 38.5 rounds to 40 as a multiple of 5, so an estimate is 40 ÷ 5 = 8.'
Daisy and Ethan are both technically correct, but whose method do you think was better? Explain your answer.

5 Chan and Dana use a calculator to work out $\dfrac{4.37 + 5.89^2}{\sqrt{68.1}}$.
Chan's answer is 47.334 96...
Dana's answer is 4.733 496...
Use estimation to help you decide who is correct. Explain your answer.

6 Which of these calculations give an estimate with the same value?

A $\dfrac{10.9}{\sqrt{78.7} + 0.86^2}$ B $\dfrac{9.9}{\sqrt{83.6} + 1.06^2}$ C $\dfrac{8.9}{\sqrt{71.2} + 1.3^2}$ D $\dfrac{14.1}{\sqrt{88.8} + 0.95^2}$

7 Shey works out an estimate for $\dfrac{3.87^2 + \sqrt{20}}{2.1}$.
Shey writes

$$\dfrac{4^2 + \sqrt{25}}{2} = \dfrac{16 + 5}{2} = 16 + 5 \div 2 = 16 + 2.5 = 18.5$$

Shey has made two mistakes. What are they?

Key point

- A number raised to a negative power is the same as the reciprocal of that number to the positive power. For example, $10^{-2} = \frac{1}{10^2}$.

△ Purposeful practice 1

1 Write 16 as a single power of 4.

2 Write 16 as a single power of 2.

3 Write 16^2 as a single power of 4.

4 Write 16^2 as a single power of 2.

5 Write 16^3 as a single power of 4.

6 Write 16^3 as a single power of 2.

7 Write 27 as a single power of 3.

8 Write 27^2 as a single power of 3.

9 Write 27^3 as a single power of 3.

10 Write 27^4 as a single power of 3.

Reflect and reason

Antony works out 32^4 as a single power of 2 like this:

$32 = 2^5$, so $32^4 = (2^5)^4$

He writes the final answer as 2^9.

What mistake has he made? What is the correct answer to 32^4 as a power of 2?

△ Purposeful practice 2

1 a Write $2^3 \div 2^3$ as a single power.

  b $2^3 \div 2^3 = 8 \div 8$. What is the answer to $8 \div 8$?

  c Use your answers to parts **a** and **b** to write the answer to $2^3 \div 2^3$.

2 a Write $3^5 \div 3^5$ as a single power.

  b $3^5 \div 3^5 = 243 \div 243$. What is the answer to $243 \div 243$?

  c Use your answers to **Q2** parts **a** and **b** to write the answer to $3^5 \div 3^5$.

3 Write each of these as an integer.

  a 4^0 **b** 6^0 **c** 9^0 **d** 15^0

Reflect and reason

Is any number raised to the power of zero always equal to 1? Explain how you know.

△ Purposeful practice 3

1 Copy and complete

  a $3^{-1} = \frac{1}{3^{\square}} = \frac{1}{\square}$

  b $3^{-2} = \frac{1}{3^{\square}} = \frac{1}{\square}$

  c $3^{-3} = \frac{1}{\square^{\square}} = \frac{1}{\square}$

  d $5^{-1} = \frac{1}{5^{\square}} = \frac{1}{\square}$

  e $5^{-2} = \frac{1}{\square^{\square}} = \frac{1}{\square}$

  f $5^{-3} = \frac{1}{\square^{\square}} = \frac{1}{\square}$

2 Write each of these as a fraction.

  a 4^{-2} **b** 9^{-2} **c** 7^{-2} **d** 2^{-2} **e** 2^{-3} **f** 2^{-4} **g** 10^{-4} **h** 10^{-6}

3 Work out each calculation, giving your answer as
   i a single power
   ii a whole number or fraction
   a $2^2 \div 2^6$ **b** $2^2 \times 2^{-5}$ **c** $2^{-3} \times 2^3$ **d** $2^4 \div 2^7$
   e $3^4 \div 3^7$ **f** $3^2 \times 3^{-4}$ **g** $5^{-3} \times 5^3$ **h** $10^4 \div 10^7$
   i $2^3 \div 2^5 \times 2^2$ **j** $2^2 \div 2^8 \times 2^3$ **k** $2^4 \times 2^2 \div 2^9$ **l** $2^4 \times 2^7 \div 2^9$
   m $3^3 \div 3^5 \times 3^2$ **n** $3^4 \div 3^5 \times 3^3$ **o** $5^3 \times 5^4 \div 5^9$ **p** $5^4 \times 5^7 \div 5^9$

Reflect and reason

Which answers in **Q3** are the same? Explain why they are the same. Write another calculation that gives the same answer.

⊠ Problem-solving practice

1 Kyle and Mia are asked to work out 7^{-2}.

Kyle writes   Mia writes

$7^{-2} = \dfrac{2}{7}$ $7^{-2} = 49$

Kyle and Mia are both incorrect. Explain what they have done wrong.

2 Copy and complete the multiplication grid for powers of 2.

×	2^{-2}		
	1	$\frac{1}{2}$	$\frac{1}{8}$
2^{-1}		$\frac{1}{16}$	
	$\frac{1}{2}$		

3 a Write $\frac{1}{8}$ as a single power of 2.
 b Use your answer to part **a** to write $\frac{1}{8} \times 2^5$ as a single power of 2.

4 Write $\frac{1}{27} \times 3^2$ as a single power of 3.

5 Write $\frac{1}{25} \div 5^4$ as a power of a single number.

6 Write three different multiplication calculations that have an answer of 7^{-3}.

7 Write three different division calculations that have an answer of $\frac{1}{100\,000}$.

8 Evie is asked to write these numbers in order of size, starting with the smallest.

$\boxed{2^{-2}}$ $\boxed{\dfrac{1}{64}}$ $\boxed{2^{-5}}$ $\boxed{2^{-4}}$ $\boxed{0.5}$

Evie writes

$2^{-5}, 2^{-4}, 2^{-2}, \frac{1}{64}, 0.5$

Is Evie correct? Explain your answer.

9 Work out the value of the letter in each calculation.

   a $2^3 \times 2^2 \div 2^a = \dfrac{1}{4}$ **b** $5^3 \times 5^b \times 5^{-7} = \dfrac{1}{5}$ **c** $10^c \times 10^5 \div 10^7 = \dfrac{1}{10\,000}$

Key points

- Multiplying by a negative power of 10 is the same as dividing by a positive power of 10. For example, $3 \times 10^{-4} = 3 \times \frac{1}{10^4} = \frac{3}{10^4} = 3 \div 10\,000 = 0.0003$
- A number written in standard form is a number between 1 and 10 multiplied by 10 to a power. Using algebra, standard form is $A \times 10^n$ where $1 \leqslant A < 10$ and n is an integer.

△ Purposeful practice 1

State whether each number is written in standard form.

1 1.7×10^4	**2** 0.7×10^4	**3** 17×10^4	**4** 7×10^4
5 10×10^4	**6** 7×10^{-4}	**7** 0.17×10^{-4}	**8** 1.7 million

Reflect and reason

For the numbers not in standard form, explain why they are not in standard form. Rewrite them so they are in standard form.

△ Purposeful practice 2

Write these numbers in standard form.

1 83 000	**2** 8 300 000	**3** 8 350 000	**4** 1 350 000
5 92 000 000	**6** 920 000	**7** 123 000	**8** 123 000 000

Reflect and reason

Which number in Purposeful practice 2 is the largest? Explain how you compared the numbers in standard form to determine that this is the largest.

△ Purposeful practice 3

Write each number as an ordinary number.

1 2.6×10^4	**2** 2.6×10^6	**3** 2.61×10^6	**4** 2×10^6
5 2.1×10^3	**6** 2.14×10^1	**7** 2.17×10^7	**8** 2.7×10^0

Reflect and reason

How do you know how many zeros, if any, to use in the number?

△ Purposeful practice 4

Write these numbers using standard form.

1 0.000 083	**2** 0.0083	**3** 0.000 83	**4** 0.000 125
5 0.000 001 25	**6** 0.000 005	**7** 0.000 000 59	**8** 0.000 000 005 9

Reflect and reason

Which number in Purposeful practice 4 is the smallest? Explain how you know this is the smallest number when all the numbers are written using standard form.

△ Purposeful practice 5

Write each number as an ordinary number.

1 2.6×10^{-4} **2** 2.6×10^{-6} **3** 2.61×10^{-6} **4** 2×10^{-6}

5 2.1×10^{-3} **6** 2.1×10^{-1} **7** 2.17×10^{-7} **8** 2.7×10^{-9}

Reflect and reason

How do you know how many zeros, if any, to use in the number?

⊠ Problem-solving practice

1 The table shows the approximate diameter of some planets, in standard form.

  a Write the diameter of each planet as an ordinary number.

  b Write the planets in order of diameter, starting with the smallest.

Planet	Diameter (m)
Mercury	4.9×10^6
Venus	1.2×10^7
Earth	1.3×10^7
Mars	6.8×10^6
Jupiter	1.4×10^8
Saturn	1.2×10^8
Uranus	5.1×10^7
Neptune	4.9×10^7

2 Jess is asked to write 7.48×10^5 as an ordinary number.
She writes
$7.48 \times 10^5 = 74\,800\,000$
Explain what Jess has done wrong.

3 Yuri and Emily are asked to write 0.000 038 using standard form.

Yuri writes   Emily writes
$0.000\,038 = 3.8 \times 10^{-6}$ $0.000\,038 = 0.38 \times 10^{-4}$
Explain what Yuri and Emily have each done wrong.

4 An electron microscope can be used to see objects as small as 1×10^{-10} m.

  a Which of the objects in the table can be seen using the microscope?

  b Write the objects in the table in order of size, starting with the smallest.

Object	Diameter (m)
carbon atom	1.5×10^{-10}
strand of hair	8×10^{-5}
nucleus of an atom	1.75×10^{-15}
oxygen molecule	1.2×10^{-10}
protein molecule	5×10^{-9}

5 An estimate for the average distance between Jupiter and Saturn is 6.5×10^8 km.
An estimate for the average distance between Earth and Mars is 7.834×10^7 km.
Which two planets are closer, Jupiter and Saturn or Earth and Mars?
Explain how you know.

6 Write these numbers in order, starting with the smallest.

3×10^4 3100 3.4×10^3 390

7 Write these numbers in order, starting with the smallest.

4.6×10^{-7} 0.000 000 42 4.55×10^{-6} 4.5×10^{-6}

2 Expressions and formulae

2.1 Solving equations

> ### Key point
> - In the balancing method, you solve equations by doing the same operations to both sides.

⚠ Purposeful practice 1

1 Solve these equations. The first one has been started for you.

a
$$\frac{5a}{2} = 20$$
$\times 2 \left(\right) \times 2$
$$5a = \square$$
$\div 5 \left(\right) \div 5$
$$a = \square$$

b $\dfrac{2b}{5} = 20$

c $\dfrac{3c}{5} = 20$

2 Solve these equations. The first one has been started for you.

a
$$\frac{3d}{2} = 9$$
$\div 3 \left(\right) \div 3$
$$\frac{d}{2} = \square$$
$\times 2 \left(\right) \times 2$
$$d = \square$$

b $\dfrac{2e}{3} = 8$

c $\dfrac{2h}{5} = 8$

3 Solve the equation $\dfrac{4x}{5} = 8$ by multiplying first, as in **Q1**, or by dividing first, as in **Q2**.

> ### Reflect and reason
> The function machines show two ways of combining functions to get $\dfrac{4x}{5}$.
>
> $x \longrightarrow \boxed{\times 4} \longrightarrow \boxed{\div 5} \longrightarrow \dfrac{4x}{5}$ $\qquad$ $x \longrightarrow \boxed{\div 5} \longrightarrow \boxed{\times 4} \longrightarrow \dfrac{4x}{5}$
>
> Draw the inverse function machines and use these to explain why you can either multiply first or divide first to solve $\dfrac{4x}{5} = 8$.

⚠ Purposeful practice 2

1 Solve

a $\dfrac{x}{3} + 1 = 5$ $\qquad$ **b** $\dfrac{x}{3} - 1 = 5$ $\qquad$ **c** $\dfrac{x}{5} + 3 = 6$

d $\dfrac{x}{5} - 3 = 1$ $\qquad$ **e** $\dfrac{x}{4} + 7 = 2$ $\qquad$ **f** $\dfrac{x}{7} + 4 = 2$

2 Solve

a $\dfrac{x+1}{3} = 5$ $\qquad$ **b** $\dfrac{x-1}{3} = 5$ $\qquad$ **c** $\dfrac{x+3}{5} = 6$

d $\dfrac{x-3}{5} = 1$ **e** $\dfrac{x+7}{4} = 2$ **f** $\dfrac{x+4}{7} = 2$

Reflect and reason

Explain what is the same and what is different when you solve these two equations:

$\dfrac{x}{3} + 2 = 8$ $\dfrac{x+2}{3} = 8$

You could draw function machines to help you explain.

⊠ Problem-solving practice

1 Emma thinks of a number.
She doubles it and then divides it by 5.
Her result is 20.

  a Write an equation for Emma's number.
  b What is Emma's number?

2 Tom thinks of a number.
He divides it by 4 and then subtracts 3.
His result is 7.

  a Write an equation for Tom's number.
  b What is Tom's number?

3 Show that the solution to $\dfrac{x}{5} + 11 = 7$ is $x = -20$.

4 Ava is asked to solve the equation $\dfrac{x+3}{5} = 12$.
Ava writes

$$\dfrac{x+3}{5} = 12$$
$$-3 \Big(\Big) -3$$
$$\dfrac{x}{5} = 9$$
$$\times 5 \Big(\Big) \times 5$$
$$x = 45$$

Ava is incorrect. Explain why.

5 Solve

  a $\dfrac{a}{2} + 3 = 15$ **b** $\dfrac{a}{2} + 4 = 16$ **c** $\dfrac{a}{2} + 13 = 25$ **d** $\dfrac{a}{2} + 18 = 30$

  e $\dfrac{a}{2} - 3 = 9$ **f** $\dfrac{a}{2} - 5 = 7$ **g** $\dfrac{a}{2} - 1 = 11$ **h** $\dfrac{a}{2} - 8 = 4$

What do you notice about your answers to parts **a–h**? Explain why.
Is this also the case for the equation $\dfrac{a}{3} - 5 = 7$? Explain why.

6 Here are six equations.

$\dfrac{2n}{5} = 10$ $\dfrac{n}{5} + 4 = 10$ $\dfrac{n}{5} - 4 = 10$

$\dfrac{n+4}{5} = 10$ $\dfrac{n-4}{5} = 10$ $\dfrac{n+2}{5} = 10$

Which equation has
  a the smallest value of n
  b the largest value of n?

Key point

- The priority of operations is
  Brackets → Indices → Division and → Addition
  (or powers) multiplication and
  subtraction

⚠ Purposeful practice 1

1 Work out the value of each expression when $x = 1$.
  a x^2 **b** $2x^2$ **c** $(2x)^2$ **d** $(3x)^2$

2 Work out the value of each expression when $y = 2$.
  a $2y^2$ **b** $(2y)^2$ **c** $(3y)^2$ **d** $3y^2$

3 Work out the value of each expression when $z = 3$.
  a $(3z)^2$ **b** $3z^2$ **c** $4z^2$ **d** $(4z)^2$

4 Work out the value of each expression when $n = -2$.
  a n^2 **b** $2n^2$ **c** $(2n)^2$ **d** $(3n)^2$

5 Work out the value of each expression when $m = -3$.
  a $(2m)^2$ **b** $2m^2$ **c** $4m^2$ **d** $(4m)^2$

6 Work out the value of each expression when $k = 0$.
  a k^2 **b** $2k^2$ **c** $(2k)^2$ **d** $3k^2$

Reflect and reason

Is $(3t)^2$ sometimes, always or never equal to $9t^2$? Explain your answer.

⚠ Purposeful practice 2

1 Work out the value of each expression when
  i $a = 3, b = 5$ **ii** $a = 4, b = 2$ **iii** $a = -1, b = 3$ **iv** $a = -2, b = -5$
  a $(a + b)^2$ **b** $a^2 + b^2$ **c** $(a - b)^2$ **d** $a^2 - b^2$

2 Work out the value of each expression when
  i $a = 3, b = 5$ **ii** $a = 4, b = 2$ **iii** $a = -1, b = 3$ **iv** $a = -2, b = -5$
  a a^3 **b** $a^3 + b^3$ **c** $(a - b)^3$ **d** $a^3 - b^3$

3 Work out the value of each expression when $x = 2$ and $y = 6$.
  a $\dfrac{x^2}{y^2}$ **b** $\dfrac{(x + 1)^2}{y^2}$ **c** $\dfrac{x^2 + 1}{y^2}$ **d** $\dfrac{x^2 + 1}{y^2 - 1}$

Reflect and reason

Look at your answers to **Q1**. Which of the expressions in parts **a** to **d** always have a positive value? Explain your answer.

What kind of expression can have a positive or negative value? Use examples from Purposeful practice 2 to show this.

Problem-solving practice

1 Four small squares are put together to form a larger square, as shown.
   a Which is the correct expression for the area of the larger square?

   A $2x^2 + 2x$ B $2x^2$ C $8x$

   D $(4x)^2$ E $(2x)^2$ F $4x$

   b Work out the area of the larger square when
        i $x = 5$ ii $x = 8$ iii $x = 10$

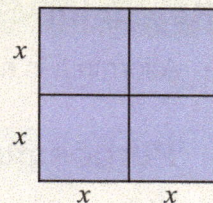

2 Ewan and Zach are asked to work out the value of $(2a)^2$ when $a = -3$.
   a Ewan writes
   $(2a)^2 = 2(-3)^2 = 2 \times 9 = 18$
   This is incorrect. What is Ewan's mistake?
   b Zach writes
   $(2a)^2 = (2 \times -3)^2 = (-6)^2 = -36$
   This is incorrect. Explain Zach's mistake.

3 Four students are given the following question in an exam.

   > Work out the value of $x^2 - (2y)^2$ when $x = 3$ and $y = -5$.

   The working and answers of the students are shown in the table.

Student	Working and answers
A	$3^2 - (2 \times -5)^2 = 6 - -20 = 26$
B	$3^2 - (2 - 5)^2 = 9 - (-3)^2 = 9 - 9 = 0$
C	$3^2 - (2 \times -5)^2 = 9 - -(10)^2 = 9 + 100 = 109$
D	$3^2 - (2 \times -5)^2 = 9 - (-10)^2 = 9 - 100 = -91$

   Which student has the correct working and answer?
   Explain why the other students are wrong.

4 Which expression/expressions give a negative value when $t = 4$ and $u = 10$?

   $(t - u)^2$ $(u + t)^2$ $(u - t)^2$

   $t^2 - u^2$ $t^2 + u^2$ $u^2 - t^2$

5 Which expression does not give the same value as the others when $p = 4$ and $q = 5$?

   $q - p$ $(q - p)^2$ $(p - q)^2$ $p^2 - q^2$

6 Here are six expressions.

   ab a^2 $2a - b^2$ b^2 $4a$ $a^2 - b^2$

   Substitute the values $a = 3$ and $b = -4$ into each expression.
   a Which expression has the smallest value?
   b Which expression has the largest value?

7 Suggest values of x and y that make the value of the expression $x^2 - y^2$ zero.

8 What values of a can Aida substitute in the equation $2a = a^2$ to make it true?

Key point

- A formula is a rule that shows a relationship between two or more variables (letters).

△ Purposeful practice 1

1 Write an expression for the total cost in pounds (£) of
   - **a** 5 hours at £12 per hour
   - **b** n hours at £12 per hour
   - **c** n hours at £x per hour
   - **d** n hours at £x per hour plus £20 tips
   - **e** n hours at £x per hour plus £30 tips
   - **f** n hours at £x per hour plus £y tips

2 Write a formula to calculate, in pounds (£),
   - **a** pay, P, for n hours at £y per hour plus £z tips
   - **b** total pay, T, for h hours at £m per hour plus £k tips
   - **c** earnings, E, for x hours at £t per hour minus £w tips

3 Write a formula for T, the total cost, in pounds (£),
   - **a** of 3 tickets at £y each
   - **b** of 5 tickets at £x each
   - **c** of 3 tickets at £y each and 5 tickets at £x each
   - **d** of a tickets at £y each and 5 tickets at £x each
   - **e** of a tickets at £y each and b tickets at £x each

Reflect and reason

Adult tickets cost £m and child tickets cost £k.
Rav writes this formula for the total cost in pounds (£) of a adult and b child tickets:

$ak + bm$

Explain what Rav has done wrong.

△ Purposeful practice 2

The graph shows the amounts three plumbers charge their customers.
Copy and complete this table.

Plumbers' charges

Plumber	Call-out fee	Hourly rate (£/h)	Formula
A	£50		$P = \square h + 50$
B			$P = \square h + \square$
C			$P = \square h + \square$

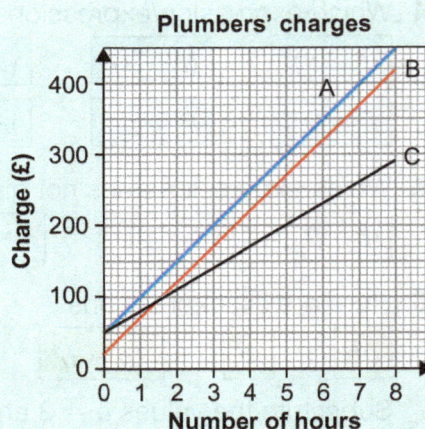

Reflect and reason

Which two plumbers have the same hourly rate? How is this shown
   - **a** on the graph
   - **b** in the formula?

Which two plumbers have the same call-out fee? How is this shown
   - **c** on the graph
   - **d** in the formula?

1   Wooden decking costs £21 per square metre.
    Emily wants to deck part of her garden with area A.
    Emily says, 'The total cost in pounds, C, of my decking is given by $C = 21 + A$.'
    Emily is incorrect. Explain why.

2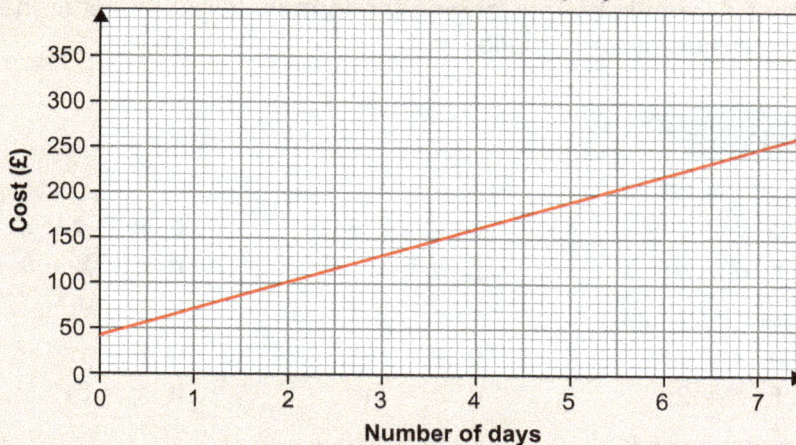

Costs for a car hire company

The graph shows the costs for a car hire company.
    a   How much does it cost to hire a car for 1 day?
    b   How much does it cost to hire a car for 4 days?
    c   The car hire company charges a fixed fee. How much is it?
    d   Write a formula for the total cost in pounds, C, to hire a car for d days.
    e   Use your formula to work out the cost of hiring a car for 12 days.

3   The graph shows the amount an electrician charges her customers.

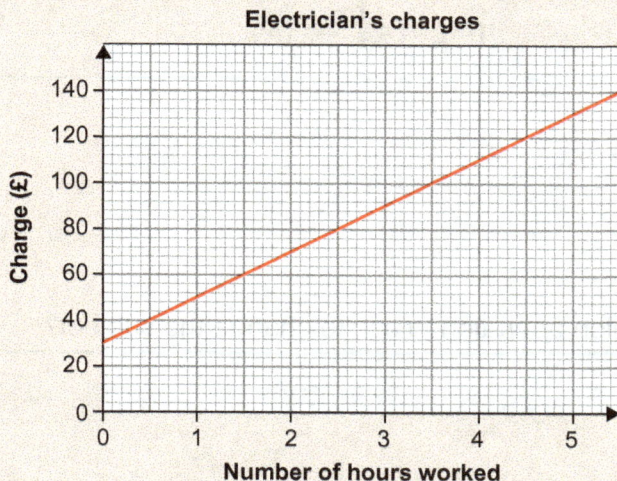

Electrician's charges

    a   Write a formula for the total charge, C, for the electrician to work h hours.
    b   Use your formula from part **a** to work out the charge for a job that takes 15 hours.

4   To cook a turkey weighing 4.5 kilograms or less, it takes 20 minutes plus 45 minutes per kilogram.
    a   Write a formula for the cooking time, T, of a turkey that weighs w kg, where w is less than 4.5 kg.
    b   Use your formula to work out the amount of time it takes to cook a 4 kg turkey.

Key points

- The subject of a formula is always the letter on its own on one side of the equation. For example, the subject of $k = \frac{1}{2}mv^2$ is k.
- You change the subject of a formula by rearranging the formula to get the letter that you want on its own on one side of the equation.

△ Purposeful practice 1

1 Make x the subject of each formula.

  a $y = x + 2$ **b** $y = x + 5$ **c** $y = 2 + x$ **d** $w = z + x$

  e $a = z + x$ **f** $a = b + x$ **g** $a = x + b$ **h** $c = x + b$

2 Make y the subject of each formula.

  a $x = yz$ **b** $x = ya$ **c** $x = zy$ **d** $a = yz$

  e $a = by$ **f** $a = 2y$ **g** $a = 5y$ **h** $x = 5y$

3 Make P the subject of each formula.

  a $N = \dfrac{P}{2}$ **b** $N = \dfrac{P}{T}$ **c** $N = \dfrac{2}{P}$ **d** $a = \dfrac{2}{P}$

  e $a = \dfrac{x}{P}$ **f** $a = \dfrac{y}{P}$ **g** $x = \dfrac{y}{P}$ **h** $x = \dfrac{a}{P}$

4 Make the letter in the brackets the subject of each of these formulae.

  a $M = DV$ (V) **b** $M = DV$ (D)

  c $a = b + c$ (b) **d** $a = b + c$ (c)

  e $p = q - t$ (q) **f** $p = q + t$ (t)

  g $L = \dfrac{M}{N}$ (M) **h** $L = \dfrac{M}{N}$ (N)

Reflect and reason

Alix and Seb make m the subject of $h = mx$.

Alix writes   Seb writes

$h = mx$ $h = mx$

$hx = m$ $\dfrac{h}{x} = m$

Who is correct? How do you decide which operation to use to change the subject?

△ Purposeful practice 2

1 Make a the subject of each formula.

  a $y = a + 2b$ **b** $y = a + 5b$ **c** $y = 5b + a$ **d** $y = a + bc$

  e $p = a - 4c$ **f** $p = a - 9u$ **g** $p = a - xy$ **h** $c = a - tx$

2 Make x the subject of each formula.

  a $p = 2x$ **b** $p = 2x - a$ **c** $p = 2x + b$ **d** $p = 2x + 3b$

e $p = 2x - 5b$ **f** $p = mx - 5$ **g** $p = mx + 4$ **h** $y = mx + c$

Reflect and reason

Are these two statements equivalent? $x = 5$ and $5 = x$.

Are these two formulae equivalent? $4x + c = y$ and $y = 4x + c$.

Do all your answers to Purposeful practice 2 have the subject on the left-hand side?
If not, rewrite them so they do.

⊠ Problem-solving practice

1 Sophie and Jordan are asked to make x the subject of the formula $y = 3x + 5$.

Sophie writes   Jordan writes

$x = \dfrac{y}{3} - 5$ $x = y - 5 \div 3$

Both Sophie and Jordan have written the wrong answer.
Explain why each of them is incorrect.

2 You can use this formula to work out the distance travelled.

$d = st$

where d = distance
       s = average speed
       t = time taken

Rearrange the formula to make s the subject.

3 You can use this formula to work out the finishing speed of an object.

$v = u + at$

where v = finishing speed
       u = initial speed
       a = acceleration
       t = time taken

Rearrange the formula to make u the subject.

4 You can use this formula to work out the density of a material.

$D = \dfrac{m}{V}$

where D = density
       m = mass
       V = volume

Which of these formulae are the density formula with m or V as its subject?

$V = Dm$	$V = \dfrac{m}{D}$	$V = \dfrac{D}{m}$	$m = DV$	$m = \dfrac{D}{V}$	$m = \dfrac{V}{D}$

5 Here are some equations of straight lines.

$y = 2x - 7$	$7 - y = 2x$	$y = 2x + 7$	$x = \dfrac{y - 7}{2}$	$x = \dfrac{y}{2} - 7$

Which two equations are the same line?

Key points

- When multiplying powers of the same letter, you add the indices.
- When dividing powers of the same letter, you subtract the indices.
- To factorise an expression completely, take out the highest common factor (HCF) of its terms.

△ Purposeful practice 1

1 Simplify

  a $x \times x$ **b** $x \times x^2$ **c** $x \times x^3$ **d** $x^2 \times x^3$

  e $2x \times x^2$ **f** $x \times 2x^2$ **g** $3x^2 \times x^3$ **h** $3x \times 5x$

  i $3x^2 \times 5x$ **j** $3x^2 \times 5x^3$ **k** $4x^2 \times 3x$ **l** $4x^2 \times 3x^2$

2 Simplify

  a $n^2 \div n$ **b** $n^5 \div n$ **c** $n^5 \div n^2$ **d** $n^6 \div n^2$ **e** $\dfrac{2n^3}{n}$ **f** $\dfrac{2n^3}{2}$

  g $\dfrac{2n^3}{2n}$ **h** $\dfrac{2n^3}{2n^2}$ **i** $\dfrac{6n^4}{6}$ **j** $\dfrac{6n^4}{n}$ **k** $\dfrac{6n^4}{6n}$ **l** $\dfrac{6n^4}{6n^2}$

  m $\dfrac{6n^4}{2n^2}$ **n** $\dfrac{6n^4}{12n^2}$ **o** $\dfrac{6n^8}{3n^4}$ **p** $\dfrac{3n^8}{6n^4}$ **q** $\dfrac{2n^6}{6n^4}$ **r** $\dfrac{6n^4}{2n^4}$

Reflect and reason

Each student A–D has made an error. Explain the error and write the correct answer.

A: $x^2 \times x^4 = x^8$ B: $3x^2 \times 5x^4 = 8x^6$ C: $\dfrac{x^6}{x^2} = x^3$ D: $\dfrac{6x^5}{2x^3} = 4x^2$

△ Purposeful practice 2

1 Expand the brackets in each expression.

  a $x(x^2 + 3)$ **b** $x^2(x^2 + 3)$ **c** $x^2(x^2 + 3x)$

  d $5x^2(x^2 + 3x)$ **e** $5x^2(2x^2 + 3x)$ **f** $5x^2(2x^3 + 3x^2)$

2 Expand the brackets in each expression.

  a $y^3(y - 1)$ **b** $y^3(2y - 1)$ **c** $y^3(2y - 3)$ **d** $4y^3(2y - 3)$

  e $4y^3(2y - 3y^2)$ **f** $-y(y^2 - 2)$ **g** $-y(3y^2 - 2y)$ **h** $-4y(3y^2 - 2y)$

3 Factorise each expression completely.

  a $n^3 + n$ **b** $n^3 + 5n$ **c** $n^3 + 5n^2$ **d** $5n^3 + 5n^2$

  e $10n^3 + 5n^2$ **f** $5n^3 + 10n^2$ **g** $2n^3 + 10n^2$ **h** $4n^3 + 10n^2$

4 Factorise each expression completely, using only one pair of brackets.

  a $m^5 - m^3$ **b** $-m^5 + m^3$ **c** $3m^5 - m^3$ **d** $3m^5 - 3m^3$

  e $9m^5 - 3m^3$ **f** $8m^2 - 2m$ **g** $2m^5 - 8m^2$ **h** $6m^5 - 8m^2$

Reflect and reason

How can you tell whether or not these expressions are fully factorised?

$2(3x + x^2)$ $x^2(2x - 4)$ $2x^2(x - 1)$ $5x(4x + 2x^2)$

1 Copy and complete the multiplication grid for powers of x.

×	**2x**		**4x³**
3x		$3x^3$	
	$6x^3$		
			$8x^6$

2 The term in each rectangle comes from multiplying the terms in the two circles that are linked to the rectangle. Copy and complete the diagram.

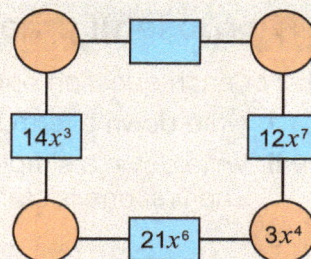

(diagram contains: $14x^3$, $12x^7$, $21x^6$, $3x^4$)

3 Copy and complete

a $4x \times \square x^{\square} = 12x^4$

b $\dfrac{8y^6}{\square y^{\square}} = 2y^4$

c $\dfrac{\square z^{\square}}{5z} = 5z^7$

4 Write three different multiplications involving powers of x that simplify to $20x^4$.

5 Write three different divisions involving powers of x that simplify to $3x^2$.

6 Copy and complete

a $2x^2(x^2 + \square) = \square + 6x^2$ **b** $5y^3(4y^4 - \square) = \square - 25y^3$

7 Alesha and Ryan are asked to expand $2x^3(4x - 5)$.

Alesha writes   Ryan writes

$2x^3(4x - 5) = 6x^4 - 7x^3$ $2x^3(4x - 5) = 8x^4 - 5$

Both Alesha and Ryan are incorrect.

a Explain what Alesha has done wrong.

b Explain what Ryan has done wrong.

c Write the correct answer.

8 Match these expressions into equivalent pairs.

$24p^5 + 8p^3$	$24p^5 + 16p^3$	$8p^3(3p^2 + 1)$	$12p^3(2p^3 + 1)$
$24p^6 + 12p^3$	$24p^5 + 12p^3$	$8p^3(3p^2 + 2)$	$12p^3(2p^2 + 1)$
$24p^6 + 8p^3$	$24p^6 + 16p^3$	$8p^3(3p^3 + 2)$	$8p^3(3p^3 + 1)$

9 Sameer is asked to factorise $24x^8 - 36x^5$.

Sameer writes

$24x^8 - 36x^5 = 4x^2(6x^6 - 9x^3)$

Write two mistakes that Sameer has made.

10 Isaak says, 'Factorising $15a^3 - 25a^2$ and factorising $18a^6 - 30a^5$ both result in having the same expression in brackets.'

Is Isaak correct? Explain why.

Key points

- When you expand double brackets, you multiply each term in one set of brackets by each term in the other brackets.
- A quadratic expression contains a squared term (e.g. x^2) and no higher power.

⚠ Purposeful practice 1

1 For each question part,
   - **i** write down a term for the area of each of the four parts of the rectangle
   - **ii** write down a simplified expression for the total area of the whole rectangle.
   The first one is started for you.

a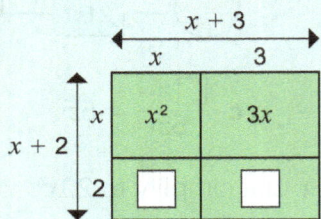

b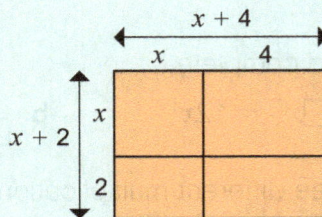

c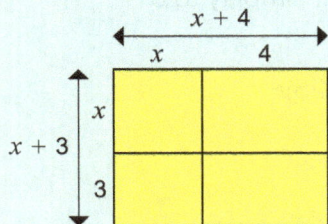

d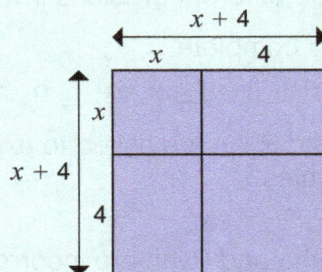

e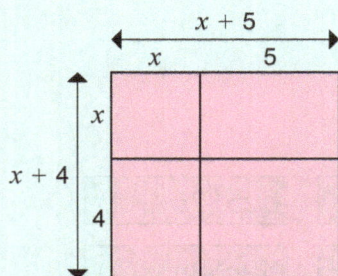

f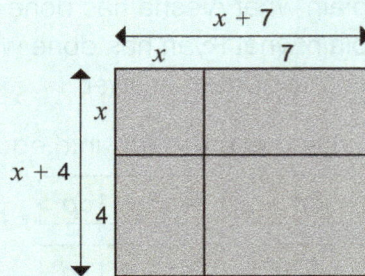

2 You can expand and simplify brackets to multiply the length and width of the rectangle in **Q1a**.
   Use this method to expand and simplify each expression.

   $$(x + 2)(x + 3) = x^2 + \underline{3x + 2x} + 6$$
   $$= x^2 + 5x + 6$$

   a $(x + 3)(x + 5)$ **b** $(x + 3)(x + 6)$ **c** $(x + 4)(x + 6)$
   d $(x + 5)(x + 6)$ **e** $(x + 6)(x + 7)$ **f** $(x + 7)(x + 8)$

Reflect and reason

When you multiply $(x + 4)(x + 2)$:

How many terms in x will there be **before** you simplify the expression?

How many terms will there be **after** you simplify the expression?

Expand and simplify

1 $(x - 2)(x + 3)$ **2** $(x - 2)(x + 5)$ **3** $(x - 2)(x + 8)$

4 $(x - 3)(x + 8)$ **5** $(x - 5)(x + 8)$ **6** $(x - 7)(x + 8)$

7 $(x - 7)(x + 1)$ **8** $(x - 7)(x + 3)$ **9** $(x - 7)(x + 6)$

10 $(x - 2)(x + 6)$ **11** $(x - 3)(x + 6)$ **12** $(x - 3)(x + 4)$

13 $(x - 3)(x - 4)$ **14** $(x - 3)(x - 5)$ **15** $(x - 3)(x - 7)$

Reflect and reason

Explain why the expansions of **Q1–12** all have a negative number term but the expansions of **Q13–15** have a positive number term.

Explain why **Q1–6** and **Q10–12** all have a positive x term but **Q7–9** and **Q13–15** have a negative x term.

⊠ Problem-solving practice

1 Maisy and Alfie both expand and simplify the quadratic expression $(x + 9)(x - 4)$.
Maisy writes   Alfie writes
$(x + 9)(x - 4) = x^2 - 36$ $(x + 9)(x - 4) = x^2 - 5x - 36$
Maisy and Alfie are both incorrect. Explain the mistake each of them has made.

2 The length of a rectangle is $n + 7$ and the width is $n + 4$.
Show that the area of the rectangle can be written as $n^2 + 11n + 28$.

3 Abdul says, '$(n - 2)(n + 5)$ simplifies to the same answer as $(n + 5)(n - 2)$.'
Ben says, '$(n - 2)(n + 5)$ simplifies to the same answer as $(n - 5)(n + 2)$.'
Which of them is correct? Explain your answer.

4 a Expand and simplify $(x + 5)(x - 5)$.
   b Is this a quadratic expression? Explain your answer.

5 Show that $(n + 2)(n - 3) = n(n - 3) + 2(n - 3)$.

6 The diagram shows a rectangle with a rectangular hole cut out of it.
Write a simplified expression for the shaded area.
You must show your working.

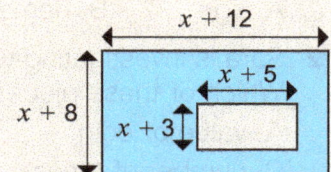

7 The diagram shows a square picture surrounded by a shaded square mount.
Write a simplified expression for the area of the shaded mount.
You must show your working.

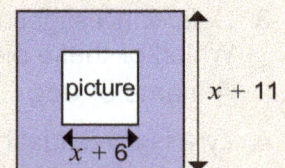

8 Write a simplified expression for the area of the rectangle.
You must show your working.

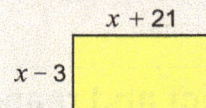

3 Dealing with data

3.1 Planning a survey

Key points

- The total number of items a survey relates to is called the population.
- A hypothesis is a statement that you can test by collecting data using a questionnaire, survey or experiment.

△ Purposeful practice 1

1 A mayor organises a survey to find out what people under 25 think of the leisure facilities in the city. Which of these is the population for this survey?

   A the population of the city   B people under 25 in the city

   C people under 25 in the country

2 A biologist organises a survey of the number of different insect species in a pond. What is the population for this survey?

3 A factory takes a sample of all the chocolate bars it produces one Friday. What population is this sample taken from?

4 A newspaper organises a survey to find out how people all over the country might vote in the next election. What is the population for this survey?

Reflect and reason

In everyday English, a population is 'all the people that live in a particular place'. How is the mathematical definition of a survey population different to the everyday definition?

△ Purposeful practice 2

1 James is investigating whether teenagers sleep more than adults.
   Which of these pieces of information should he collect?

   A age   B name   C occupation   D hours of sleep per 24 hours

2 Sara is investigating whether a coin is unbiased when flipped.
   Which of these pieces of information should she collect?

   A value of coin   B material coin is made of

   C number of times coin is flipped   D number of times the coin lands on 'heads'

3 Dale is investigating the hypothesis 'one syllable names are the most popular for dogs'.
   Which of these pieces of information should he collect?

   A name of dog   B name of owner   C age of dog   D age of owner

4 Lyra is investigating attitudes towards bullying across different age groups in her school. Which of these pieces of information is it most appropriate to collect?
   A name   B name of tutor group   C key stage

Reflect and reason

In a survey, do you always need to collect data on names and ages? Use your answers to Purposeful practice 2 to explain.

Problem-solving practice

1 A headteacher organises a survey to find out what students think of the school's uniform.
Kelly says, 'The population for this survey is all children who live in the same town as the school.'
Anish says, 'The population for this survey is every person in school today.'
Freya says, 'The population for this survey is all students who are registered at the school.'
Who is correct? Explain why.

2 A teacher wants to investigate how students in different year groups travel to school.
   a What is the population for her survey?
   b What information should she collect?

3 Jack is investigating how long teenagers in his town spend playing games on consoles.
   a What is the population for his survey?
   b What information should he collect?

4 Look at the survey the manager of a leisure centre gives to her members.
What might the manager be investigating?

> Write in each box how many hours per week you use each facility.
> Gym ☐
> Swimming pool ☐
> Fitness classes ☐

5 Aarav carries out a survey.
He displays his data in this table.

Age group	Football	Netball	Tennis	Athletics	Other
0–10	22	1	5	3	14
11–20	32	35	17	28	33
21–30	44	22	13	15	24
31–40	38	19	14	8	28
41–50	29	15	12	3	18
Over 50	57	3	7	2	23

What might Aarav be investigating?

6 Ava wants to find out how long the students at her school spend on their homework.
She asks her friends to record how long they spend on homework over the next week.
Explain why this is not a fair way to collect the data.

7 A politician wants to find out what percentage of people in a town would support closing their library.
The politician decides not to survey the whole population of everyone living in the town.
   a Why is it a good idea that the politician does not survey the whole population?
   b Which method should the politician use to decide who to survey? Explain why.
      A Everyone who enters the library that week.
      B The children at her local primary school.
      C Everyone living in her street.
      D Every 50th person registered as living in the town.
      E Everyone she works with.

Key points

- A grouped frequency table has 4 or 5 equal width classes.
- A data collection sheet is a table or chart for collecting data.
- Discrete data can only take particular values. For example, dress sizes can only be whole numbers.
- Continuous data is measured and can take any value. For continuous data there are no gaps between the groups.

△ Purposeful practice 1

1 Write down 5 groups of equal class width, e.g. 1–☐, ☐–☐, ... for
  a test marks between 1 and 25
  b test marks between 1 and 50
  c test marks between 1 and 100

2 Write down 4 groups of equal class width, e.g. 1–☐, ☐–☐, ... for
  a number of shirts sold between 1 and 20
  b number of shirts sold between 1 and 40
  c number of shirts sold between 1 and 100

3 Write down 5 groups of equal class width, e.g. $0 \leqslant x < ☐$, $☐ \leqslant x < ☐$, ... for
  a rainfall between 0 mm and 25 mm
  b rainfall between 0 mm and 40 mm
  c rainfall between 0 mm and 75 mm

4 **a** Is the number of pages in a book discrete or continuous data?
  b A series of books have between 101 and 300 pages each.
    Write down 5 groups of equal class width for this data.

5 **a** Is the length of a long jump discrete or continuous data?
    Long jump results in a school competition are between 300 and 450 cm.
  b Write down 5 groups of equal class width for this data.
  c Write down 4 groups of equal class width for this data.

Reflect and reason

How do you decide whether to use groups like this: 1–10, 11–20, ... or like this: $0 \leqslant x < 10$, $10 \leqslant x < 20$, ... for a set of data?

Look at your answers to **Q5**. Is it better to group this data into 4 groups or 5 groups? Explain.

△ Purposeful practice 2

1 Design a grouped frequency table to record people's ages.
  Start your first group at 0.
  Make the last group 'over 75'.

2 Design a grouped frequency table to record people's daily 'screen time' in hours.
  Make the last group '8+'.

3 Design a two-way grouped frequency table to record people's ages and daily 'screen time'.

Reflect and reason

Drashma collects the data for **Q3** in a table like this:

Name	Age	Screen time

Look at your table for **Q3**. Which table is better for showing the number of 26 to 50-year-olds with between 4 and 8 hours screen time? Explain your answer.

⊠ Problem-solving practice

1 These are the test results for a group of students.

> 28, 35, 19, 44, 8, 17, 23, 37, 31, 34,
> 41, 26, 33, 29, 40, 35, 38, 37, 24, 32

Test results	Tally	Frequency
1–☐		
☐–☐		
☐–☐		
☐–☐		
☐–50		

  a Copy and complete the grouped frequency table for his data.

  b How many students are in the group?

  c What is the modal class?

2 Nia measures the height, in cm, of some plants in her greenhouse.

> 5.8, 18.7, 9.3, 14.2, 4.5, 12.1, 8.9, 16.1,
> 11.2, 16.8, 13.2, 12.7, 15.4, 10.8, 11.6

Height (cm)	Tally	Frequency

  a Use the information to copy and complete the grouped frequency table.

  b How many plants did Nia measure?

  c What is the modal class in your table?

3 Each of the tables is incorrect. Explain why in each case.

a

Height (cm)	Frequency
30–40	
40–50	
50–60	

b

Mass (g)	Frequency
$0 < m \leqslant 5$	
$5 < m \leqslant 8$	
$8 < m \leqslant 12$	

c

Number of children	Frequency
$0 \leqslant c < 20$	
$20 \leqslant c < 40$	
$40 \leqslant c < 60$	

d

Time (s)	Frequency
$0 < t < 2$	
$2 < t < 4$	
$4 < t < 6$	

Key points

- The median of n values in order is the $\frac{n+1}{2}$th value.
- You can calculate an estimate of the mean from a grouped frequency table. Use the midpoint of each class to represent the values in that class.

△ Purposeful practice 1

1 **a** Find the median of these data values.

0, 2, 3, 1, 3, 2, 3, 1, 0, 1, 3

b Fill in a table for the values. Give your table two columns, with the headings 'Value' and 'Frequency'.

c Find the median from the table.

2 The table shows the numbers of children in some families.

a Copy and complete this list of the numbers of children.

0, 0, 0, 0, 1, ...

b Find the median from your list in part **a**.

c Find the median from the table.

Check that your answers to parts **b** and **c** are the same.

Number of children	Frequency
0	4
1	6
2	10
3	1

3 The table shows the ages of children living in one street.

Find the class that contains the median.

Age of child (years)	Frequency
0–6	15
7–13	7
14–20	3

4 The table shows the masses of tomatoes from one plant.

Find the class that contains the median.

Mass of tomato (grams)	Frequency
$10 < m \leqslant 20$	3
$20 < m \leqslant 30$	4
$30 < m \leqslant 40$	2
$40 < m \leqslant 50$	8

Reflect and reason

What do you do first when you have to find the median from a list of values?

Why don't you need to do this to find the median from a table?

△ Purposeful practice 2

1 Calculate the mean of the data in Purposeful practice 1 **Q1** and **Q2**.
Round your answers to 1 d.p.

2 Calculate an estimate for the mean of the data in Purposeful practice 1 **Q3** and **Q4**.
Round your answers to 1 d.p.

Reflect and reason

Look at the mean values you found in Purposeful practice 2. Does the mean have to be one of the data values? Can it be larger than or smaller than all the data values?

Problem-solving practice

1 The table shows the number of pets belonging to children in a class.

Number of pets	Frequency
0	2
1	15
2	5
3	4
4	1

Ryan, Seth and Tia work out the median number of pets.

Ryan writes

$\emptyset, \not{1}, 2, \not{3}, \not{4}$

median = 2

Seth writes

$2 + 15 + 5 + 4 + 1 = 27$

$\frac{27 + 1}{2} = 14$

median = 14

Tia writes

$2 + 15 + 5 + 4 + 1 = 27$

$\frac{27 + 1}{2}$th = 14th

median = 1

a Who is correct? Explain your answer.

b Work out the mean number of pets.
Write your answer to 1 d.p.

2 A company records how many hours of overtime each member of staff works during a month. The table shows the results.

A director of the company works out an estimate of the mean. She writes

Estimate of mean = 80 ÷ 4 = 20

a The director is incorrect. Explain why.

b Work out a correct estimate for the mean.

c Which class contains the median?

Overtime (hours)	Frequency
$0 \leqslant h < 5$	26
$5 \leqslant h < 10$	17
$10 \leqslant h < 15$	24
$15 \leqslant h < 20$	13
Total	80

3 For his homework, Toby is asked to work out an estimate of the mean of this set of data. He smudges one of the frequencies given in the table after he works out that the total of the midpoint multiplied by the frequency is 375.

a Work out the missing frequency.

b Work out an estimate of the mean.

c Which class contains the median?

Length (cm)	Frequency
$0 \leqslant l < 10$	1
$10 \leqslant l < 20$	●
$20 \leqslant l < 30$	6
$30 \leqslant l < 40$	5

Key point

- You can use a line of best fit to predict values from a scatter diagram.

△ Purposeful practice 1

1 Two students plot the same data of the French and Spanish marks for their class on a scatter diagram and draw a line of best fit.

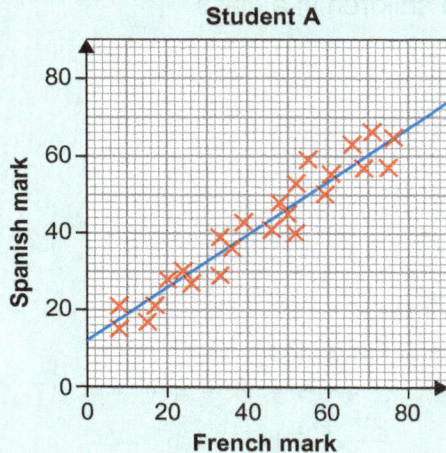

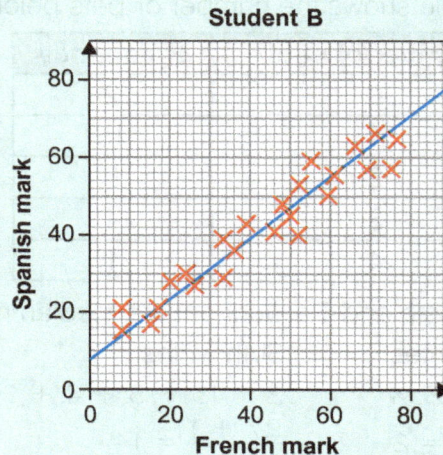

From each graph, use the line of best fit to predict

a the Spanish mark when the French mark is 62

b the Spanish mark when the French mark is 24

c the French mark when the Spanish mark is 34

d the French mark when the Spanish mark is 60

Reflect and reason

Do both students' scatter graphs give the same predicted marks? Explain.

△ Purposeful practice 2

1 The table shows the height and hand span of 10 people.

Height (cm)	144	180	160	200	170	150	168	156	188	203
Hand span (cm)	11	19	16	24	20	14	15	14	26	26

a Draw a scatter diagram of this data.

b Draw a line of best fit.

c Use your line of best fit to predict

  i the hand span of a person with height 174 cm

  ii the height of a person with hand span 21 cm

Reflect and reason

Will every student who answers **Q1b** draw their line of best fit in exactly the same position? How will this affect their answers to part **c**?

1 The scatter graph shows the height and arm span of some students.

Arm span and height of students

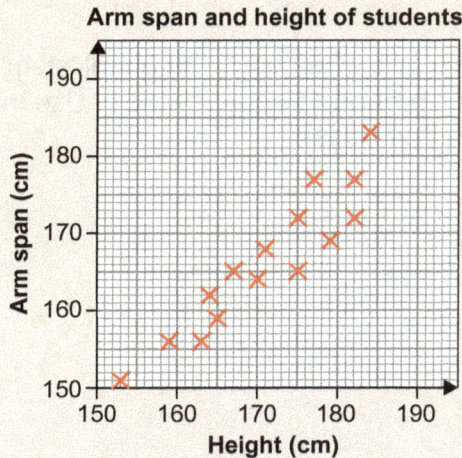

Another student measures their height.
They are 172 cm tall.
Estimate the arm span of this student.

2 The table shows the scores of two maths test papers for eight students.

Paper 1	32	20	30	18	44	28	37	45
Paper 2	29	19	31	20	40	29	40	44

   a Draw a scatter graph of this data.
   b Another student scores 25 on Paper 1.
      Estimate the score that this student will achieve on Paper 2.

3 The scatter graph shows the mass and diameter of some apples.

Mass and diameter of apples

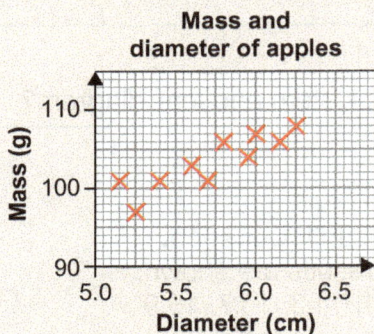

Clare estimates the mass of another apple with a diameter of 5.5 cm.
Clare says, 'This apple will have a mass of 95 grams.'
Use the scatter graph to explain why Clare is unlikely to be correct.

4 The table shows the lengths and widths of leaves from a tree.

Length (cm)	11.6	14.1	10.2	9.7	13.4	13.8	12.6	12.9
Width (cm)	8.3	11.5	7.8	7.1	10.2	10.7	9.5	9.9

A leaf has a length of 13.7 cm and a width of 7.8 cm.
Is this leaf likely to be from the same type of tree? Explain your answer.

Key points

- A back-to-back stem and leaf diagram shows two sets of data with a central 'stem'.
- You can calculate an estimate of the mean from a grouped frequency table. Use the midpoint of each class to represent the values in that class.
- A report could include
  the hypothesis or what you are investigating
  the data shown in a graph or chart
  averages and range
  a conclusion
  what else you could investigate

△ Purposeful practice 1

20 students tested their typing speed in words per minute.
The 20 students then took a typing course and tested their typing speeds again.
The stem and leaf diagrams show their typing speeds before and after the course.

Typing speed before course

```
1 | 7 9
2 | 1 5 6 6 9
3 | 0 2 5 5 6 8 8
4 | 1 1 2 4 5 7
```
Key: 1|7 means 17

Typing speed after course

```
2 | 1 2 4
3 | 5 7 7 9
4 | 0 2 2 6 8
5 | 1 1 2 4 4 5 7
6 | 3
```
Key: 2|1 means 21

1 Draw a back-to-back stem and leaf diagram to show the typing speeds.

Reflect and reason

Why do you need two titles and two keys for a back-to-back stem and leaf diagram?

△ Purposeful practice 2

A gardener grows sunflowers from two different types of sunflower seed.
He measures the diameter of each sunflower, in cm. His results are shown.
Type A: 16.5, 14.9, 14.1, 16.3, 12.6, 14.0, 15.7, 13.6, 13.4, 14.3, 13.7, 15.9
Type B: 18.4, 17.6, 19.2, 16.1, 18.2, 19.3, 16.2, 16.4, 19.8, 18.6, 19.5, 18.9

1 Draw a back-to-back stem and leaf diagram for the data.

2 Copy and complete this grouped frequency table for the data.

Diameter (cm)	Type A	Type B
$12 < d \leq 14$		
$14 < d \leq 16$		
$16 < d \leq 18$		
$18 < d \leq 20$		

3 Draw line graphs for the grouped data on the same axes.

4 Calculate the mean, median and range of the data. Give your answers to 1 d.p.

5 Calculate an estimate for the mean from the grouped data.
Give your answer to 1 d.p.

6 Write two sentences comparing the diameters of the two types of sunflower.

> ### Reflect and reason
> Which method for displaying data do you think best shows the differences between the two sets of data? Explain.
>
> Did you find it easier to calculate the mean from the data or the grouped data? Explain.

⊠ Problem-solving practice

1 Some students record how long it takes them to get to school on a dry day, to the nearest minute.
3, 3, 4, 4, 4, 5, 5, 6, 6, 8, 9, 10, 10, 10, 11, 11, 13, 14, 18, 21
They also record how long it takes on a rainy day, to the nearest minute.
4, 5, 6, 6, 7, 9, 9, 10, 10, 11, 12, 15, 17, 19, 19, 22, 25, 27, 28, 31

  a Draw a back-to-back stem and leaf diagram to display the data.
  b Write a sentence comparing the median for the time taken on the two days.
  c Write a sentence comparing the range for the time taken on the two days.

2 A group of Year 9 and Year 11 students recorded their heights.
The back-to-back stem and leaf diagram shows the results.
Compare the heights of the two groups of students, making reference to the median and range.

Heights of Year 9   Heights of Year 11

7	14	
8 5 4 2	15	5 7
8 8 7 6 4 3	16	2 3 5 8 8
8 5 2 0	17	1 2 4 4 9
	18	0 3 4

Key:
7|14 means 147 cm

Key:
15|5 means 155 cm

3 A biologist records the heights of some plants grown with and without fertiliser.
The table shows the results.

The biologist says, 'My hypothesis is that plants grown with fertiliser grow taller.'
Write a report based on this data.
Make sure you conclude with whether the biologist is correct or not.

Height (cm)	Number of plants grown with fertiliser	Number of plants grown without fertiliser
$40 < h \leqslant 45$	1	6
$45 < h \leqslant 50$	2	14
$50 < h \leqslant 55$	15	4
$55 < h \leqslant 60$	7	1

4 The table shows the finish times of some 3 km races that Anya and Dina ran.

Anya says, 'When we run, our times are about the same.'
Is Anya's hypothesis correct? Write a report to explain why.

Time (minutes)	Anya	Dina
$20 < t \leqslant 25$	7	4
$25 < t \leqslant 30$	14	9
$30 < t \leqslant 35$	7	17
$35 < t \leqslant 40$	4	2

Mixed exercises A

Mixed problem-solving practice A

1 These are the ages, in years, of 15 females at a tennis club.
17, 19, 19, 20, 24, 24, 25, 27, 30, 34, 37, 43, 44, 48, 51
The stem and leaf diagram shows the distribution of the ages of the males at the tennis club.
Compare the distributions of the ages of the females and the distributions of the ages of the males.

1	7 8
2	1 3 4 8 9
3	1 1 2 2 5 8
4	0 5 5 7
5	0 2 3 6
6	2

Key: 1|7 means 17 years old

2 This formula is used to work out the body mass index, BMI, for a person of mass m kg and height h m.

$$\text{BMI} = \frac{m}{h^2}$$

A 'healthy' BMI for an adult is generally considered to be between 18.5 and 25.
Harry has a mass of 86 kg. He has a height of 1.85 m.
Is Harry's BMI considered 'healthy' by this definition? You must show your working.

3 $A = b^3 \times c$
Estimate A when $b = 412.95$, $c = 8.9 \times 10^7$.
Give your answer in standard form.

4 In the diagram, all angles are in degrees.
Angle POR = angle QOR.
Work out the value of x.

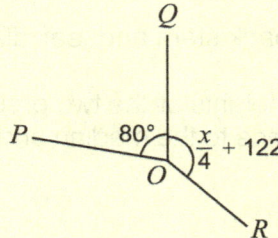

Q

P —— 80° $\frac{x}{4} + 122$

O

R

5 The first table gives some information about the masses, in kg, of a sample of 50 suitcases for flight A at an airport check-in desk.
   a What is the modal class?
   b Work out an estimate for the mean mass.

Mass, m (kg)	Frequency
$0 < m \leqslant 10$	5
$10 < m \leqslant 20$	28
$20 < m \leqslant 30$	16
$30 < m \leqslant 40$	1

The second table gives some information about the masses, in kg, of a sample of 50 suitcases for flight B at an airport check-in desk.
   c Compare the masses of the suitcases for flights A and B.

Mass, m (kg)	Frequency
$0 < m \leqslant 10$	1
$10 < m \leqslant 20$	7
$20 < m \leqslant 30$	28
$30 < m \leqslant 40$	14

6 1000^x can be written as 10^A
   a Show that $A = 3x$.
   b Make x the subject of $A = 3x$.

7 **a** Match each shape X–Z with the area expression A–F that describes it.

A: $2x^2 + 2xy$ B: $2x^2$ C: $x^2 + 2x + 2y + y^2$

D: $x^2 + y^2$ E: $x^2 + 2xy + y^2$ F: $(2x)^2$

X y Y y Z x
x x x
x y x x x x

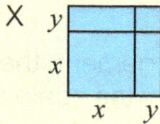

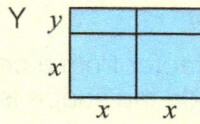

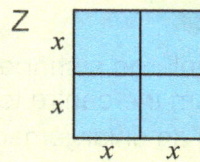

b Work out the area of each shape when $x = 8\,\text{cm}$ and $y = 3\,\text{cm}$.

8 Simplify each calculation.
Give each answer as a number written in standard form raised to a power.

a $(4.7 \times 10^5)^{-4} \times (4.7 \times 10^5)^{11}$ **b** $\dfrac{(3.5 \times 10^7)^{-5}}{(3.5 \times 10^7)^3}$

9 Mr White wants to compare the test scores of students who revise using his revision list, with students who revise without the revision list.

The scatter diagram gives some information about the test scores and how long students spend revising.

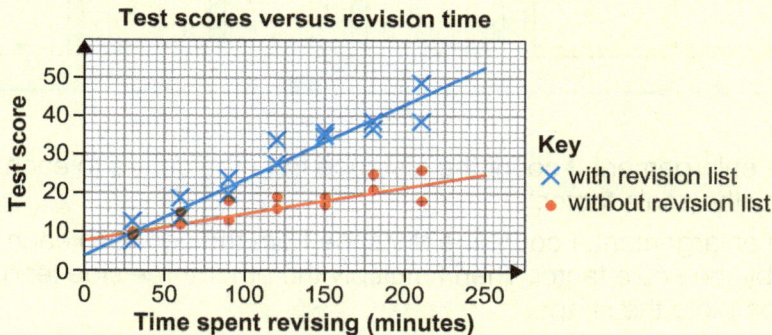

Test scores versus revision time

Key
$\times$ with revision list
• without revision list

a Beth revises for $1\frac{1}{4}$ hours using Mr White's revision list.
Find an estimate for Beth's score.

b Yanah is revising without the revision list.
Work out an estimate for how much Yanah's score increases for every hour she revises.

c Write a formula for the test score, S, after h hours of revision for each set of students.

d Write a sentence comparing the test scores of students who revise from Mr White's revision list, with students who revise without it.

10 The diagram shows shape A.
All the measurements are in centimetres.

a Find an expression in terms of x for the area, in cm^2, of shape A.
You must simplify your answer.

b Shape B is a rectangle.
Shape B has the same area as shape A.
Shape B has a length of $(x + 12)$ centimetres.
Sarah says, 'Shape B has a width of $(x + 3)\,\text{cm}$.'
Is Sarah correct? Show your working to explain your answer.

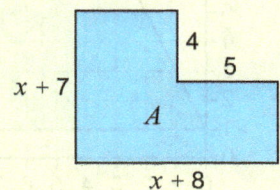

4
5
$x + 7$
A
$x + 8$

4 Multiplicative reasoning

4.1 Enlargement

Key points

- When you enlarge a shape by a scale factor from a centre of enlargement, the distance from the centre to each point on the shape is multiplied by the scale factor.
- To describe an enlargement, give the scale factor and the coordinates of the centre of enlargement.

△ Purposeful practice 1

Copy each shape onto a square grid. Enlarge each shape by the scale factor given above it in each case, using the cross as the centre of enlargement.

scale factor 2

A, B, C, D

scale factor 3

E, F, G, H

Reflect and reason

Taran says, 'To draw each enlargement, I count the distance from the centre to each vertex and then multiply by the scale factor.'

Hana says, 'To draw each enlargement, I count the distance from the centre to each base vertex and multiply by the scale factor. Then I multiply the other three side lengths by the scale factor and complete the shape.'

Whose method do you prefer? Explain your answer.

△ Purposeful practice 2

Describe the enlargement that takes shape X to shape Y in each of these diagrams.

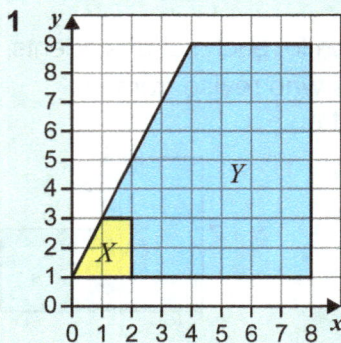

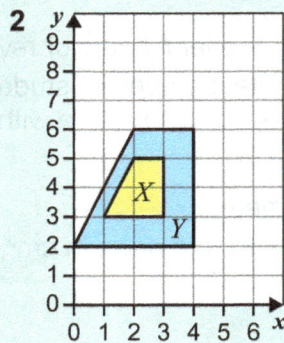

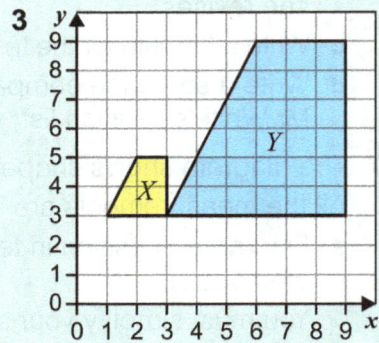

Reflect and reason

When describing an enlargement, why is it important to include the coordinates of the centre of enlargement, as well as the scale factor?

Copy each shape onto a square grid. Then enlarge the shapes by scale factor 2, using the cross as the centre of enlargement.

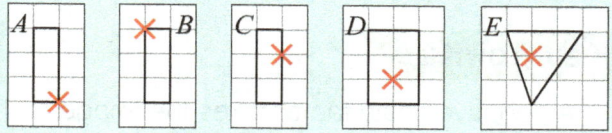

Reflect and reason

What is the same and what is different when the centre of enlargement is on the shape (A–C) and inside the shape (D and E)?

⊠ Problem-solving practice

1 Match each enlargement of triangle A to triangle B with its description D to F.

a

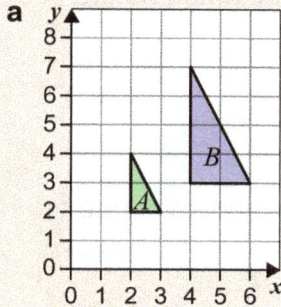

b

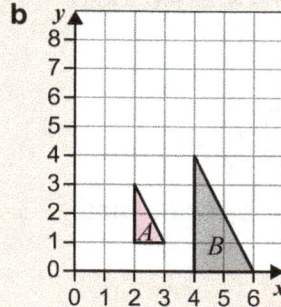

c

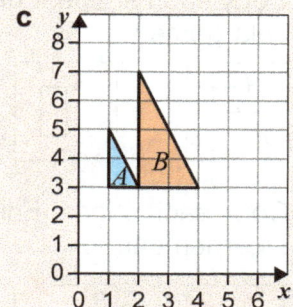

D An enlargement by scale factor 2 with centre of enlargement (0, 3).

E An enlargement by scale factor 2 with centre of enlargement (0, 2).

F An enlargement by scale factor 2 with centre of enlargement (0, 1).

2 Use the diagram to copy and complete each sentence.

a Shape ☐ is an enlargement of shape ☐ by scale factor 3 with centre of enlargement (4, −5).

b Shape ☐ is an enlargement of shape ☐ by scale factor 3 with centre of enlargement (3, 1).

c Shape ☐ is an enlargement of shape ☐ by scale factor 3 with centre of enlargement (4, −2).

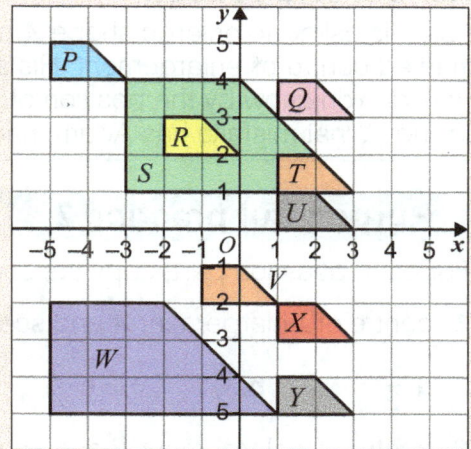

3 Josh is asked to enlarge shape A by scale factor 2 and centre of enlargement (10, 1).

His answer is shown as shape B on the diagram.

Is Josh correct? Explain your answer.

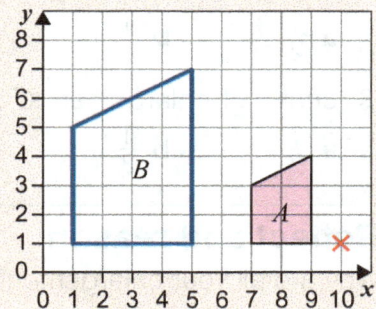

Unit 4 Enlargement   **34**

4.2 Negative and fractional scale factors

Key points

- A negative scale factor takes the image to the opposite side of the centre of enlargement.
- You can enlarge a shape using a fractional scale factor. Use the same method of multiplying the length of each side by the scale factor.
- The word 'enlarge' is used for fractional scale factors, even though the image may be smaller.

△ Purposeful practice 1

1 Copy each shape. Enlarge them by scale factor −2, using the marked centre of enlargement.

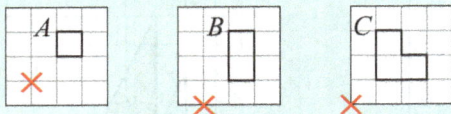

2 Copy each shape. Enlarge them by scale factor −3, using the marked centre of enlargement.

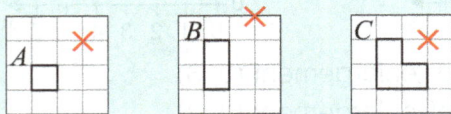

Reflect and reason

Adam is asked to enlarge shape A by scale factor −2, using the marked centre of enlargement. His answer is shape B.
How do you know by the position of shape B that Adam's answer is wrong? What mistake has Adam made?

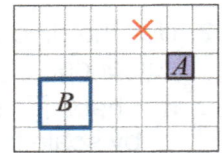

△ Purposeful practice 2

For each question part, copy the shape onto a new grid and then enlarge it using

1 centre of enlargement A and scale factor

   a $\frac{1}{2}$ **b** $\frac{1}{3}$ **c** $\frac{1}{4}$

2 centre of enlargement B and scale factor

   a $\frac{1}{2}$ **b** $\frac{1}{3}$ **c** $\frac{1}{4}$

3 centre of enlargement C and scale factor

   a $\frac{1}{2}$ **b** $\frac{1}{3}$ **c** $\frac{1}{4}$

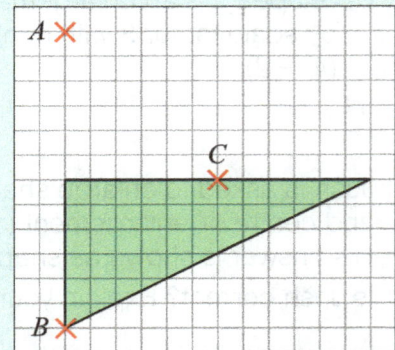

Reflect and reason

Why are all your enlargements smaller than the original shape?
Which answers give shapes with the same length sides? Explain why.

1 Which shape is an enlargement of shape P with a scale factor -2 and a centre of enlargement $(0, 0)$?

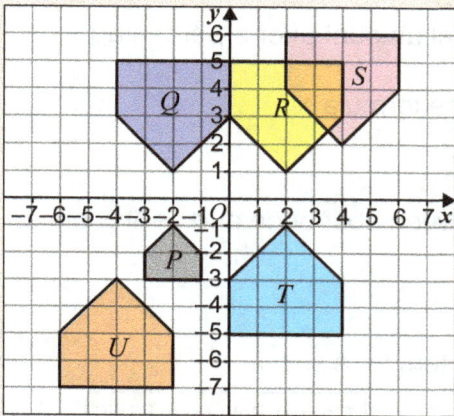

2 Use the diagram to copy and complete each sentence.

   a Shape A is an enlargement of shape B by scale factor ☐ with centre of enlargement (☐, ☐).

   b Shape C is an enlargement of shape A by scale factor ☐ with centre of enlargement (☐, ☐).

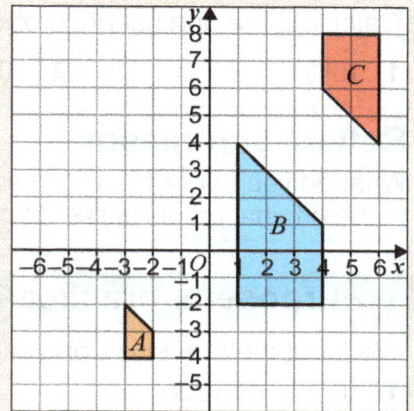

3 Georgia is asked to enlarge shape X by scale factor $\frac{1}{2}$ using the centre of enlargement $(4, 3)$.
   Her answer is shown in the diagram.
   Is Georgia correct? Explain your answer.

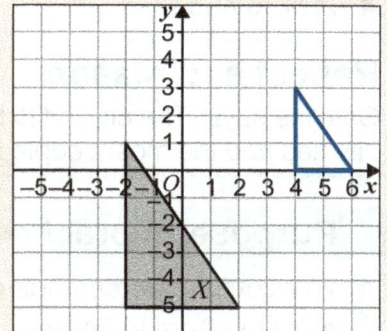

4 Joe says, 'The transformation that maps triangle A onto triangle B is an enlargement by scale factor -2, centre of enlargement $(0, 0)$.'
   Joe is incorrect.
   What two mistakes has Joe made?

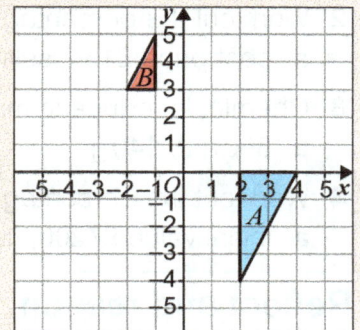

Key points

- You can use inverse operations to find the original amount after a percentage increase or decrease.
- You can calculate a percentage change using the formula

$$\text{percentage change} = \frac{\text{actual change}}{\text{original amount}} \times 100$$

- Percentage profit is the percentage change between cost price and selling price.

▲ Purposeful practice 1

A shop is holding a sale. The sale prices on some items are shown.

| Coat: Sale price £90 | | Jeans: Sale price £54 | | T-shirt: Sale price £3.60 |

Calculate the original price of each item if everything has been discounted by

1 10%   **2** 20%   **3** 40%   **4** 55%

Reflect and reason

What do you notice about the original prices of the coat, jeans and T-shirt in **Q1** compared to the original prices in **Q2**? Explain your answer (using maths).

▲ Purposeful practice 2

Work out the previous population of a city if, since then, it has increased by

1 10% to 486 200   **2** 15% to 920 115   **3** 20% to 800 790

4 22% to 483 974   **5** 28% to 353 920   **6** 5% to 705 600

Reflect and reason

Caroline says, 'The city in **Q5** has increased by the largest percentage. This means that this city has had the most people moving there in the given period.' Is she correct? Explain.

▲ Purposeful practice 3

1 Work out the percentage change in the growth of a plant
   a from 40 cm to 54 cm   **b** from 128 cm to 160 cm

2 Work out the percentage profit made on an item with
   a cost price £154, selling price £231   **b** cost price £63.50, selling price £88.90

3 Chemicals reduce in mass during a reaction. Work out the percentage change from
   a 560 g to 140 g   **b** 400 g to 280 g

4 Work out the percentage loss made on an investment with
   a initial value £7200, final value £6300   **b** initial value £2000, final value £1900

Reflect and reason

Ali says, 'I always divide by the bigger number when working out percentage change.' Is this a good method? Explain your answer.

1 A car dealer sells a car for £21 390.
This is 15% more than the car dealer paid for the car.

   a Which is the correct function machine to work out how much the car dealer paid for the car?

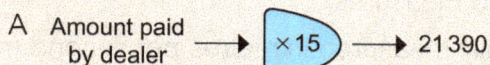

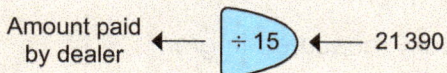

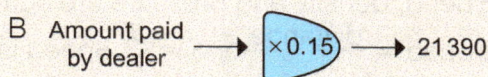

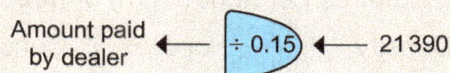

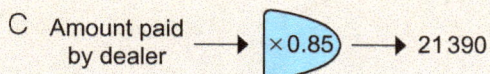

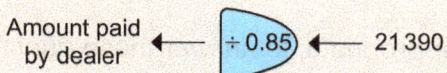

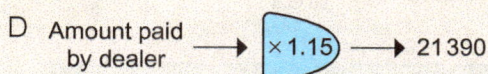

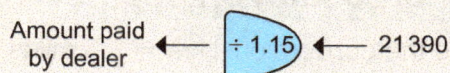

     A   Amount paid by dealer → ×15 → 21390

          Amount paid by dealer ← ÷15 ← 21390

     B   Amount paid by dealer → ×0.15 → 21390

          Amount paid by dealer ← ÷0.15 ← 21390

     C   Amount paid by dealer → ×0.85 → 21390

          Amount paid by dealer ← ÷0.85 ← 21390

     D   Amount paid by dealer → ×1.15 → 21390

          Amount paid by dealer ← ÷1.15 ← 21390

   b How much did the car dealer pay for the car?

2 Alesha's wage increased by 5% over the last year.
Alesha now gets paid £10.08 per hour.
What was Alesha's wage last year?

3 Karl buys a TV that is reduced by 25% in a sale. He pays £420 for the TV.

   a What was the original price of the TV?

   Chris pays £580 for a TV that was discounted by 20%.

   b Who saved the most money in buying a TV and how much more did they save?

4 During a 10 year period, the number of people living in Town A increased by 5% to 22 890.
In the same period, the number of people living in Town B increased by 8% to 14 688.
In which town was the actual increase (i.e. number of people) the largest?

5 Kalini buys a multipack containing 6 bags of crisps. The multipack costs £1.75.
Kalini sells the 6 bags of crisps for 50p each.
Work out Kalini's percentage profit, giving your answer correct to 1 decimal place.

6 Sean buys and sells antiques.
He aims to make at least 30% profit on each antique he sells.
On Monday, Sean buys an antique for £380.
On Tuesday, he sells the antique for £500.
Show that Sean reached his profit target for this antique.

7 Sanjit is asked to work out the percentage profit made on an item bought for £236 and sold for £295.
Sanjit writes

$$\frac{236}{295} \times 100 = 80\%$$

Sanjit is incorrect.

   a What two mistakes has Sanjit made?

   b What is the actual percentage profit?

Key points

- Compound measures combine measures of two different quantities.
- Speed, density and pressure are compound measures.
- Speed = $\frac{\text{distance}}{\text{time}}$ or $S = \frac{d}{t}$. Speed is usually measured in metres per second (m/s), kilometres per hour (km/h) or miles per hour (mph).
- Density = $\frac{\text{mass}}{\text{volume}}$ or $D = \frac{m}{V}$. Density is usually measured in g/cm^3.
- Pressure = $\frac{\text{force}}{\text{area}}$ or $P = \frac{F}{A}$. Pressure is usually measured in N/m^2.

Purposeful practice 1

Use the conversion 1 km = 1.6 miles, where appropriate, to answer these questions.

1 Convert 20 m/s into
  a m/min (metres per minute)   b m/hour (metres per hour)
  c km/h (kilometres per hour)   d mph (miles per hour)

2 Convert 72 mph into
  a km/h (kilometres per hour)   b m/hour (metres per hour)
  c m/min (metres per minute)   d m/s (metres per second)

3 Work out the average speed, in km/h, for a distance of 240 km covered by a
  a train in 2 hours   b car in 4 hours
  c cyclist in 16 hours   d plane in 15 minutes

4 Work out the distance, in km, for a car travelling at an average speed of 45 km/h for
  a 2 hours   b 4 hours   c 16 hours   d 15 minutes

5 Work out the time taken, in hours, by a long distance runner running at an average speed of 12 km/h, for a distance of
  a 12 km   b 24 km   c 30 km   d 6 km

Reflect and reason

How do you know when to divide and when to multiply when using the formula connecting speed, distance and time?

Purposeful practice 2

1 Work out the density, in g/cm^3, of each metal or alloy with volume 2 cm^3.
  a tin, mass = 14.6 g   b zinc, mass = 14.26 g
  c brass, mass = 17.5 g   d nickel, mass = 17.78 g

2 Work out the mass, in g, of each metal or alloy with volume 2 cm^3.
  a iron, density = 7.2 g/cm^3 b lead, density = 11.33 g/cm^3
  c bronze, density = 8.8 g/cm^3 d copper, density = 8.94 g/cm^3

3 Work out the volume, in cm^3, of
  a aluminium with density 2.71 g/cm^3 and mass 10.84 g
  b silver with density 10.49 g/cm^3 and mass 31.47 g

4 Work out the pressure, in N/m², of a force on an area 4 m² that is

   a 20 N   **b** 36 N   **c** 52 N   **d** 120 N

5 Work out the force, in N, on an area 6 m² when the pressure is

   a 7 N/m²   **b** 12 N/m²   **c** 15 N/m²   **d** 21 N/m²

Reflect and reason

How can you use the units of measure for density (g/cm³) and pressure (N/m²) to help you to remember the formulae for density and pressure?

(Did you know 'per' in maths can mean divide?)

Problem-solving practice

1 Which speed is faster, 360 km/h or 105 m/s? Show your working.

2 2 cm³ of gold has a mass of 38.64 g. 2 cm³ of platinum has a mass of 42.9 g.
Which metal has the greater density? Show your working.

3 Silver has a density of 10.49 g/cm³.
Javid has a piece of silver with mass 41.96 g.
Moira has a piece of silver with volume 3.5 cm³.
Whose piece of silver has the greater mass? Show your working.

4 The diagram shows a solid iron cuboid. Iron has a density of 7.87 g/cm³.
Work out the mass of the iron cuboid.

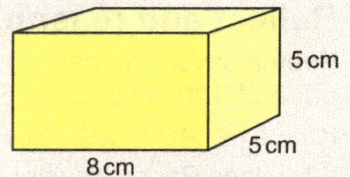

5 Will and Silas are asked to work out the average speed, in km/h, for a 5 km run that takes 30 minutes.
Will writes

$$Speed = \frac{distance}{time} = \frac{5}{30} = 0.17 \text{ km/h (to 2 d.p.)}$$

Silas writes

$$Speed = \frac{distance}{time} = \frac{5000}{0.5} = 10\,000 \text{ km/h}$$

   a Both Will and Silas are wrong. Explain why.

   b What is the average speed?

6 Clare leaves for work at 8 am. She travels 36 miles at an average speed of 45 mph.
Darren leaves for work at 8.15 am. He travels 20 miles at an average speed of 30 mph.
Who gets to work first? Show your working.

7 Sophie travels from Birmingham to Manchester, then to Hull.
The total distance is 203 miles.
Sophie takes 1 hour and 33 minutes to travel from Birmingham to Manchester.
It takes her 1 hour and 57 minutes to travel from Manchester to Hull.
What is Sophie's average speed across the entire journey?

8 Seth is driving on a road with a speed limit of 60 mph.
He drives on the road at this speed limit for 42 miles.
The speed limit then drops to 40 mph.
Seth then drives at this speed for a further 12 miles.
How long does the total journey take?

Key points

- You can use direct proportion to work out the best value for money.
- When the quantities are in inverse proportion, as one increases, the other decreases at the same rate. This means that when one doubles, the other halves; when one triples, the other is divided by 3; and so on.

Purposeful practice 1

A newsagent sells A4 envelopes in different size packs.

Pack A	Pack B	Pack C	Pack D	Pack E
5 envelopes	20 envelopes	25 envelopes	50 envelopes	100 envelopes
£1.40	£4.80	£7.50	£10.50	£22

1 Work out the price of one envelope in
  a Pack A   **b** Pack B   **c** Pack C   **d** Pack D   **e** Pack E

2 Which pack is
  a the best value for money   **b** the worst value for money?

Reflect and reason

Reema says, 'You can work out the best and worst value for money by working out the price of 100 envelopes.' She writes

Pack A: £1.40 × 20, Pack B: £4.80 × 5, Pack C: £7.50 × 4, Pack D: £10.50 × 2

Why does Reema multiply by 20, 5, 4 and 2?

Which method do you prefer, working out the price of one envelope or 100 envelopes? Explain your answer.

Purposeful practice 2

A supermarket sells kitchen rolls with different numbers of sheets, and in differently sized packs.

Pack A	Pack B	Pack C
A pack of 2 kitchen rolls each with 150 sheets	A pack of 4 kitchen rolls each with 200 sheets	A pack of 6 kitchen rolls each with 100 sheets
£3.60	£8.80	£7.80

1 Work out the price of one kitchen roll in
  a Pack A   **b** Pack B   **c** Pack C

2 Work out the price of 50 sheets in
  a Pack A   **b** Pack B   **c** Pack C

3 Which pack is
  a the best value for money   **b** the worst value for money?

Reflect and reason

Why do you think **Q2** asked you to work out the price of 50 sheets and not 1 sheet?

1 2 builders can build a wall in 4 days. How long would it take
  a 1 builder   **b** 4 builders   **c** 8 builders?

2 **a** 4 decorators can paint all the Year 9 classrooms in 6 days. How long would it take
    i 2 decorators   **ii** 8 decorators   **iii** 6 decorators?

  b There are 6 Year 9 classrooms. The decorators are asked to paint an additional 3 Year 10 classrooms. Assuming each classroom takes the same time to paint, how long would it take to paint all Year 9 and Year 10 classrooms if there are
    i 4 decorators   **ii** 2 decorators   **iii** 3 decorators?

Reflect and reason

How do you know when to multiply and when to divide when working out inverse proportion problems like those in Purposeful practice 3?

⊠ Problem-solving practice

1 Milk is sold in three sizes of bottle.
A 2-pint bottle of milk costs £0.80.
A 4-pint bottle of milk costs £1.12.
A 6-pint bottle of milk costs £1.50.
Which bottle of milk is the best value for money? You must show your working.

2 Paperclips are sold in tubs.
A small tub has 200 paperclips and costs £2.71.
A large tub has 1000 paperclips and costs £9.99.
Which tub of paperclips is better value for money?
You must show your working.

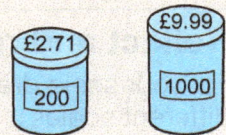

3 Washing powder is sold in three box sizes.
A 1.5 kg box of washing powder costs £2.40.
A 2.9 kg box of washing powder costs £3.77.
A 4.5 kg box of washing powder costs £5.94.
Which size box is the best value for money?
You must show all your working.

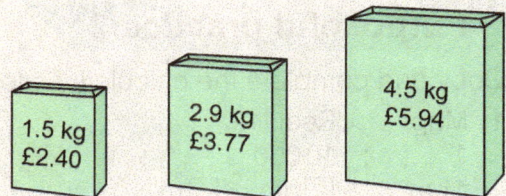

4 Tea bags are sold in three box sizes.
A small box of 30 tea bags costs £1.20.
A medium box of 80 tea bags costs £2.64.
A large box of 240 tea bags costs £8.16.
Which size box is the best value for money?
You must show all your working.

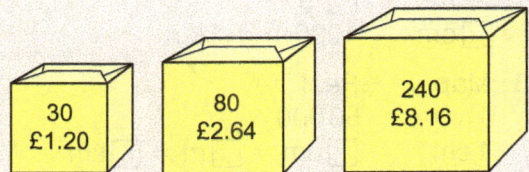

5 A supermarket sells lemonade in 2-litre bottles and 330 ml cans.
A multipack of 4 bottles of lemonade costs £2.60.
A multipack of 6 cans of lemonade costs £1.65.
Which is the better value for money? You must show all your working.

6 It takes 3 people 6 hours to dig a hole.
James says, 'It will take 6 people 12 hours to dig another hole of the same size.'
Is James correct? Explain why.

7 It takes 2 shredders 30 minutes to shred 96 metres of paper.
How long will it take 5 shredders to shred 96 metres of paper?

5 Constructions

5.1 Using scales

△ Purposeful practice 1

1 Here is a rectangle.

Make an accurate scale drawing of this rectangle on centimetre squared paper, using a scale of

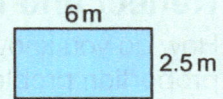

a 1 cm to 1 m   **b** 1 cm to 2 m   **c** 1 : 50

6 m / 2.5 m

2 Here is the plan for the stage at a festival.

Make accurate scale drawings of this plan on centimetre squared paper, using a scale of

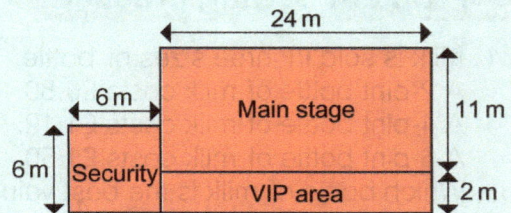

a 1 cm to 2 m
b 1 cm to 4 m
c 1 : 100

24 m, 6 m, Main stage, 11 m, 6 m, Security, 6 m, VIP area, 2 m

Reflect and reason

For your scale drawings in **Q1** and **Q2**, list the advantages and disadvantages of using different scales.

△ Purposeful practice 2

Copy and complete the calculations for each map scale.

1

Map		Real life
1	:	10 000
1 cm		□ cm = □ m
3 cm		□ m
□ cm		1000 m = 1 km

2

Map		Real life
1	:	20 000
1 cm		□ cm = □ m
3 cm		□ m
□ cm		1000 m = 1 km

3

Map		Real life
1	:	50 000
1 cm		□ cm = □ m = □ km
3 cm		□ km
□ cm		1 km

4

Map		Real life
1	:	100 000
1 cm		□ cm = □ m = □ km
3 cm		□ km
□ cm		5 km

Reflect and reason

For **Q3** Dershna works out

$$\times 3 \begin{pmatrix} \text{Map} & & \text{Real life} \\ 1\,\text{cm} & \text{is} & 50\,000\,\text{cm} \\ 3\,\text{cm} & \text{is} & 150\,000\,\text{cm} \end{pmatrix} \times 3$$

$$150\,000\,\text{cm} \div 100 = 1500\,\text{m}$$
$$1500\,\text{m} \div 1000 = 1.5\,\text{km}$$

Look at how you worked out what 3 cm represents in **Q3**. Which method do you prefer? Explain why.

1 The length of a car is 3.2 metres.
   Jed makes a scale model of the car.
   He uses a scale of 1 cm to 40 cm.
   Work out the length of the scale model of the car. Give your answer in centimetres.

2 The dimensions of the downstairs rooms in Brooke's house are
   kitchen: 3 m by 3.5 m
   hall: 1.5 m by 3 m
   living room: 5 m by 4.5 m

   A scale diagram is drawn on centimetre squared paper as shown.

   a The scale diagram is incorrect. Explain why.
   b Draw a correct scale diagram on centimetre squared paper.

   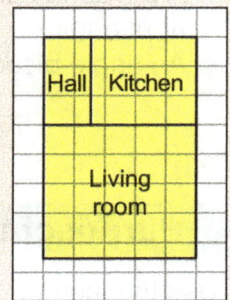

   Scale 1 : 50

3 This section of a map has a scale of 1 : 500 000.
   What is the total distance if you travel in a straight line from Town A to Town B, and then return to Town A?

   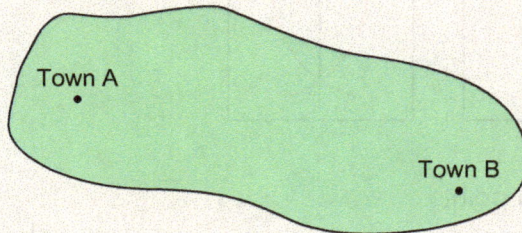

4 The city map shown uses a scale of 1 cm to 500 m.
   Use the map to measure as accurately as possible the real distance (in a straight line) in metres between
   a the aquarium and the museum
   b the football stadium and the museum
   c the university and the aquarium

   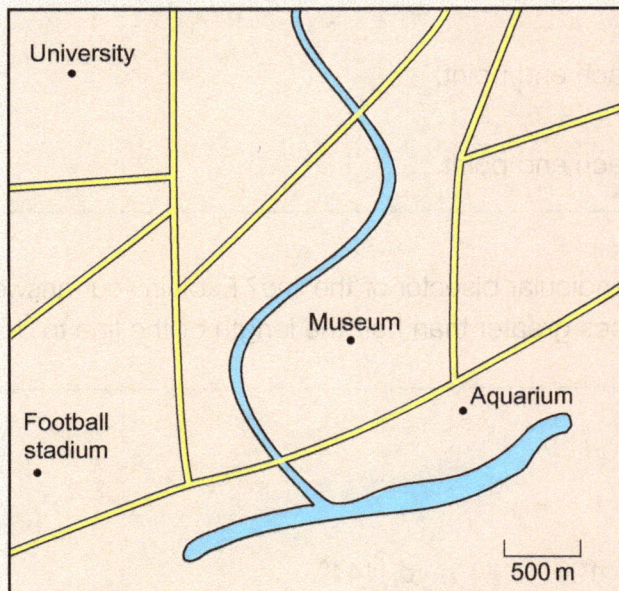

   500 m

Key points

- Construct means draw accurately using a ruler and compasses.
- A perpendicular bisector is a line that cuts another line in half at right angles.
- An angle bisector cuts an angle in half.

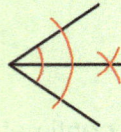

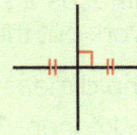

Purposeful practice 1

Use the method shown to complete each question.

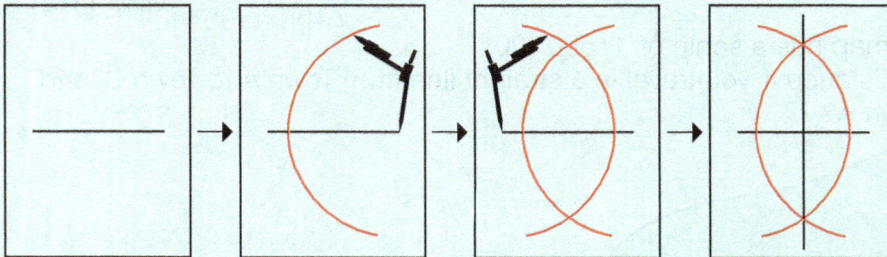

1 a Draw a straight line 10 cm long.
   b Draw arcs of radius 8 cm from each end point.
   c Draw the perpendicular bisector of the line.

2 a Draw a straight line 10 cm long.
   b Draw arcs of radius 7 cm from each end point.
   c Draw the perpendicular bisector of the line.

3 a Draw a straight line 10 cm long.
   b Draw arcs of radius 6 cm from each end point.
   c Draw the perpendicular bisector of the line.

4 a Draw a straight line 10 cm long.
   b Draw arcs of radius 5 cm from each end point.

5 a Draw a straight line 10 cm long.
   b Draw arcs of radius 4 cm from each end point.

Reflect and reason

In **Q4** and **Q5** could you draw the perpendicular bisector of the line? Explain your answer.

Why do you need to open the compasses greater than half the length of the line to draw a perpendicular bisector?

Purposeful practice 2

1 Draw each angle with a protractor.
   Construct its angle bisector.

   a 40°   **b** 65°   **c** 120°   **d** 144°

2 a Draw an angle of 100° with a protractor. Draw the arms of the angle 6 cm long.

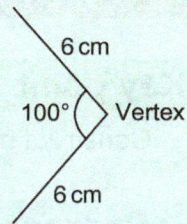

6 cm

100° Vertex

6 cm

  b Draw arcs of radius 4 cm to construct the angle bisector.

3 Repeat **Q2** but use arcs of radius 5 cm to construct the angle bisector.

4 Repeat **Q2** but draw the first pair of arcs with radius 5 cm, and the second pair of arcs with radius 4 cm, to construct the angle bisector.

5 Repeat **Q2**, but draw each arc with a different radius. Does this construct the angle bisector?

Reflect and reason

Does it matter what length arcs you draw to construct an angle bisector? Use your diagrams from Purposeful practice 2 to explain your answer.

⬚ Problem-solving practice

1 Sara and Felix are asked to bisect the line AB.

Sara draws

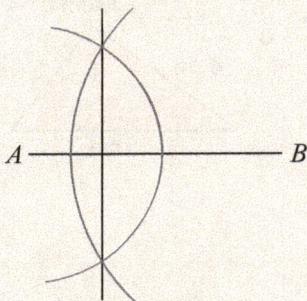

Felix draws

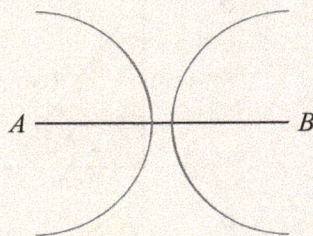

  a Is Sara correct? Explain why.
  b Is Felix correct? Explain why.

2 Eva is asked to bisect the angle. Eva draws the diagram shown.
Eva's diagram is incorrect. Explain why.

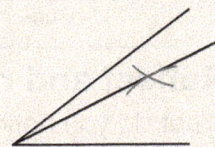

3 a Draw a straight line 8 cm long.
  b Construct the perpendicular bisector to form a right angle.
  c Construct the angle bisector of one of the right angles.
  d Without using a protractor, what is the size of the two angles you have created in part **c**?

4 a Copy or trace the triangle.
  b Find the point S where the perpendicular bisector of line PQ intersects the bisector of angle PRQ.

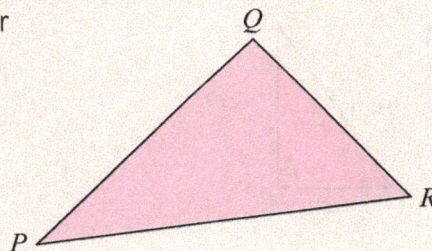

Q

R

P

Key point

• Construct means draw accurately using a ruler and compasses.

△ Purposeful practice 1

Construct these triangles accurately.

1 a 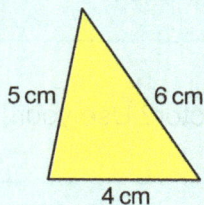 **b** 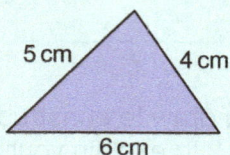 **c**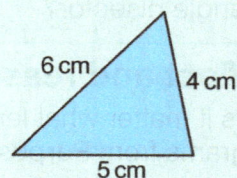

2 a 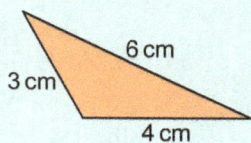 **b** 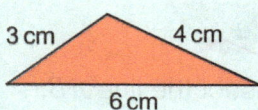 **c**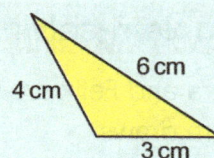

3 a 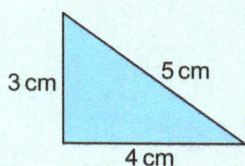 **b** 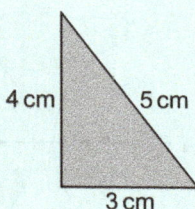 **c**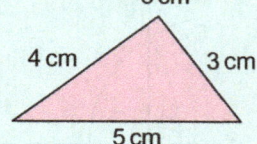

4 a 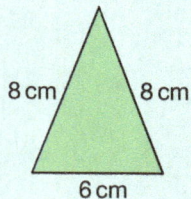 **b**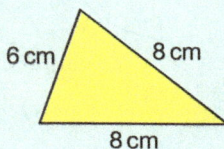

Reflect and reason

What do you notice about all the triangles you constructed in **Q1**?

Do you get the same result for the other questions?

Does it matter which side you choose for the base when you construct a triangle using the measurements of its sides? Explain your answer.

△ Purposeful practice 2

Construct these right-angled triangles accurately.

1 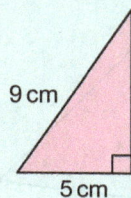 **2**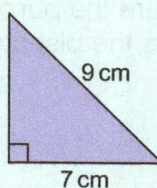

3

6 cm   9 cm

4

6 cm
11 cm

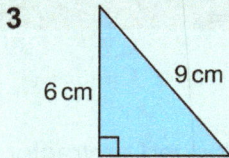

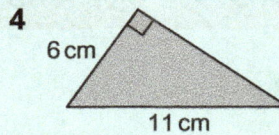

Reflect and reason

In Purposeful practice 2, which triangles did you have to 'rotate' before you could construct them?

To construct right-angled triangles, does it matter which side you choose for the base? Explain your answer.

Problem-solving practice

1 Construct a triangle with the given sides, and state whether it is scalene, isosceles or right-angled.

   a 5 cm, 6 cm and 7 cm

   b 7 cm, 6 cm and 6 cm

2 Construct an equilateral triangle with sides of length 5 cm.

3 A pyramid with a square base is shown.
The sloping faces are identical isosceles triangles.
Construct an accurate drawing of one of the triangular sloping faces of the pyramid.

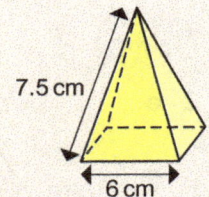

7.5 cm

6 cm

4 Sofia is asked to construct a triangle with sides 10 cm, 11 cm and 12 cm.
Sofia says, 'I will need to set my compasses up three times, first to 10 cm, then to 11 cm and finally to 12 cm.'
Is Sofia correct? Explain.

5 Alex is asked to construct the triangle shown accurately.
Alex starts his construction like this:

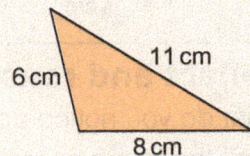

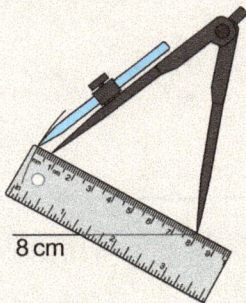

11 cm
6 cm
8 cm

8 cm

   a Alex is incorrect. Explain why.
   b Construct the triangle correctly.

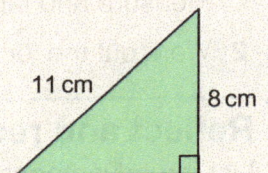

6 Explain why a triangle cannot be constructed with sides 4 cm, 6 cm and 12 cm.

7 Millie is asked to construct the right-angled triangle shown.
Millie starts by drawing a horizontal line 8 cm long.
She then sets her compasses to 11 cm to draw an arc.

   a Millie is incorrect. Explain why.
   b Construct the triangle correctly.

11 cm
8 cm

Key point

- Accurate drawings are drawn to scale with accurate angles. Use a ruler and protractor to make accurate drawings.

△ Purposeful practice 1

Make accurate drawings of these triangles.
Measure and label all the sides and angles.

1 a 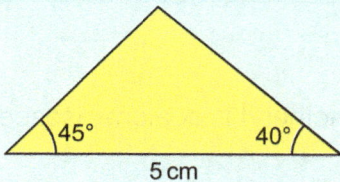   **b** 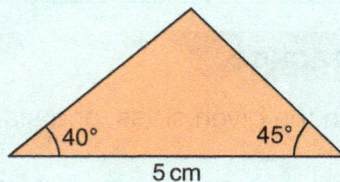   **c**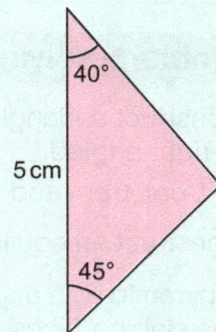

2 a 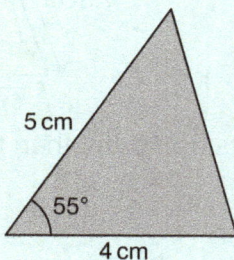   **b** 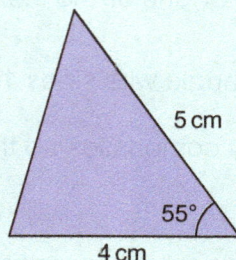   **c**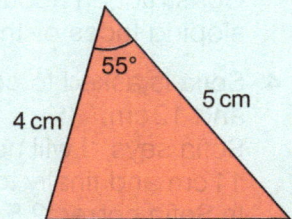

Reflect and reason

What do you notice about
    all the triangles you drew in **Q1**
    all the triangles you drew in **Q2**?
Does it matter which side you choose for the base?

△ Purposeful practice 2

1 Construct an accurate drawing of this triangle using a scale of
  a 1 : 5
  b 1 : 10
  c 1 : 20
Measure and label the sides and angles in your scale drawings.

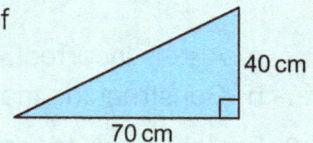

2 Work out the length of the third side in real life.

Reflect and reason

List the advantages and disadvantages of using each scale in **Q1**.

1 Here is a pyramid with a square base.
The sloping faces are identical isosceles triangles.

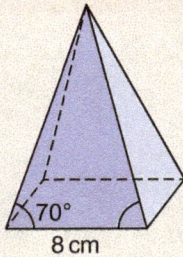

70°
8 cm

  a Construct an accurate drawing of one of the triangular sloping faces of the pyramid.

  b Oliver makes the outline of this pyramid using metal rods.
    What is the total length of the rods that he uses?

2 Draw triangle ABC when $AB = 6\,cm$, $AC = 7\,cm$ and angle $BAC = 50°$.

3 Jade is asked to draw this triangle accurately.

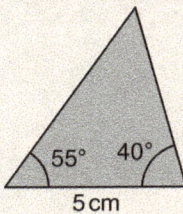

55° 40°
5 cm

Jade starts her drawing like this:

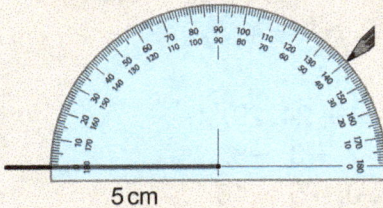

5 cm

  a Jade is incorrect. Explain why.

  b Draw the triangle correctly.

4 A sketch of the side view of a frame for swings is shown.
The triangle in the top part of the frame is an equilateral triangle.

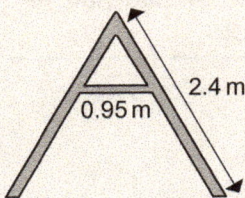

2.4 m
0.95 m

  a Jake is making a wire model of the swing. Construct an accurate scale drawing of the side view of the frame using an appropriate scale.

  b Jake says, 'I already know the distance on the ground between the two feet of the frame, without making any measurements or calculations.'
    Explain how Jake knows this, and state the distance between the two feet.

6.1 *n*th term of arithmetic sequences

Key points

- To find the *n*th term of an arithmetic sequence,
  1. find the common difference
  2. if the common difference is 3, compare with the sequence for $3n$
     if the common difference is 4, compare with the sequence for $4n$
     …and so on.

◬ Purposeful practice 1

1 Write the first five terms of the sequence with *n*th term

   a $2n$ **b** $-2n$ **c** $2n - 1$ **d** $2n + 3$

   e $2n + 10$ **f** $-2n + 1$ **g** $-2n + 2$ **h** $-2n + 7$

2 Find the *n*th term of each sequence.

   a $3, 5, 7, 9, 11, \ldots$ **b** $0, 2, 4, 6, 8, \ldots$

   c $-3, -5, -7, -9, -11, \ldots$ **d** $2, 0, -2, -4, -6, \ldots$

   e $6, 4, 2, 0, -2, \ldots$ **f** $5, 3, 1, -1, -3, \ldots$

3 Find the *n*th term of each sequence.

   a $3, 6, 9, 12, 15, \ldots$ **b** $-3, -6, -9, -12, -15, \ldots$

   c $4, 7, 10, 13, 16, \ldots$ **d** $-4, -7, -10, -13, -16, \ldots$

   e $-4, -1, 2, 5, 8, \ldots$ **f** $8, 5, 2, -1, -4, \ldots$

4 Find the *n*th term of each sequence.

   a $1, 6, 11, 16, 21, \ldots$ **b** $9, 14, 19, 24, 29, \ldots$

   c $-3, -8, -13, -18, -23, \ldots$ **d** $12, 7, 2, -3, -8, \ldots$

   e $-7, -2, 3, 8, 13, \ldots$ **f** $10, 5, 0, -5, -10, \ldots$

Reflect and reason

The sequence with *n*th term $5n + 8$ is $13, 18, 23, 28, \ldots$

Lewis notices that in this sequence, the ones digit alternates between two values: 3 and 8. Lewis says, 'All sequences with $5n$ in the *n*th term have digits that alternate between two values.' Use your answers to **Q4** to show he is incorrect.

◬ Purposeful practice 2

For each sequence of patterns made from tiles,

a write the sequence of numbers of tiles in the first three patterns

b work out the *n*th term

c find the number of tiles in the 6th pattern   **d** work out which pattern has 37 tiles

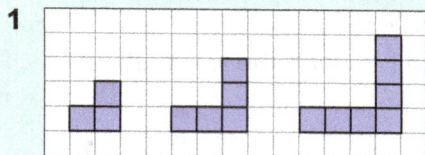

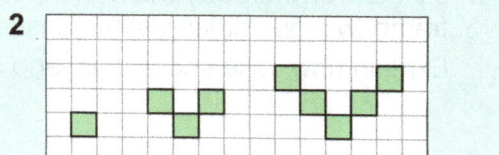

1

2

3

4

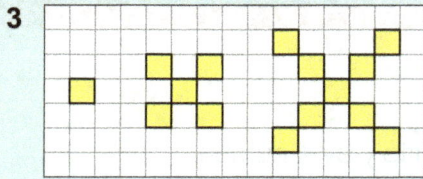

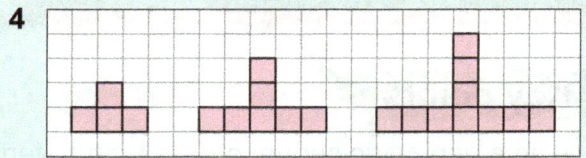

Reflect and reason

For part **c** of each question, Sam draws the first six patterns to find the number of tiles in the 6th pattern. Is this the most efficient method? Explain your answer.

⊠ Problem-solving practice

1 A sequence of patterns is made from triangular tiles and square tiles.
The first three patterns in the sequence are shown.
Tom says, 'When the pattern number is odd, an odd number of square tiles are needed to make the pattern.'
Is Tom right? Explain your answer.

Pattern number 1   Pattern number 2   Pattern number 3

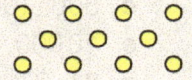

2 Here is a sequence of patterns made with counters.

a Find an expression, in terms of n, for the number of counters in pattern number n.

b Priya has 50 counters.
Which pattern number can she make in order to use as many of her counters as possible?

Pattern number 1   Pattern number 2   Pattern number 3

3 The first four terms of a number sequence are shown.
5, 9, 13, 17, …

a Work out the difference between the 10th term and the 15th term in the sequence.

The 50th term of this number sequence is 201.

b Write the 51st term of this sequence.

4 The first four terms of an arithmetic sequence are shown.
3, 7, 11, 15, …
Is 121 a term of this arithmetic sequence? Explain your answer.

5 Here is a sequence of patterns made with white squares and grey rectangles.
Brodie says, 'There is a pattern in this sequence with exactly 60 white squares.'

Pattern number 1   Pattern number 2   Pattern number 3

a Is Brodie right? Explain your answer.

A pattern in the sequence has exactly 20 grey rectangles.

b How many white squares does this pattern have?

6 A sequence of rectangles is made up of squares.
Each square has a perimeter of 12 cm.
Find an expression for the perimeter, in centimetres, of rectangle n.

Rectangle 1   Rectangle 2   Rectangle 3

Key points

- In a geometric sequence, the term-to-term rule is 'multiply by a number'.
- In an arithmetic or linear sequence, the term-to-term rule is 'add (or subtract) a number.'

△ Purposeful practice 1

1 Generate the first four terms of each sequence.

   a 1st term 1, term-to-term rule × 4   **b** 1st term 2, term-to-term rule × 4

   c 1st term 64, term-to-term rule ÷ 4   **d** 1st term 64, term-to-term rule × $\frac{1}{4}$

   e 1st term 64, term-to-term rule ÷ 2   **f** 1st term 64, term-to-term rule × $\frac{1}{2}$

   g 1st term 7, term-to-term rule × 2   **h** 1st term 0, term-to-term rule × 2

2 Work out the term-to-term rule for each sequence.

   a 0, 5, 10, 15, …   **b** 1, 5, 25, 125, …

   c 500, 100, 20, 4, …   **d** 25, 20, 15, 10, …

   e 10000, 1000, 100, 10, …   **f** 10000, 1000, −8000, −17000, …

   g 81, 27, 9, 3, …   **h** 0, 3, 6, 9, …

3 **a** Which sequences in **Q2** are linear?

   b Which sequences in **Q2** are geometric?

Reflect and reason

Rae says, 'The sequence 16, 8, 4, 2, … is not geometric because the term-to-term rule is divide by 2.' Explain why Rae is incorrect.

△ Purposeful practice 2

1 Generate the first four terms of each sequence.

   a 1st term 1, term-to-term rule × −1   **b** 1st term 1, term-to-term rule × −2

   c 1st term 16, term-to-term rule × $-\frac{1}{2}$ **d** 1st term −16, term-to-term rule × $-\frac{1}{2}$

   e 1st term −1, term-to-term rule × 5   **f** 1st term −1, term-to-term rule × −5

   g 1st term 500, term-to-term rule × $-\frac{1}{5}$ **h** 1st term −500, term-to-term rule × $\frac{1}{5}$

2 For each sequence,

   i write the next term   **ii** find the term-to-term rule

   a 3, −3, 3, −3, …   **b** −7, 7, −7, 7, …

   c 1, 3, 9, 27, …   **d** 1, −3, 9, −27, …

   e −1, 3, −9, 27, …   **f** −1, −3, −9, −27, …

   g −2000, 1000, −500, 250, …   **h** −2000, −1000, −500, −250, …

   i 2000, −1000, 500, −250, …   **j** 2000, 1000, 500, 250, …

Reflect and reason

How can you tell whether a geometric sequence has term-to-term rule 'multiply by a negative number'? Use examples from Purposeful practice 2 to explain.

1 Look at the sequence 1, 2, 4, 8, 16, ...
Cara says, 'The term-to-term rule for this sequence is + 1 because 1 + 1 = 2.'
  a Cara is incorrect. Explain why.
  b What is the term-to-term rule for the sequence?

2 Amil is asked to write the term-to-term rule for the sequence −3, −6, −12, −24, −48.
Amil writes
Term-to-term rule = × −2
Is Amil correct? Explain.

3 Emily is asked to generate the first five terms of the sequence with 1st term 64 and
term-to-term rule × $-\frac{1}{2}$. Emily writes
64, −32, −16, −8, −4
Is Emily correct? Explain.

4 The first four terms of a sequence are 1, 5, 25, 125.
Is 1500 in the sequence? Explain how you know.

5 The term-to-term rule of a sequence is × −3. The first term of the sequence is 1.
  a What is the fourth term of the sequence?
  b Which term in the sequence is −243?

6 The first five terms of a sequence are 1, 3, 9, 27, 81.
What is the difference between the 6th and 8th terms of the sequence?

7 The first five terms of a sequence are 96, 48, 24, 12, 6.
Write the first term in the sequence that is less than 1.

8 The 1st term of a sequence is 1, and the term-to-term rule is × −5.
What term in the sequence is closest to 2000?

9 Here are the first five terms of some geometrical sequences.
Copy and complete the missing values.
  a ☐, ☐, 100, 50, 25   **b** 1, ☐, 25, 125, ☐
  c ☐, 250, −50, 10, ☐   **d** ☐, 12, 48, ☐, 768

10 The first five terms of a sequence are 100, 50, 25, 12.5, 6.25.
Will any of the terms in the sequence be negative? Explain why.

11 The first term of a geometric sequence is 1.
The fourth term of the geometric sequence is 1000.
What is the term-to-term rule of the sequence?

12 Write a first term and a term-to-term rule for a geometric sequence that includes the
term 20 and is
  a an ascending sequence of positive numbers with all first five terms less than 100
  b a descending sequence
  c a sequence that includes both positive and negative numbers

13 Louis opens a savings account.
Louis starts by saving £10 in the first month he opens the savings account.
He is then going to double how much he saves each month until he is saving over
£500 per month. After this, he will continue to put the same amount in each month.
  a In which month will Louis first save over £500?
  b How much will he save in the first year of opening the savings account?

Key points

- $<$ means less than $>$ means greater than
  $\leq$ means less than or equal to $\geq$ means greater than or equal to
- You can show inequalities on a number line.
  An empty circle $\circ$ shows that the value is not included.
  A filled circle $\bullet$ shows that the value is included.
  An arrow shows that the values continue towards infinity or negative infinity.

- 'Satisfy' means 'make the statement true'.

Purposeful practice 1

1 Write an inequality for each statement.

  a 3 is less than x.

  b x is less than 3.

  c x is greater than 3.

  d 3 is greater than x.

  e 3 is less than or equal to x.

  f x is greater than or equal to 3.

2 Write an inequality for each statement.

  a x is less than 2 and greater than -1.

  b x is less than or equal to 2 and greater than -1.

  c x is less than 2 and greater than or equal to -1.

  d x is between -1 and 2, excluding 2.

  e x is between -1 and 2, excluding -1.

Reflect and reason

Look at **Q1** and **Q2**. Which words or phrases tell you which sign ($<$, $>$, $\leq$, $\geq$) to write in the inequality?

Purposeful practice 2

1 Draw a number line to represent each inequality.

  a $x > 2$ **b** $x \geq 2$ **c** $x \leq 2$

  d $x < 2$ **e** $x < -2$ **f** $x \geq -2$

2 Draw a number line to represent each inequality and write all the integer values that satisfy it.

  a $0 < x < 3$ **b** $0 < x \leq 3$ **c** $0 \leq x \leq 3$ **d** $0 \leq x < 3$

  e $-1 \leq x < 3$ **f** $1 \leq x < 3$ **g** $1 < x \leq 3$ **h** $-3 < x \leq 3$

  i $-3 \leq x < 1$ **j** $-3 < x \leq 1$ **k** $-3 < x \leq 0$ **l** $-2 \leq x < 0$

3 Write the inequality for each number line. The first one is started for you.

  a

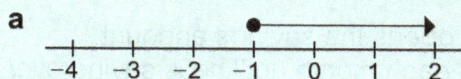

$x \geq \square$

  b

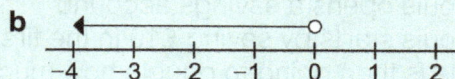

  c

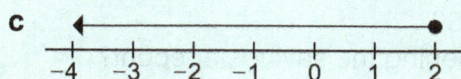

  d

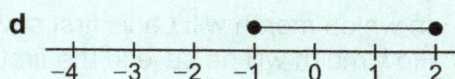

e

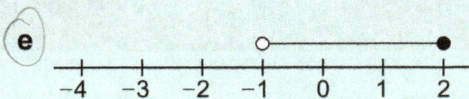

f

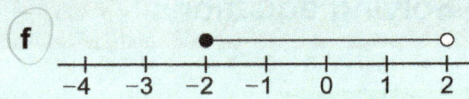

g

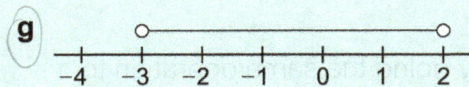

h

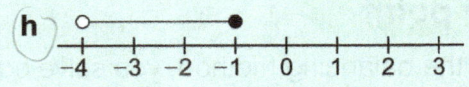

Reflect and reason

Doug says, 'This number line represents $-2 \leqslant x \leqslant -5$.'
Explain why Doug is incorrect.

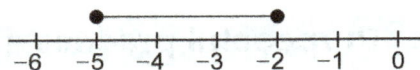

⊠ Problem-solving practice

1 a Match each inequality to the correct statement. One statement is missing.

　i $x \leqslant 2$　**ii** $x \geqslant -2$　**iii** $x \geqslant 2$　**iv** $x > -2$　**v** $x < 2$　**vi** $x \leqslant -2$

　A: x is greater than -2　　　　　B: x is less than or equal to -2
　C: x is greater than or equal to -2　D: x is less than 2
　E: x is less than or equal to 2

b Write a statement for the inequality that has not been used.

2 Jess and Rashid are asked to write the inequality for the number line shown.

Jess writes　　　　　Rashid writes

$-2 < x \leqslant 3$　　　　$-2 \geqslant x > 3$

Jess and Rashid are both incorrect. Explain why.

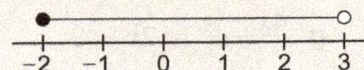

3 Clare thinks of a number.
When 9 is subtracted from her number, the answer is less than 4.

a Write an inequality to show this.

b What is the largest whole number that Clare's number could be?

4 a Draw a number line to represent the inequality $-3 < x < 2$.

b Write all the possible integer values of x.

5 Each number line A–F represents an inequality, using integers only.

A
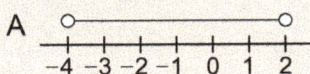
B
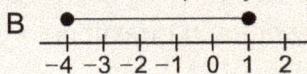
C
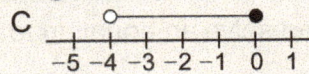

D
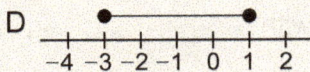
E
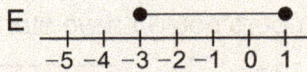
F
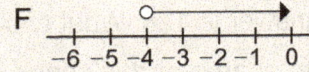

a Which two number lines represent the same inequality?

b Which inequality includes the smallest possible value of x? Explain why.

c Which inequality includes the greatest possible value of x? Explain why.

6 Look at each statement. Assume x can take only integer values.

　A: x is less than 4 and greater than -5.
　B: x is less than or equal to 4 and greater than -5.
　C: x is less than 4 and greater than or equal to -5.
　D: x is between -5 and 4, excluding 4 and -5.

a Which two statements represent the same inequality?

b Which statement includes the smallest possible value of x? Explain why.

c Which statement includes the greatest possible value of x? Explain why.

Key point

- In the balancing method, you solve equations by doing the same operation to both sides.

△ Purposeful practice 1

1 Solve these equations.

a $\dfrac{2x + 5}{3} = 7$

b $\dfrac{2x - 5}{3} = 7$

c $\dfrac{2x - 5}{7} = 3$

d $\dfrac{5 - 2x}{7} = 3$

e $\dfrac{3 - 2x}{7} = 5$

f $\dfrac{3x + 2}{7} = 5$

g $\dfrac{3x - 5}{7} = 2$

h $\dfrac{7 - 3x}{5} = 2$

i $\dfrac{7x - 3}{5} = -1$

2 Solve these equations.

a $\dfrac{2x + 3}{5} = x$

b $\dfrac{2x + 3}{4} = x$

c $\dfrac{2x + 3}{4} = x - 1$

d $\dfrac{5x + 3}{4} = x + 2$

e $\dfrac{5x + 6}{4} = 2x$

f $\dfrac{5x + 6}{4} = 2x + 3$

g $\dfrac{4x - 1}{5} = 2x + 3$

h $\dfrac{4x - 1}{5} = 2x - 1$

i $\dfrac{2x - 1}{4} = 5x - 2$

3 Look back at the equations in **Q1** and **Q2** that have fraction solutions.
For each one, write the fraction as a decimal to 2 decimal places.
Substitute the decimal value into the equation. Does it satisfy the equation?

Reflect and reason

When is it more accurate to give a solution as a fraction rather than converting it to a decimal?

△ Purposeful practice 2

Write and solve an equation to answer each question.

1 I think of a number, square it and add 7.
My answer is 128. What two numbers could I have started with?

2 The total area of this shape is 173 cm². What is length x?

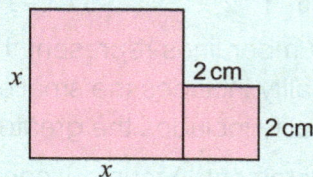

3 Steve worked out his height squared to calculate his BMI.
(height, in m)² = 2.8224
What is Steve's height, in metres?

Reflect and reason

In Purposeful practice 2, which question had a negative and a positive solution?
Which questions had only positive solutions? Explain your answer.

1 Candice is asked to solve the equation $\dfrac{3x-4}{2}=5$
She writes

$$+4\left(\begin{array}{c} \dfrac{3x-4}{2}=5 \\[4pt] \dfrac{3x}{2}=9 \\[4pt] 3x=18 \\[4pt] x=6 \end{array}\right)\begin{array}{l} +4 \\[8pt] \times 2 \\[8pt] \div 3 \end{array}$$

$\times 2$ $\div 3$

a Candice is incorrect. What mistake has she made?

b What is the correct value of x?

2 In the diagram, lines AB and CD are equal in length (cm).

a Show that $5x + 8 = 6x$

b Solve $5x + 8 = 6x$

c Work out the length of AB.

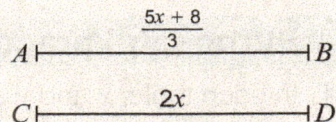

3 Faisal and Jay write the same number.
Faisal multiplies the number by 4, adds 1 and then divides the result by 3.
Jay multiplies the number by 2 and then subtracts 7.
Faisal's answer is the same as Jay's answer.
Work out the number that Faisal and Jay started with.

4 The side lengths of a rectangle are shown in the diagram.

a Work out the length of the rectangle.

b Work out the perimeter of the rectangle.

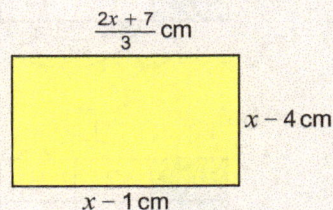

5 Work out the size of each angle in the isosceles triangle.

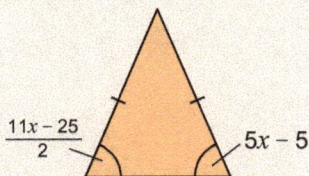

6 I think of a positive number, square it and subtract 5.
The answer is 59.
Taylor is trying to work out my number and writes

$$+5\left(\begin{array}{c} x^2-5=59 \\[4pt] x^2=64 \\[4pt] x=32 \end{array}\right)\begin{array}{l} +5 \\[6pt] \div 2 \end{array}$$

$\div 2$

Taylor is incorrect. Explain why.

7 Kate has a square piece of card with side length x cm.
Kate cuts a smaller square from her card with side length 2 cm.
The area of the card Kate has left is 320 cm².
Work out the length of the square Kate started with.

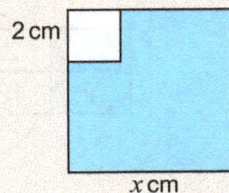

Key points

- For two quantities, x and y, in direct proportion,
  $\frac{y}{x}$ has constant value, k
  the graph of y against x has gradient k
  the relationship between x and y is $y = kx$
- For two quantities, x and y, in inverse proportion,
  xy has constant value k
  the relationship between x and y is $y = \frac{k}{x}$

△ Purposeful practice

1 In each table, x and y are in direct proportion.

  i Use the multiplication patterns to find the missing values in the tables.

  ii Write the formula connecting x and y in the form $y = \ldots$

a

×2 ×3

x	1	2	3	5
y	7	14		

×2 ×3

x	1	2		3	5
y	7	14			

×□ ×□

b

×□

x	2	3	5	7
y	4	6		

×□

x	2	3	5	7
y	4	6		

×□

2 In each table, x and y are in inverse proportion.

  i Use the multiplication patterns to find the missing values.

  ii Write the formula connecting x and y in the form $y = \dfrac{\square}{\square}$

a

×2 ×3

x	1	2	3	5
y	30	15		

÷2 ÷3

x	1	2	3	5
y	30	15		
xy	30	30	30	

b

×2 ×5

x	2	4	10	16
y	16			

÷2 ÷5

x	2	4	10	16
y	16			
xy				

c

×1.5

x	2	3	5	7
y	10.5			

÷☐

x	2	3	5	7
y	10.5			
xy				

Reflect and reason

For the table in **Q2b**, Lou writes

×8

x	2	4	10	16
y	16			

$y = \dfrac{8}{x}$

Explain the mistake Lou has made in finding the constant value k in $y = \dfrac{k}{x}$.

⊠ Problem-solving practice

1 In the table, x and y are in direct proportion.

x	2	4	10	16
y	5	10	25	40

Casey is asked to write a formula connecting x and y.
Casey writes
$y = x + 3$
a Casey is incorrect. Explain why.
b Write the correct formula connecting x and y.

2 y is directly proportional to x.
When $x = 10$, $y = 400$.

a Find a formula for y in terms of x.
b Calculate the value of y when $x = 70$.

3 y is directly proportional to t.
$y = 32$ when $t = 5$.
Work out the value of y when $t = 8$.

4 The price of apples, P, is directly proportional to the mass, m, of apples sold.
The price of 0.6 kg of apples is £1.11.

a Write a formula connecting P and m.
b Work out the price of 2.2 kg of apples.

5 The number of builders it takes to build a house is inversely proportional to the time it takes in days.
A house is built in 14 days by 6 builders.

a Write a formula connecting the number of builders, b, and number of days, d.
b How long would it take 8 builders to build the same house?

6 y is inversely proportional to x.
$y = 36$ when $x = 5$.
Work out the value of y when $x = 8$.

7 Circles, Pythagoras and prisms

7.1 Circumference of a circle

Key points

- The circumference C is the perimeter of a circle. To find the circumference you can use the formula $C = \pi d$ or $C = 2\pi r$. Use the π key on your calculator.
- The Greek letter π (pronounced pi) is a special number, $3.141\,592\,6535\ldots$
- Half a circle is called a semicircle.

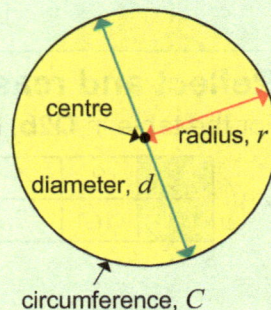

circumference, C

Purposeful practice 1

1 Work out the diameter, in cm, of a circle with radius
   a 3 cm   **b** 3.5 cm   **c** 33 mm   **d** 0.3 m

2 Work out the radius, in cm, of a circle with diameter
   a 8 cm   **b** 9 cm   **c** 98 mm   **d** 8.9 m

Reflect and reason

Copy and complete these formulae connecting diameter (d) and radius (r).

$$d = \square\, r \qquad\qquad r = \frac{d}{\square}$$

Purposeful practice 2

1 Estimate the circumference of a circle with
   a diameter 10 cm   **b** radius 10 cm
   c diameter 12.2 cm   **d** radius 12.2 cm

2 Write the circumference of each circle in **Q1** in terms of π.

3 Use a calculator to work out the circumference of each circle in **Q1**. Give your answers to 2 decimal places.

4 Work out, to the nearest cm, the perimeter of a semicircle with
   a diameter 7 cm   **b** radius 4 cm

Reflect and reason

In **Q1**, how did you work out your estimates? Did you use the same method to estimate the answers for **Q1** parts **a** and **c** as for **Q1** parts **b** and **d**?

Purposeful practice 3

1 Work out, to 2 significant figures, the diameter of a circle with circumference
   a 27 cm   **b** 2.7 m   **c** 270 mm

2 Work out, to 2 significant figures, the radius of a circle with circumference
   a 38 cm   **b** 3.8 m   **c** 380 mm

Reflect and reason

What extra step did you have to take to work out your answers to **Q2** compared to **Q1**? Explain why you needed the extra step.

Problem-solving practice

1 Mark and Zara are asked to work out the circumference of this circle.
    Mark writes   Zara writes
    $C = 6 \times \pi$ $C = 12 \times \pi$
    Who is correct? Explain why.

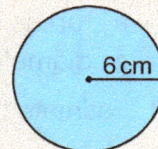
6 cm

2 Which circle A–C will have the largest circumference? Explain your answer without working out the actual circumference of each circle.
    A: a circle with radius 4 cm
    B: a circle with diameter 10 cm
    C: a circle with radius 5.5 cm

3 A circular shaped wedding cake has a diameter of 35 cm.
    A ribbon is going to be wrapped around the side of the wedding cake.
    A 2 cm overlap is needed to glue the ribbon together.
    Ribbons are sold in lengths of 50 cm.
    The ribbon for the wedding cake costs £1.18 per 50 cm.
    How much does the ribbon for the wedding cake cost?
    You must show your working.

4 Seth is rolling a coin in a straight line from one end of a table to the other.
    The diameter of the coin is 2.45 cm.
    The length of the table is 180 cm.
    How many full rotations will the coin complete before reaching the other end of the table?

5 AB is the diameter of the circle.
    Calculate the distance around the circumference from A to B.
    Give your answer to 3 significant figures.

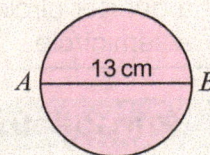
A 13 cm B

6 Tariq walks in a circle with diameter 150 m.
    There are four points equally spaced on the walk.
    Work out the distance Tariq walks between two of the points.
    Give your answer correct to 1 decimal place.

7 A bicycle travels 223.4 cm for each full turn of its wheels.
    Calculate the diameter of the wheel.
    Give your answer correct to 3 significant figures.

8 The circle fits exactly inside the square.
    The area of the square is 49 cm².
    Work out the circumference of the circle.
    Give your answer to 3 significant figures.

7.2 Area of a circle

Key point

- The formula for the area A of a circle with radius r is $A = \pi r^2$.

▲ Purposeful practice 1

1 Work out the area in cm², in terms of π, of a circle with
   a radius 2 cm   b radius 3 cm   c radius 5 cm   d radius 10 cm
   e diameter 2 cm   f diameter 10 cm   g diameter 20 cm   h diameter 1 m

2 Estimate the area of each of the circles in **Q1**. Give your answers in cm².

3 Use a calculator to work out the area of each circle in **Q1**. Give your answers in cm² to 1 decimal place.

Reflect and reason

Li gets the same answer for **Q2** parts **a** and **e**. What mistake has Li made?

▲ Purposeful practice 2

Work out the area of these fractions of circles. Give your answers to a sensible degree of accuracy.

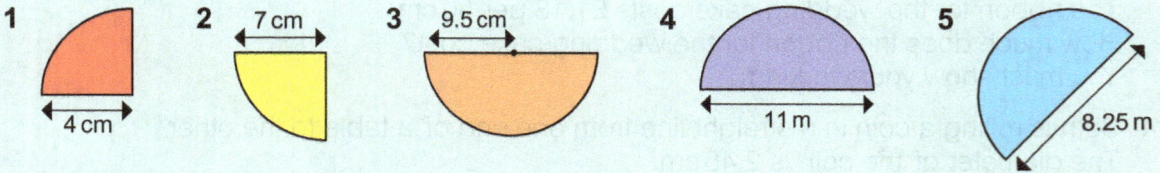

1   4 cm

2   7 cm

3   9.5 cm

4   11 m

5   8.25 m

Reflect and reason

Write the formula for the area of
   a quarter circle
   a semicircle

▲ Purposeful practice 3

1 Giving your answer to a sensible degree of accuracy, work out the radius of a circle with area
   a 100 mm²   b 10 cm²   c 0.1 m²

2 Giving your answer to a sensible degree of accuracy, work out the diameter of a circle with area
   a 200 mm²   b 20 cm²   c 0.2 m²

Reflect and reason

The areas in **Q2** are double the areas in **Q1**.
When the area doubles, does the radius double? Explain your answer.

1 Part of a garden is in the shape of a circle with radius 10 m.
This part of the garden is to be covered with grass seed to make a lawn.
Each box of grass seed covers 35 m² of garden.
How many boxes of grass seed are needed?

2 Work out the shaded area.
Give your answer correct to 1 decimal place.

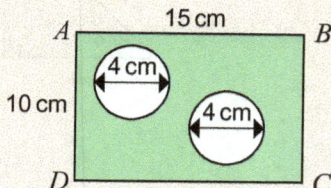

3 Jamie is asked to work out the area of a circle with diameter 7 cm.
Jamie writes

$$A = \pi \times 7^2$$

a Jamie is incorrect. Explain why.

b Calculate the area of the circle, giving your answer correct to 3 significant figures.

4 Farrah draws a circle with radius 8 cm.
She shades 25% of the circle blue.
What area of the circle, in cm², is shaded blue?
Give your answer correct to 3 significant figures.

5 *OABC* is a square.
OAC is a quarter circle.
Calculate the area of the shaded region.
Give your answer correct to 3 significant figures.

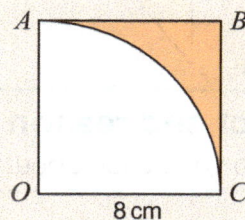

6 The diagram shows a semicircle drawn inside
a rectangle.
Work out the area of the shaded region.
Give your answer correct to 3 significant figures.

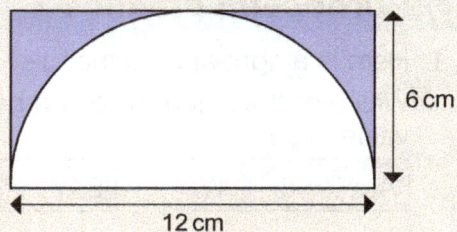

7 The diagram shows two circles.
The centre of both circles is marked with a cross '×'.
Ben says, 'Exactly half of the diagram is shaded.'
Is Ben correct? Show your working to explain.

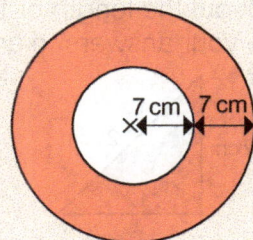

8 A pony is tied with a length of rope to a post in the middle of a field.
The pony can graze a circular area of grass with an area of 1960 m².
How long is the rope?
Give your answer to 1 decimal place.

Key points

- The longest side of a right-angled triangle is called the hypotenuse.
- Pythagoras' theorem shows the relationship between the lengths of the three sides of a right-angled triangle.
  $c^2 = a^2 + b^2$

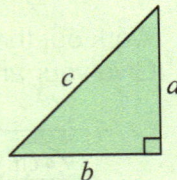

△ Purposeful practice 1

1 Write the length of the hypotenuse of each right-angled triangle.

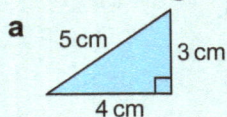

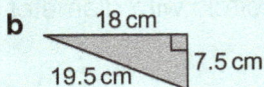

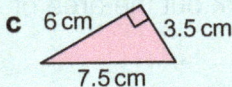

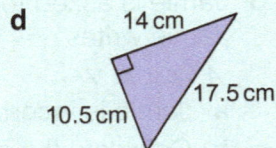

a 5 cm, 3 cm, 4 cm

b 18 cm, 7.5 cm, 19.5 cm

c 6 cm, 3.5 cm, 7.5 cm

d 14 cm, 17.5 cm, 10.5 cm

2 Work out the length of the hypotenuse in each of these right-angled triangles, correct to the nearest mm.

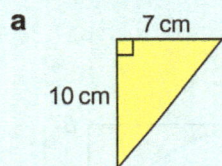

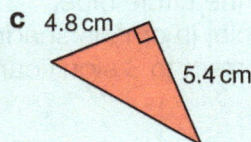

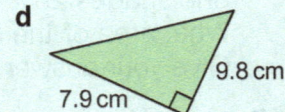

a 7 cm, 10 cm

b 22 cm, 25 cm

c 4.8 cm, 5.4 cm

d 7.9 cm, 9.8 cm

Reflect and reason

What do you notice about the hypotenuse and the right angle in a right-angled triangle?

△ Purposeful practice 2

1 Here is a right-angled triangle.

Which of these formulae can be used to correctly work out the value of x?

8 cm, 17 cm, x

A: $x^2 = 8^2 + 17^2$

B: $x^2 + 8^2 = 17^2$

C: $x^2 + 17^2 = 8^2$

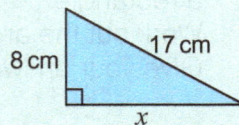

2 Work out the length of the side labelled x in each of these right-angled triangles. Give your answers to an appropriate degree of accuracy.

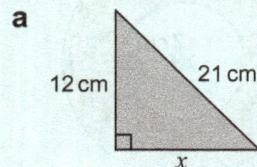

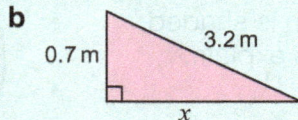

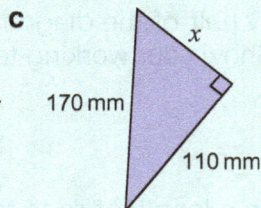

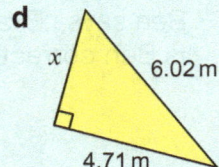

a 12 cm, 21 cm, x

b 0.7 m, 3.2 m, x

c x, 170 mm, 110 mm

d x, 6.02 m, 4.71 m

Reflect and reason

In each triangle in **Q2**, would you expect the missing side to be smaller or larger than each of the other two sides, or is it not possible to predict?

Work out the missing side in each right-angled triangle.
Give your answers to an appropriate degree of accuracy.

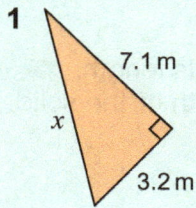

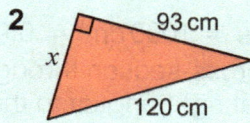

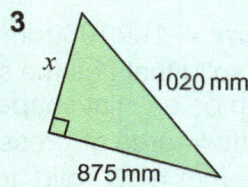

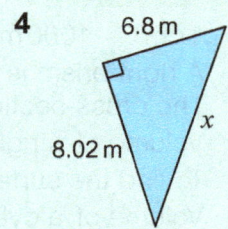

1
7.1 m
x
3.2 m

2
93 cm
x
120 cm

3
x
1020 mm
875 mm

4
6.8 m
8.02 m
x

Reflect and reason

What was the same and what was different when finding the missing sides in the triangles in **Q1** and **Q2**?

▦ ⊠ **Problem-solving practice**

1 The diagram shows the positions of phone masts A, B and C.
Mast A is 26 km due north of mast B.
Mast C is 25 km due east of mast B.
Calculate the distance AC.
Give your answer correct to 3 significant figures.

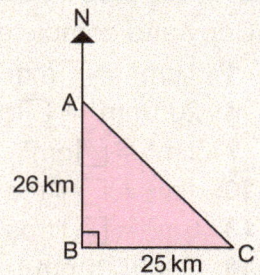

N
A
26 km
B
25 km C

2 Work out the perimeter of the triangle.
Give your answer correct to 1 decimal place.

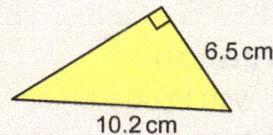

6.5 cm
10.2 cm

3 A rectangular frame is made from five straight pieces of metal, as shown.
The mass of the metal is 1.2 kg per metre.
Work out the total mass of the metal in the frame.
Give your answer correct to 3 significant figures.

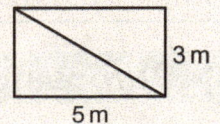

3 m
5 m

4 Pablo says, 'As $8^2 + 15^2 = 17^2$, then the triangle with sides 8 cm, 15 cm and 17 cm is a right-angled triangle.' Is Pablo correct?

5 Triangle *ABC* is a right-angled triangle.
Two of the sides are length 6 cm and 10 cm.
Work out the two possible lengths of the other side.

6 Harry has 50 m of fence and he wants to put a fence all the way around the edge of this garden. The outline of the garden is shown.
Does he have enough fence? You must show all your working.

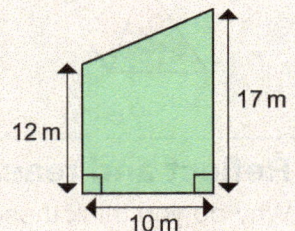

17 m
12 m
10 m

7 The diagram shows a quadrilateral *ABCD*.
Calculate the length of *CD*.
Give your answer correct to 3 significant figures.

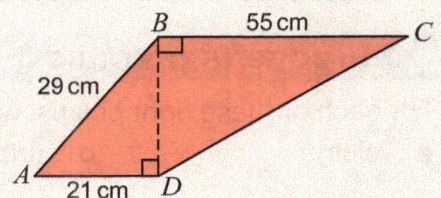

B   55 cm   C
29 cm
A 21 cm D

Key points

- $1\,cm^3 = 1000\,mm^3$, $1\,m^3 = 1\,000\,000\,cm^3$, 1 litre $= 1000\,cm^3 = 0.001\,m^3$
- A right prism is a 3D solid that has the same cross-section throughout its length. The cross-section can be any flat shape. It is at right angles to the length of the solid.
- Volume of a right prism = area of cross-section × length.
- To find the surface area of a 3D solid, total the area of all its faces.
- Volume of a cylinder = $\pi r^2 h$
  Surface area of a cylinder = $2\pi r^2 + 2\pi rh$

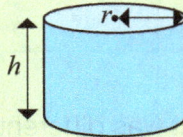

◭ Purposeful practice 1

Copy and complete these measurement conversions.

1 $1\,cm^3 = \square\,mm^3$	**2** $0.1\,cm^3 = \square\,mm^3$	**3** $0.2\,cm^3 = \square\,mm^3$
4 $200\,mm^3 = \square\,cm^3$	**5** $2100\,mm^3 = \square\,cm^3$	**6** $210\,mm^3 = \square\,cm^3$
7 $1\,m^3 = \square\,cm^3$	**8** $0.1\,m^3 = \square\,cm^3$	**9** $0.01\,m^3 = \square\,cm^3$
10 $1\,m^3 = \square$ litres	**11** $0.1\,m^3 = \square$ litres	**12** $0.01\,m^3 = \square$ litres
13 $5\,m^3 = \square$ litres	**14** $0.5\,m^3 = \square$ litres	**15** $0.05\,m^3 = \square$ litres
16 $7\,000\,000\,cm^3 = \square\,m^3$	**17** $7\,500\,000\,cm^3 = \square\,m^3$	**18** $7500\,cm^3 = \square\,m^3$

Reflect and reason

Why do **Q1–3** ask you to convert cm^3 measures to mm^3, not mm or mm^2?

Why is it possible to convert cm^3 or m^3 to litres?

◭ Purposeful practice 2

1 Here are some 3D solids. Name those that are right prisms.

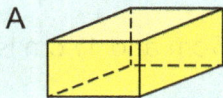

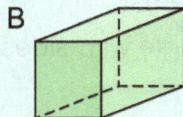

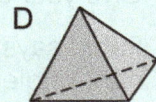

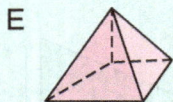

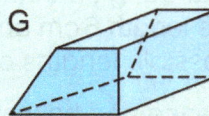

A   B   C   D

E   F   G   H

Reflect and reason

Why do you think these are called **right** prisms? (There is a mathematical reason.)

◭ Purposeful practice 3

For each of these right prisms, work out its
a volume   **b** surface area

1

4 cm
9 cm
3 cm

2

4 cm
9 cm
3 cm

3

4 cm
6 cm
9 cm

4

3 cm
4 cm
6 cm
9 cm

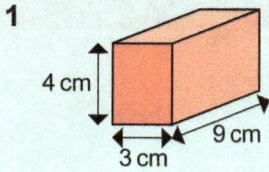

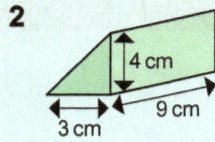

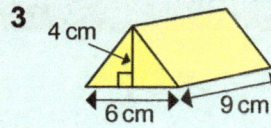

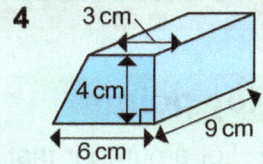

Reflect and reason

Write a sentence explaining how you worked out the volume for **Q2** and **Q3**.
Explain a different method for working out the volumes of these right prisms.

Purposeful practice 4

For each of these cylinders, work out its

a volume   **b** surface area

Give your answers to an appropriate degree of accuracy.

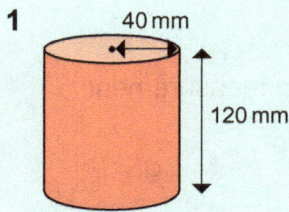

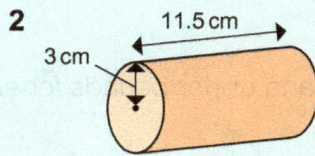

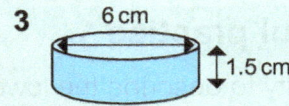

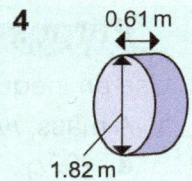

1

40 mm
120 mm

2

11.5 cm
3 cm

3

6 cm
1.5 cm

4

0.61 m
1.82 m

Reflect and reason

How is the curved surface area of a cylinder related to the area of a rectangle?

Problem-solving practice

1 Work out the volume of the cuboid.
Give your answer in cm³.

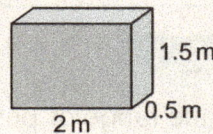

1.5 m
2 m
0.5 m

2 The two solids shown are the foam insides of two soft-play blocks.

106 cm
56 cm
90 cm
108 cm
68 cm
120 cm
120 cm

   a Work out the total volume of foam used for these two blocks.

Both blocks are covered in material.
The material costs £12.50 per square metre.

   b What is the lowest possible cost of covering both blocks?

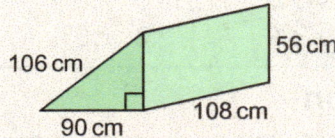

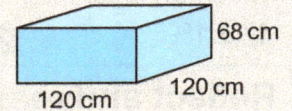

3 The volume of the triangular prism shown is 714 cm³.
Work out the length of the triangular prism.

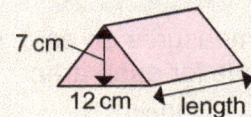

7 cm
12 cm
length

4 The whole of the outside of the metal drum shown is to be painted.
Each tin of paint covers 1.25 m².

57 cm
97 cm

   a How many tins of paint are needed to cover the metal drum?

The drum is filled with water so it is 5 cm from the top of the drum.

   b How many litres of water are in the drum? (Assume the sides have negligible thickness.)
Give your answer correct to 1 decimal place.

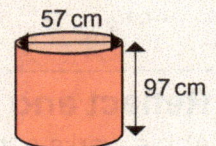

Key points

- For a number that is rounded
  the lower bound is the smallest possible value that rounds up to that number
  the upper bound is the smallest possible value that rounds up to the next number
  This can be shown as an inequality. In the example shown
  the lower bound is 4.5 cm
  the upper bound is 5.5 cm

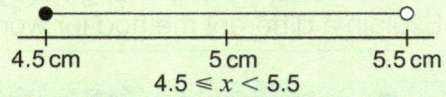

$$4.5 \leq x < 5.5$$

- An error interval tells you the minimum and maximum possible measurements.
- An error interval can be written using a 'plus–minus' sign $\pm$.
  For example, $\pm 1\%$ means the maximum possible measurement is $+1\%$ and the minimum possible measurement is -1%.

△ Purposeful practice 1

Use an inequality to describe the lower and upper bounds for each measurement.

1 A mass, m, of 200 g to the nearest
  a 100 g **b** 10 g **c** 20 g **d** 1 g **e** 5 g **f** 2 g

2 A length, l, of 30 m to the nearest
  a 10 m **b** 1 m **c** 5 m **d** 2 m **e** 1 cm

Reflect and reason

Why are different inequality signs ($\leq$ and $<$) used for the lower and upper bound?

△ Purposeful practice 2

Use an inequality to describe the range of possible values for a mass, m, that is 200 g to within an error interval of

1 $\pm 1\%$ **2** $\pm 2\%$ **3** $\pm 5\%$ **4** $\pm 2.5\%$ **5** $\pm 25\%$

Reflect and reason

What do you notice about your answers to Purposeful practice 1 **Q1** parts **a–c** and Purposeful practice 2 **Q3–5**? Explain. Is this still true if working with 100 g?

△ Purposeful practice 3

The measures on each shape are to the nearest cm. Work out the lower and upper bounds for each area.

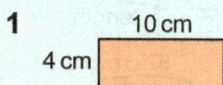

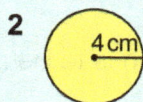

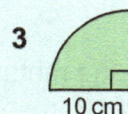

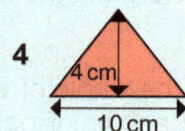

Reflect and reason

Abbie works out the lower and upper bounds for the area, A, of the shape in **Q1**.
Area = $4 \times 10 = 40$ cm²
Minimum area to nearest cm = 39.5 cm²; maximum area to nearest cm = 40.5 cm²
Therefore, 39.5 cm² $\leq A <$ 40.5 cm²
Explain why Abbie is incorrect.

Problem-solving practice

1 Phil measures the height, h, of a table as 70 cm to the nearest centimetre.
He writes the inequality to describe the lower and upper bounds for the measurement as
$69 \leqslant h < 71$
Phil is incorrect. Explain why.

2 Louise makes 10 chocolate bars.
Each of these chocolate bars has a mass of 51 grams.
Write an inequality to describe the range of possible values for the total mass, m, of all 10 chocolate bars within a $\pm 5\%$ error interval.

3 A machine puts drinks into cups.
The capacity of a cup is 200 ml, correct to the nearest 1 ml.

a What is the lower bound for the capacity of a cup?

The machine puts 24 ml of cordial and 175 ml of water into each cup, both measured correct to the nearest ml.

b Is it possible that the total volume of cordial and water put in a cup is greater than the capacity of the cup? Explain your answer.

4 The length of a rectangle is 20 cm within a $\pm 1\%$ error interval.
The width of a rectangle is 10 cm within a $\pm 1\%$ error interval.
Use an inequality to describe the range of possible values for the perimeter, P, of the rectangle.

5 $s = kt$
$k = 16$ to the nearest whole number
$t = 40$ within a $\pm 1\%$ error interval

a Work out the least possible value of s.
b Work out the greatest possible value of s.

6 A cyclist rides at an average speed of 12 m/s within a $\pm 2.5\%$ error interval.
During a race, the cyclist rides at this speed for 44 seconds to the nearest second.
The formula for working out the distance cycled is
distance = speed $\times$ time
Use the formula to work out the least and greatest possible distances cycled.

7 A solid sphere has a density of 7.2 g/cm³ within a $\pm 1\%$ error interval and a volume of 30 cm³ to the nearest cubic centimetre.
The formula for working out the mass of an object is
mass = density $\times$ volume
Use the formula to work out the greatest possible mass of the solid sphere.

8 The length of a rectangle is 16 cm correct to the nearest centimetre.
The width of a rectangle is 7 cm correct to the nearest centimetre.
Work out the lower and upper bounds for the area of the rectangle.

9 The measures of the cuboid are given to the nearest centimetre.
Calculate the lower and upper bounds for the volume of the cuboid.

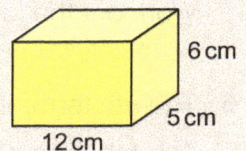
6 cm
5 cm
12 cm

10 Grant is working out the lower bound for the volume of a cube.
The length of the cube is 125 mm rounded to the nearest 5 mm.
Grant writes
$V = 120 \times 120 \times 120 = 1728000 \text{ mm}^3$
Grant is incorrect. Explain why.

Mixed exercises B

Mixed problem-solving practice B

1 The diagram shows a sketch of triangle XYZ.

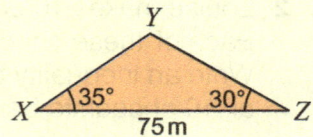

  a Make an accurate scale drawing of the triangle using a
  scale of 1 : 1000.

  b Construct the perpendicular bisector of XZ.

  c The perpendicular bisector of XZ meets the line YZ at point M.
  What is the actual distance of MZ?

2 **a** Construct a triangle with sides 6 cm, 6 cm and 6 cm.

  b What is the size of each angle?

  c What type of triangle is this?

  d Bisect one of the angles in your triangle.

  e What is the size of the two angles you created in part **d**?

3 The diagram shows triangle A drawn on a grid.

  Felix enlarges triangle A by scale factor -2 with
  centre of enlargement (0, 0) to get triangle B.

  He then reflects triangle B in the x-axis to get
  triangle C.

  Maisie reflects triangle A in the x-axis to get
  triangle D.

  She is then going to enlarge triangle D by
  scale factor -2 with centre of enlargement
  (0, 0) to get triangle E.

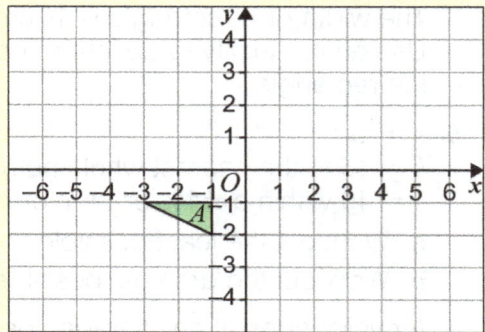

  Maisie says, 'Triangle E should be in the same position as triangle C.'

  Is she correct? You must show how you get your answer.

4 The first four terms of a geometric sequence are 3, 9, 27, 81.

  a Write the 5th term in the sequence.

  b Copy and complete the table for the sequence.

1st term	2nd term	3rd term	4th term	5th term
3	$3 \times 3 = 3^2$	$3 \times 3 \times 3 = 3^{\square}$	_____ $= 3^{\square}$	_____ $= 3^{\square}$

  c Work out the 10th term of the sequence.

  d Write the general term of the sequence.

5 Each of the sides of the triangle is measured to the nearest centimetre.
  Work out the lower and upper bound of the side labelled x.

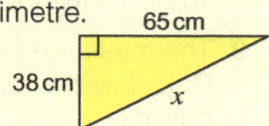

6 The nth term of sequence X is $\dfrac{5n - 6}{2}$.

  The nth term of sequence Y is $30 - n$.

  Vicki says, 'There is only one term, n, that gives the same value for both sequence
  X and sequence Y.'

  Is Vicki right? Explain.

7 A company makes a new shade of green paint by mixing yellow and blue paint.
The amount of yellow paint used, y, is directly proportional to the amount of blue paint used, b.
For a small tin of green paint, 450 ml of yellow paint is mixed with 50 ml of blue paint.
Work out how much blue paint needs to be mixed with 10 litres of yellow paint to get the same shade.
Give your answer correct to the nearest millilitre.

8 The diagram shows a solid cylinder with a mass of 513 g.
Calculate the density of the cylinder.
Give your answer correct to 2 decimal places.

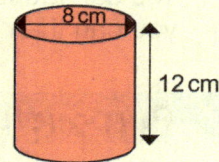
8 cm
12 cm

9 An electric car can go up to 152 miles on a single charge, to the nearest mile.
The manufacturer claims the maximum range is a 5% increase on their previous model.
What are the lower and upper bounds for the maximum range of the previous model? Give your answer to 2 decimal places.

10 Shaun drives along a road for 380 seconds, correct to the nearest second.
The speed limit for the road is 50 km/h.
Shaun drives at the speed limit rounded to the nearest 10 metres per hour.
What is the furthest distance Shaun could have driven during this time?
You must show your working.

11 PQR is a right-angled triangle.
P, Q and R are points on the circumference of a circle, centre O.
POR is a diameter of the circle.
Calculate the circumference of the circle.
Give your answer correct to 3 significant figures.

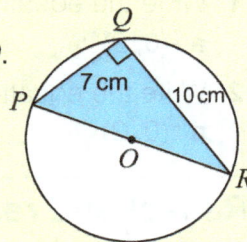
Q
7 cm
10 cm
P
O
R

12 The diagram shows a circle inside a square.
20 cm is the distance from one corner of the square to the opposite corner.
Work out the total area of the shaded regions.
Give your answer correct to 3 significant figures.

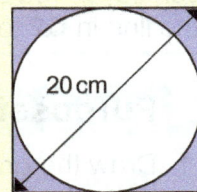
20 cm

13 $-4 \leqslant 2x < 10$
Write an inequality for
a $4x - 1$
b $3x$

14 Look at the three inequalities.

$$-3 \leqslant x < 5 \qquad -4 < 2x \leqslant 14 \qquad -4 \leqslant 3x + 2 \leqslant 20$$

a Which inequality gives the lowest integer value of x?
b Which inequality gives the greatest integer value of x?
Explain your answer in each case.

8 Graphs

Key point

- You can identify the y-intercept and gradient from the equation of a straight line, and you can then use these to draw its graph.

◭ Purposeful practice 1

For each equation, plot the y-intercept and then use the gradient to draw its graph.

1 $y = x$ **2** $y = x - 1$ **3** $y = -x - 1$ **4** $y = -x - 2$

5 $y = 2x$ **6** $y = 2x + 1$ **7** $y = -2x + 1$ **8** $y = -2x - 2$

Reflect and reason

Another method for drawing graphs is to complete a table of values, like the one shown, and then plot the points.
Which method do you prefer? Explain why.

x	−1	0	1
y			

◭ Purposeful practice 2

1 Write the equation of the line parallel to $y = x$ with y-intercept

     a (0, 2)   **b** (0, 3)   **c** (0, −2)   **d** (0, −3)

2 Write the equation of the line parallel to $y = 2x$ with y-intercept

     a (0, 2)   **b** (0, 3)   **c** (0, −2)   **d** (0, −3)

Reflect and reason

Jon says, 'You can change the equation of the line in **Q1** to $y = x + 1$ and the equation of the line in **Q2** to $y = 2x + 1$, and all the answers are the same.' Is Jon correct? Explain.

◭ Purposeful practice 3

1 Draw the graphs of each pair of equations on the same axes.
Write the coordinates where they cross.

     a $y = x + 1$ **b** $y = x + 2$ **c** $y = 2x + 2$ **d** $y = 2x + 3$
        $y = 3$ $y = 1$ $x = 1$ $x = -1$

2 Blake says, 'You don't have to draw the graphs in **Q1** to work out where they cross.
You can use algebra.' For **Q1a** Blake writes

$y = x + 1$ and $y = 3$
substitute $y = 3$ into $y = x + 1$: $3 = x + 1$
        then solve to work out x: $x = 2$
The graphs cross at coordinates (2, 3).
Show Blake's algebra method also works for **Q1** parts **b**, **c** and **d**.

Reflect and reason

Do you prefer the method in **Q1** or **Q2** for working out where graphs cross? Explain why.

1 Draw the graph of $y = \frac{1}{2}x + 3$ for values of x from -4 to 4.

2 a Draw the graph of $y = \frac{1}{2}x - 1$ for values of x from -2 to 4.

   b Use your graph to find the value of x when $y = 0.5$.

3 a Draw the graph of $y = \frac{1}{2}x + 2$.

   b i Draw the line that is parallel to $y = \frac{1}{2}x + 2$ and passes through the point with coordinates $(0, -1)$.

      ii Write the equation of this line.

4 a Draw the graph of $y = x + 3$ on a set of axes from -6 to 6.

   b i Draw the line that is parallel to $y = x + 3$ and passes through the point with coordinates $(3, 1)$.

      ii Write the equation of this line.

5 The diagram shows a straight line, A, drawn on a grid. Another straight line, B, is parallel to A and passes through the point $(0, -2)$.
   Find the equation of B.

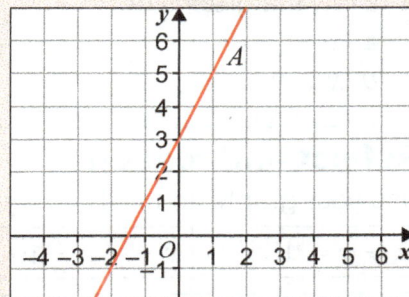

6 a Draw the graph of $y = 2x - 7$.

   b Find an equation for the straight line parallel to $y = 2x - 7$ that passes through $(1, 5)$.

7 Copy and complete
   'The line $y = \Box x - 1$ crosses the line $y = 5$ at the point $(2, 5)$.'

8 In a video game, a ship moves along the line $y = \frac{1}{2}x - 3$.
   A submarine moves along the line $x = 4$.
   At what point would the ship be directly above the submarine?

9 $ABCD$ is a parallelogram.
   The equation of line AB is $y = 10$.
   The equation of AD is $y = 3x - 2$.

   a What are the coordinates of point A?
   Points B and D lie on the line $y = x$.

   b What are the coordinates of point B?

   c Find an equation for the side BC.

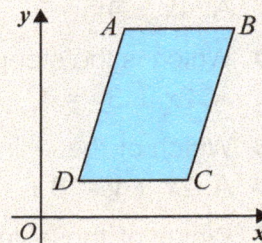

10 Here are the equations of some lines.
   Line A: $y = 2x + 3$ Line B: $y = 2x - 3$
   Line C: $y = 2x - 1$ Line D: $y = 2x + 1$
   Line E: $y = 2x + 5$ Line F: $y = 2x - 5$

   a Which of these lines crosses the line $y = 1$ at the point $(3, 1)$?

   b Which of these lines crosses the line $y = -3$ at the point $(-1, -3)$?

Key points

- Graphs with equations of the form $ax + by = c$ are linear. To find the y-intercept of a graph, find the y-coordinate where $x = 0$. To find the x-intercept of a graph, find the x-coordinate where $y = 0$.
- To find the gradient or y-intercept of a straight-line graph, rearrange its equation in the form $y = mx + c$.

△ Purposeful practice 1

1 Draw the graphs of
   a $x + y = 4$ **b** $x + y = 5$ **c** $x + y = 6$
   d $x + y = -2$ **e** $x + y = -3$ **f** $x + y = -4$

2 Draw the graphs of
   a $x - y = 4$ **b** $x - y = 5$ **c** $x - y = 6$
   d $x - y = -2$ **e** $x - y = -3$ **f** $x - y = -4$

Reflect and reason

Use your graphs to predict the y-intercept of each equation shown.

| $x + y = 15$ | $x + y = -15$ | $x - y = 15$ | $x - y = -15$ |

△ Purposeful practice 2

1 Which lines pass through $(0, 2)$? Show your working.
   A: $x + y = 2$ B: $2x + 2y = 2$ C: $x + 2y = 2$ D: $2x + y = 2$

2 Which lines pass through $(0, 3)$? Show your working.
   A: $3x + 2y = 6$ B: $2x + 3y = 6$ C: $2y - 6 = 3x$ D: $6x + 2y = 3$

3 Which is the steepest line? Show your working.
   A: $4x + 4y = 1$ B: $4y + 1 = -x$ C: $4x + y = 1$ D: $x + 4y = 4$

4 Which is the steepest line? Show your working.
   A: $2x + 3y = 1$ B: $3x + 2y = 1$ C: $2y + 3 = -x$ D: $x + 2y = 3$

5 Which of these lines are parallel? Show your working.
   A: $2x + y = 8$ B: $2x + 2y = 4$ C: $4x + 2y = 1$ D: $4x + y = 2$

6 Which of these lines are parallel? Show your working.
   A: $16 = 4x - 2y$ B: $12x = 6y - 3$ C: $4y - 12x = 8$ D: $2y - 8x = 4$

Reflect and reason

Arabee and James are comparing the two equations shown.
$2x + 3y = 1$ $2y + 3x = 1$
Arabee says, 'Their gradients are 2.'
James says, 'Their gradients are 3.'
Are either of them correct? Explain.

1 **a** Draw the graph of equation $10y - 2x = 25$.
Draw your x-axis from -15 to 15 and your y-axis from 0 to 10.

   b Use your graph to estimate the value of
   i y when $x = 5$ **ii** x when $y = 5$

2 Prisha says, 'All of these equations contain x, so all of these lines have a gradient of 1.'
Is she correct? Explain your answer.
Line A: $y = x + 5$
Line B: $y + x = 2$
Line C: $x + 2y = -3$
Line D: $2y = x + 4$

3 Put these lines in order of steepness, starting with the least steep.
Line A: $3y = 5 + 12x$
Line B: $y - 2x = 5$
Line C: $2y = x + 4$
Line D: $3y - 2 = x$

4 Put these lines in order of their y-intercepts, starting with the lowest.
Line A: $y + x = 3$
Line B: $3y + 2 = x$
Line C: $y - 2x = 1$
Line D: $2y = x + 5$

5 The equation of line A is $y = 4x - 3$.
The equation of line B is $2y - 8x = 1$.
Show that these two lines are parallel.

6 The equations of some straight lines are shown.
Line A: $y + 2x = 3$
Line B: $3y + 2 = 3x$
Line C: $2y - 4x = 7$
Line D: $2y = 2x + 5$

   Which two lines are parallel?

7 Which of these lines is the odd one out? Explain why.

| A: $3y - 6x = 12$ | B: $4y - 12 = 8x$ | C: $2y - 6x = -4$ |
| D: $5y = 10x - 25$ | E: $4y = 8x - 4$ | F: $1 = -2x + y$ |

8 Which of these lines is the odd one out? Explain why.

| A: $2y - 2x = -2$ | B: $3y + 3 = 6x$ | C: $2y + 2 = -2x$ |
| D: $3y + 6x = -3$ | E: $y - x = 1$ | F: $3y + 9x = -3$ |

9 The straight line L has equation $3x + y = 4$.
Find the equation of the straight line parallel to L that passes through $(-1, 6)$.

10 Two incomplete equations are shown.
$y = \square x + \square$ and $2y = \square x + \square$

   a Copy and complete these equations so that they are parallel.
   b Copy and complete these equations so that they have the same y-intercept.

8.3 Simultaneous equations

Key points

- The point where two (or more) graphs cross is called the point of intersection.
- Simultaneous equations are two or more equations that, when solved, have the same values for the unknowns.
- You can find the solution to a pair of simultaneous equations by
    1. drawing the graphs on the same coordinate grid
    2. then finding the point of intersection

⚠ Purposeful practice 1

For each graph,
- **a** write the coordinates of the point of intersection of the lines
- **b** write the solution for the pair of simultaneous equations shown by the lines

1

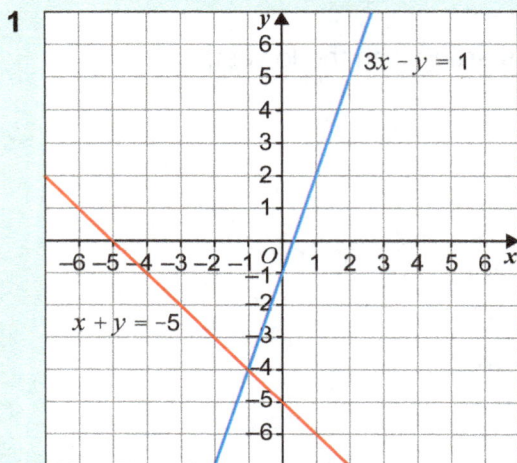

$3x - y = 1$
$x + y = -5$

2

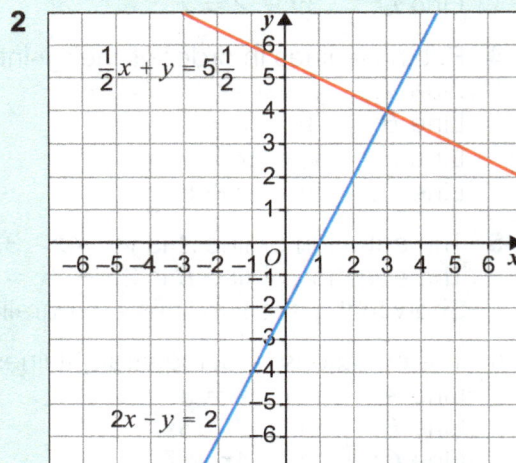

$\frac{1}{2}x + y = 5\frac{1}{2}$
$2x - y = 2$

3

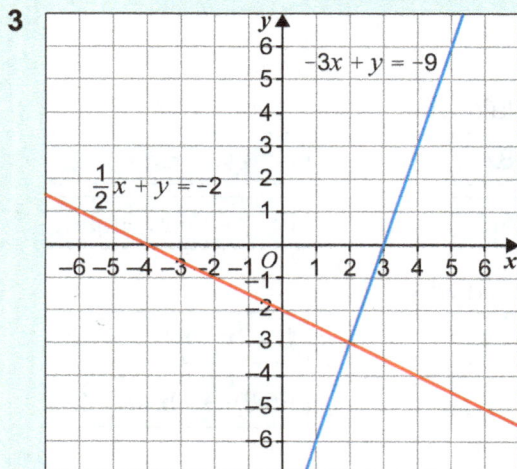

$-3x + y = -9$
$\frac{1}{2}x + y = -2$

4

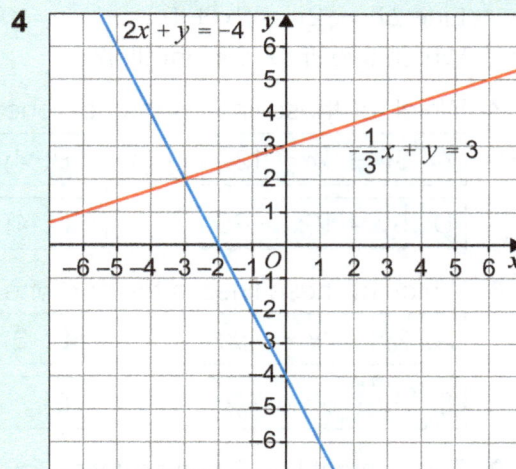

$2x + y = -4$
$-\frac{1}{3}x + y = 3$

Reflect and reason

Katherine draws graphs to solve the simultaneous equations
$$2x + y = -4$$
$$-\frac{1}{3}x + y = 3$$
She writes the solution $(-3, 2)$. What mistake has she made?

77

Draw graphs to solve each pair of simultaneous equations.

1 $y = x$
$x + y = 8$

2 $y = 3x$
$x + y = 8$

3 $2x + y = 1$
$x + y = 3$

4 $x + 2y = 0$
$x + y = 1$

5 $2x - 2y = 4$
$4x + y = -7$

6 $2x - 2y = 10$
$x - 4y = 2$

Reflect and reason

Maria says, 'I always check my solutions to simultaneous equations by substituting the values of x and y back into each equation.'
Show what she means for your solutions to **Q1–6**. Is this a useful check? Explain why.

⊠ Problem-solving practice

1 Aljaz is asked to solve the simultaneous equations $y = 2x$ and $x + y = 6$ graphically.
He draws the graph shown.
  a Aljaz is incorrect. What has he done wrong?
  b Solve the simultaneous equations $y = 2x$ and $x + y = 6$ graphically.

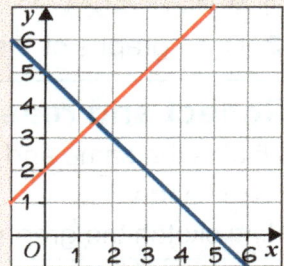

2 Use the graph to solve each pair of simultaneous equations.
  a $y - 2x = 3$
$3y + x = -12$
  b $3y + x = -12$
$3y + 15x = 30$
  c $y - 2x = 3$
$3y + 15x = 30$
  d $y - 2x = 3$
$y = x$

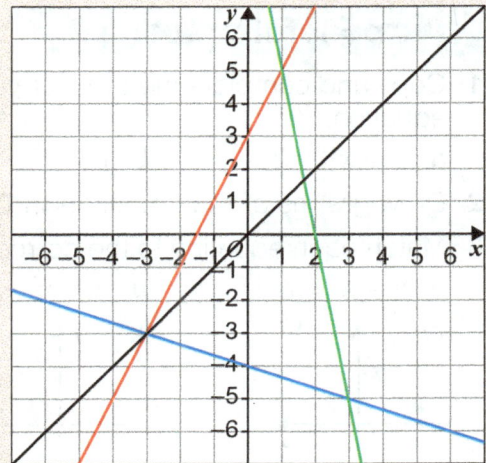

3 A square grid is placed over a map.
Two train lines on the map follow straight lines until they both reach the same station.
The equations of the lines are $2x + y = 17$ and $y - x = 2$.
Draw and use the graphs to find the coordinates of the station.

4 Draw the graphs to show that the simultaneous equations $y - 2x = 1$ and $y - 2x = -2$ have no solution.

5 Draw a graph to show two simultaneous equations that have the solution $x = 2$, $y = 3$.
Label your two lines with their equations.

6 At a cinema,
  2 adult tickets and 3 child tickets cost £34
  1 adult ticket and 2 child tickets cost £20
Draw a graph to find the cost of an adult ticket and the cost of a child ticket.

Key points

- A quadratic equation contains a term in x^2, but no higher power of x.
- The graph of a quadratic equation is a curved shape called a parabola.

△ Purposeful practice 1

1 Copy and complete the table of values for each quadratic equation.

x	−3	−2	−1	0	1	2	3
y							

   a $y = x^2$　　　　　　**b** $y = 2x^2$　　　　　　**c** $y = 3x^2$

2 Draw graphs of the equations in **Q1** on the same set of axes.

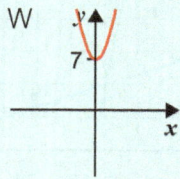

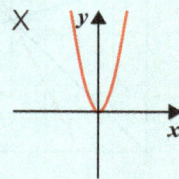

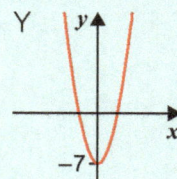

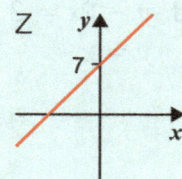

Reflect and reason

What is the same and what is different about the graphs of
$y = x^2$ and $y = x$　　　　$y = 2x^2$ and $y = 2x$　　　　$y = 3x^2$ and $y = 3x$?
Hint: sketch the graphs of $y = x$, $y = 2x$ and $y = 3x$ to help you.

△ Purposeful practice 2

1 Copy and complete the table of values in Purposeful practice 1 for each quadratic equation.
   a $y = x^2 + 2$　　　　**b** $y = x^2 + 4$　　　　**c** $y = x^2 + 6$

2 Draw graphs of the equations in **Q1** on the same set of axes.

3 Match each equation to the correct graph: W, X, Y or Z.
   a $y = x + 7$　　　**b** $y = x^2 + 7$　　　**c** $y = x^2 - 7$　　　**d** $y = 7x^2$

Reflect and reason

What is the same and what is different about the graphs of $y = 2x^2$ and $y = x^2 + 2$?

△ Purposeful practice 3

Draw the line $y = 10$ on the same set of axes as your graphs for **Q2** in Purposeful practice 2. Use the graphs to find or estimate two solutions to each of these equations.

1 $x^2 + 6 = 10$　　　　**2** $x^2 + 4 = 10$　　　　**3** $x^2 + 2 = 10$

Reflect and reason

Which solutions are exact? Which solutions are estimates? Explain why.
Could you find a more accurate solution by solving the equations using algebra?
Explain your answer.

Problem-solving practice

1 Fleur is asked to draw the graph of $y = x^2 - 2$.
Her graph is shown.
Write one thing that is wrong with Fleur's graph.

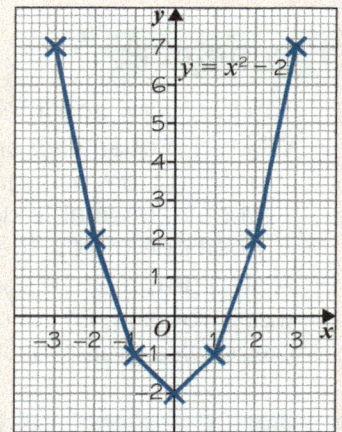

2 a Copy and complete the table of values for $y = x^2 - 3$.

x	-3	-2	-1	0	1	2	3
y	6				-2		

  b On a grid, draw the graph of $y = x^2 - 3$ for values of x from -3 to 3.
  c Find estimates for the solutions of the equation $x^2 - 3 = 0$.

3 a Copy and complete the table of values for $y = x^2 + 1$.

x	-2	-1	0	1	2
y		2			

  b On a grid, draw the graph of $y = x^2 + 1$ for values of x from -2 to 2.
  c By drawing a suitable straight line on the grid, find estimates for the solutions of
  $x^2 + 1 = 3$.

4 Yasmin is asked to complete the table of values and draw
the graph for $y = x^2 - 1$.
She fills in the table as shown.

x	-3	-2	-1	0	1	2	3
y	-10	-5	-2	-1	0	3	8

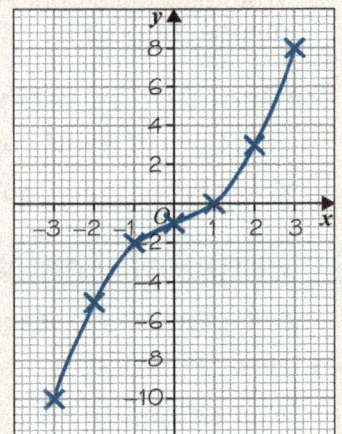

Yasmin draws the graph shown.

  a How can you tell from the graph that Yasmin has made
  at least one mistake?
  b Describe the exact mistakes Yasmin has made.
  c Draw the correct graph of $y = x^2 - 1$.

5 a Which of these graphs is a quadratic equation?

  $y = x + 3$ $y = x^2 + 3$ $y = x - 3$

  b Copy and complete the table of values for the graph you chose in part **a** and then
  draw its graph.

x	-2	-1	0	1	2
y					

Key points

- You can draw and interpret graphs showing inverse proportion.
- When two quantities are in inverse proportion,
  plotting them as a graph gives a curve
  when one variable doubles, the other halves
  when one triples, the other is divided by 3, and so on.
- A step graph has a constant value for given intervals. Empty circles ○ show
  that a value is not included in an interval. A step graph is an example of a linear
  piece-wise graph, as it is made up of pieces.

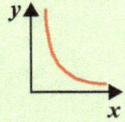

△ Purposeful practice 1

The graph shows the number of hours it takes to pick an entire field's worth of crop, based on the number of people picking the crop.

1 How many people are needed to pick it in

   a 4 hours   **b** 6 hours   **c** 8 hours?

2 How long does it take 12 people to pick the entire field?

3 Estimate how long it takes 10 people to pick the entire field.

4 The relationship can be described by $y = \frac{k}{x}$. Use the values you found in **Q1** and **Q2** to work out the value of k.

5 Write a formula connecting number of hours to number of people.

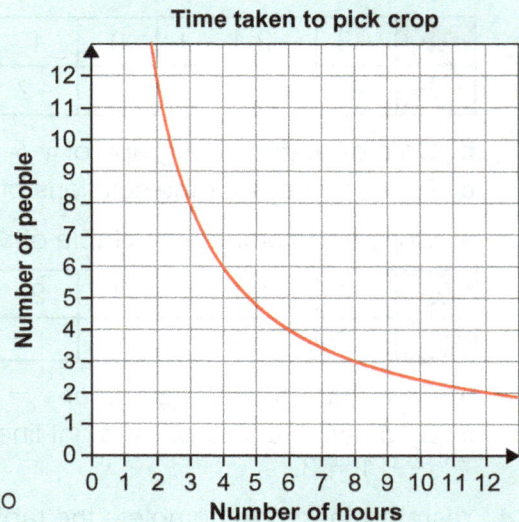

Time taken to pick crop

Reflect and reason

The farm owner wants each field to be picked in 10 hours.

Does the answer given by the graph for number of people required make sense? Explain.

△ Purposeful practice 2

The step graph shows the hire costs for a city bike hire club.

1 How much does it cost to hire a bike for

   a $3\frac{1}{2}$ days   **b** $2\frac{1}{2}$ days   **c** 1 week   **d** 5 days?

2 There is a fixed fee to join the club. Then there is the cost of hire each day.

   a How much is the cost of hire each day?

   b How much is the fixed fee?

Bike hire costs

Reflect and reason

Tarek says, 'Each step on the step graph should have a vertical line joining it.'
Why would vertical lines on the graph in Purposeful practice 2 not make sense?

1 A cup of boiling water is left to cool.
The graph shows the temperature of the water in the cup at different times.

a What is the temperature after half an hour?

b After how many minutes is the temperature 50 °C?

c How long does it take the water to cool to body temperature (37 °C)?

d Does the water temperature ever reach 0 °C? Explain.

e Does the graph show inverse proportion? Explain.

Time taken for water to cool

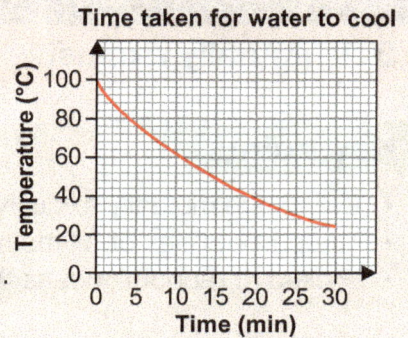

2 The graph shows how many hours it takes to clean all the bedrooms in a hotel, based on the number of cleaners working on a given day. Write a formula connecting number of hours, y, to number of cleaners, x.

Time taken to clean all rooms

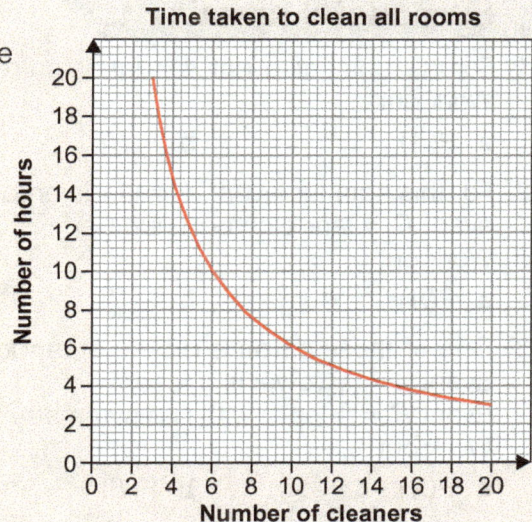

3 The step graph shows the tax rate for earnings in the UK for the 2019/2020 tax year. For each tax band, only the earnings within that band are taxed at the level shown. For Example, somebody who earns £100 000 would pay no tax on the first £12 500, 20% tax on earnings between £12 500 and £50 000, and 40% tax on all earnings beyond £50 000.

Tax rate for earnings in the UK for the 2019/2020 tax year

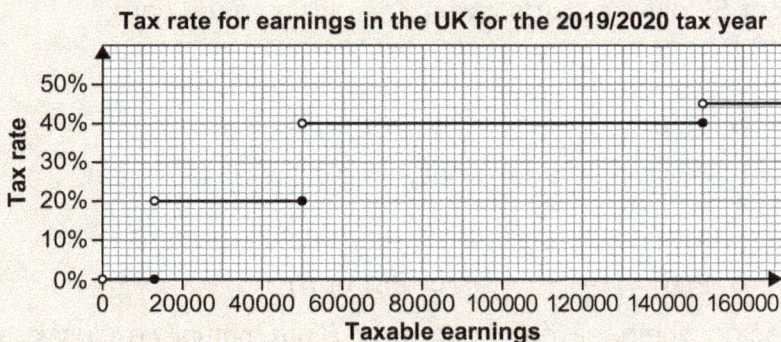

a What is the tax rate for £12 500.01 – £50 000?

b What earnings are taxed at the 40% rate?

c Paul earns £24 000 during this year.
How much tax will he pay?
Hint: remember that there is no tax on the first £12 500.

d Saisha earns £60 000 during this year.
How much tax will she pay?

9 Probability

9.1 Mutually exclusive events

Key points

- Events are mutually exclusive if they cannot happen at the same time.
- The probabilities of all the mutually exclusive outcomes of an event add to 1.
- 'Picked at random' means that each item is equally likely to be picked.

△ Purposeful practice 1

1 For this spinner, event A = lands on red, event B = lands on yellow.
Work out
    a P(A)   **b** P(B)   **c** P(A or B)

2 For this spinner, event A = lands on prime number,
event B = lands on odd number.
Work out
    a P(A)   **b** P(B)   **c** P(A or B)

3 One of these cards is picked at random.
Event A = a vowel is chosen.
Event B = a letter with line symmetry is chosen.
Work out
    a P(A)   **b** P(B)   **c** P(A or B)

4 One of these cards is picked at random.
Event A = a vowel is chosen.
Event B = a consonant is chosen.
Work out
    a P(A)   **b** P(B)   **c** P(A or B)

5 For an ordinary pack of 52 playing cards, event A = picking a red card,
event B = picking a club.
Work out
    a P(A)   **b** P(B)   **c** P(A or B)

6 For an ordinary pack of 52 playing cards, event A = picking a black card,
event B = picking a king.
Work out
    a P(A)   **b** P(B)   **c** P(A or B)

7 For each of **Q1–6**, decide whether event A and event B are mutually exclusive.
If A and B are not mutually exclusive, give an example to show why.

8 For the mutually exclusive events you determined in **Q7**, work out P(A) + P(B).
Compare P(A) + P(B) with P(A or B). What do you notice?

9 Repeat **Q8** for the events in **Q1–6** that are not mutually exclusive.

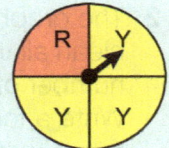

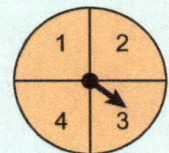

Reflect and reason

When can you work out P(A or B) by adding P(A) and P(B)?

1 Work out the probabilities for this spinner.

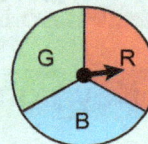

  a i P(R)   **ii** P(B)   **iii** P(G)   **iv** P(R) + P(B) + P(G)
  b i P(B)   **ii** P(not B)   **iii** P(B) + P(not B)

2 Work out the probabilities for an ordinary dice.

  a i P(6)   **ii** P(not 6)   **iii** P(6) + P(not 6)
  b i P(odd)   **ii** P(even)   **iii** P(odd) + P(even)

Reflect and reason

For a dice, are the events '6' and 'not 6' mutually exclusive? Explain how they represent all the outcomes of rolling a dice.

Use your answers to **Q1b** and **Q2a** to help you explain why:

P(event does not happen) = 1 − P(event happens)

⊠ **Problem-solving practice**

1 Here is an 8-sided spinner, where each section contains a letter.

     event A = lands on a vowel
     event B = lands on A or T
     event C = lands on a consonant

  a Which two events are mutually exclusive?
  b Work out   **i** P(A or B)   **ii** P(A or C)

2 There are only red, yellow, blue and green counters in a bag.
  A counter is taken at random from the bag.
  The table shows each of the probabilities, with one value missing.

Colour	red	yellow	blue	green
Probability	0.4	0.2	0.3	

  a Are the four outcomes, red, yellow, blue and green mutually exclusive?
  b Work out the probability that a counter will be green.

3 A 4-sided spinner is coloured blue, green, red and yellow.
  The table shows the probability that the spinner will land on blue and yellow.

Colour	blue	green	red	yellow
Probability	0.4			0.3

  The probability that the spinner will land on green is equal to the probability that the spinner will land on red.

  a Are the four outcomes on the spinner mutually exclusive?
  b Find the probability that the spinner lands on green.

4 The table shows the possible scores in a game.

Score	0	2	5	10	50
Probability	40%	2x	x	10%	5%

  A player is twice as likely to score 2 points as to score 5 points.

  a Work out the probability of scoring 5.
  b Work out the probability of scoring 2.
  c How many times should you expect to score 0 in 50 plays?

Key points

For an unbiased or fair dice or spinner,
- the theoretical probabilities are close to the experimental probabilities
- the theoretical number of expected outcomes is close to the experimental number of outcomes (for a large number of trials)

Purposeful practice 1

The table next to each spinner shows the results from spinning that spinner.

1 For each spinner,
  i calculate, as a fraction, the theoretical probability of landing on red
  ii calculate, as a fraction, the experimental probability of landing on red, using the table of results
  iii compare the theoretical probability of landing on red with the experimental probability of landing on red and decide if the spinner is fair

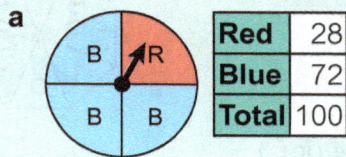

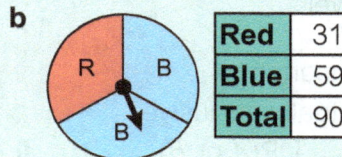

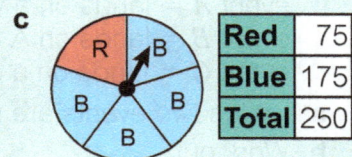

a

Red	28
Blue	72
Total	100

b

Red	31
Blue	59
Total	90

c

Red	75
Blue	175
Total	250

2 Repeat **Q1** for these spinners. Calculate the probabilities as decimals.

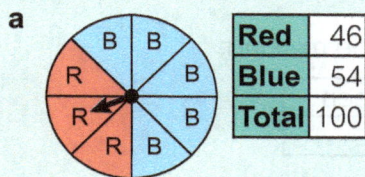

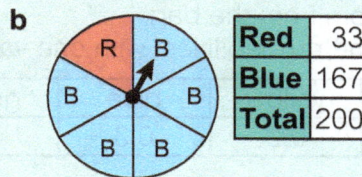

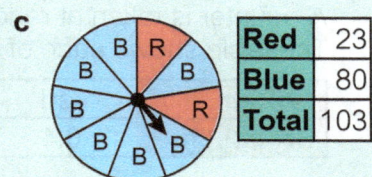

a

Red	46
Blue	54
Total	100

b

Red	33
Blue	167
Total	200

c

Red	23
Blue	80
Total	103

Reflect and reason

When is it easy to compare probabilities as fractions?
When is it easier to convert probabilities to decimals to compare them?

Purposeful practice 2

For each spinner, compare the theoretical number of times you expect it to land on 'blue' (B) to the actual number of times it landed on 'blue'. Use this to decide if the spinner is fair.

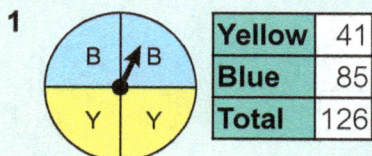

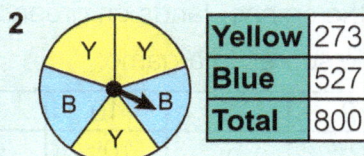

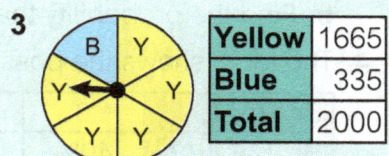

1

Yellow	41
Blue	85
Total	126

2

Yellow	273
Blue	527
Total	800

3

Yellow	1665
Blue	335
Total	2000

Reflect and reason

In Purposeful practice 1, what was the same, and what was different, about the methods you used to decide whether the spinner was fair?

1 The table shows the results when Alicia rolls a 6-sided dice.

Number on dice	1	2	3	4	5	6
Frequency	42	33	28	24	15	8

Is the dice biased? Explain your answer.

2 Yousef and Kate are playing a game.
They roll two 6-sided dice and find the difference between them.
Yousef wins if the difference is less than 3, Kate wins if the difference is 3 or more.
The table shows the results of their rolls.
Do Yousef and Kate have an equal chance of winning? Explain your answer.

Difference between dice	0	1	2	3	4	5
Frequency	52	82	65	49	34	18

3 The table shows the results when Hamid spins this spinner 200 times.

Number on spinner	1	2	3	4	5
Frequency	74	48	35	25	18

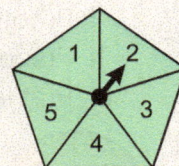

Hamid is trying to decide if the spinner is fair.
He writes

$P(1) = \frac{1}{5}$

$\frac{1}{5}$ of 200 = 40

74 is almost double 40 and 18 is less than half of 40, so the spinner is not fair.

a Do you think Hamid is correct? Explain.

b Why has Hamid written that the probability of the spinner landing on 1 is $\frac{1}{5}$?

c What does the 40 represent in Hamid's working?

4 Dan and Amelia are playing a card game where they play their first card at random.
They each start with six cards.
These are Dan's cards:

These are Amelia's cards:

Dan says, 'There are two colours, so the probability that each of us plays a red card first is $\frac{1}{2}$.'
Explain why Dan is not correct.

Key points

- A sample space diagram shows all the possible outcomes of two events.
- In a 'fair' game, all players have the same probability of winning.

⚠ Purposeful practice

For each pair of spinners in **Q1–3**,

a draw a sample space diagram like this one to show the possible outcomes. Some of the values for **Q1** have been entered for you.

	4				
Spinner 2	3	1, 3			
	1	1, 1	2, 1		
		1	**2**	**3**	**4**
		Spinner 1			

b work out

  i P(both spinners land on an even number)

  ii P(score on spinner 1 is 4)

  iii P(at least one spinner lands on 3)

1

Spinner 1   Spinner 2

2

Spinner 1   Spinner 2

3

Spinner 1   Spinner 2

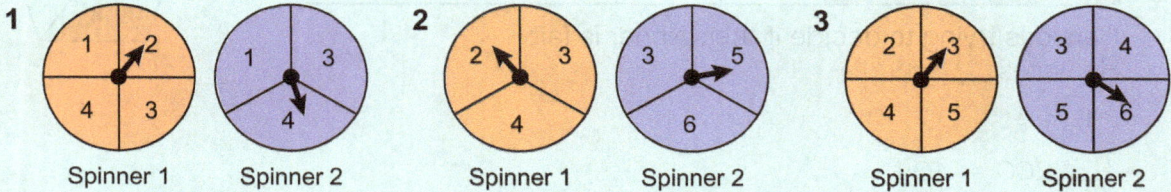

For each of the spinners in **Q4–6**, the scores are added.

a Draw a sample space diagram like this one to show the possible outcomes. Some of the values for **Q4** have been entered for you.

	2	3			
Spinner 2	1	2			
	0	1	2		
		1	**2**	**3**	**4**
		Spinner 1			

b Work out

  i P(total score is even)

  ii P(total score is less than 5)

  iii P(total score is a square number)

4

Spinner 1   Spinner 2

5

Spinner 1   Spinner 2

6

Spinner 1   Spinner 2

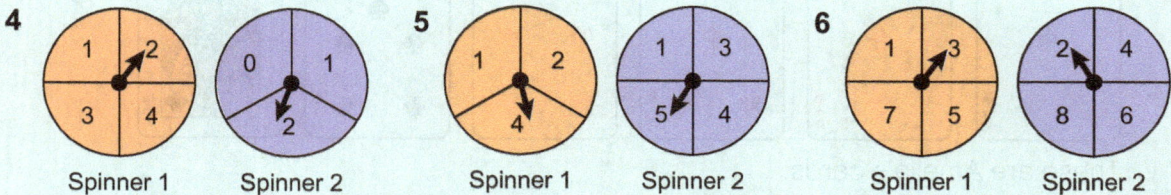

Reflect and reason

For the spinners in **Q1**, work out P(total score is even).

For the spinners in **Q5**, work out P(both spinners land on an even number).

How do you decide whether to show the two scores in your sample space diagram (as in **Q1–3**) or the total score (as in **Q4–6**)?

1 Two fair 6-sided dice are rolled.
What is the probability that both dice show the same score?

2 Steve has two fair 6-sided dice.
Steve is going to roll both dice and record the total.

    a Draw a sample space diagram to show all the possible outcomes.

    b Steve says, 'As both dice are fair, there is an equal chance of getting a total of 6 as
there is of getting a total of 7.'
Is Steve correct? Explain your answer.

3 The diagram shows a security lock on a door.
You have to enter the correct code (a letter followed by a number) to open
the door.
Noah does not know the code.
He enters one of the letters at random.
He then enters one of the numbers at random.
Work out the probability that Noah enters the correct code on his first go.

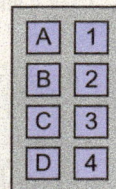

4 In a game, players need to spin the spinner shown and roll
a 6-sided dice. Both are fair.
The score is the total of the two numbers.
Work out the probability that the score is an even number.

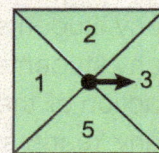

5 A game is played with the two sets of dominoes shown.
One domino is taken at random from each set.
The total numbers of dots on each domino are multiplied together.
Work out the probability that the product is an odd number.

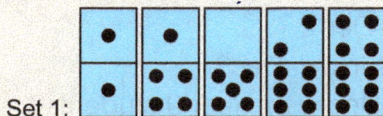

Set 1:

Set 2:

6 Rina plays a game with two sets of cards, as shown.

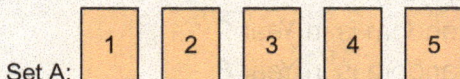

Set A: | 1 | 2 | 3 | 4 | 5 |

Set B: | 6 | 7 | 8 | 9 |

Rina takes one card at random from each set.

    a What is the probability that Rina's total score will be greater than 12?

Rina's year group are raising money for a charity.
120 students are each going to play Rina's card game once.
Each student pays £1 to play.
Rina pays £2 to any player getting a total of 8, as well as returning their £1 entry.

    b Work out how much money for charity Rina should expect to make from her game.

Key point

- When the outcomes of an experiment or survey are pairs of results, you can show the results in a two-way table.

△ Purposeful practice

1 Noor surveyed all the students in Year 8 and Year 9. She recorded the year group and birthday month of each student.

	Jan–Mar	Apr–Jun	Jul–Sep	Oct–Dec	Total
Year 8	13	16	18	11	
Year 9	10	21	21	10	
Total					

   a Copy and complete the table by working out the total of each row and column.
   b How many students were surveyed in total?
   c How many students surveyed had birthdays in Jan–Mar?
   d What fraction of the students surveyed had birthdays in Jan–Mar?
   e How many Year 8 students surveyed had birthdays in Jan–Mar?
   f What fraction of the students surveyed were Year 8 students with birthdays in Jan–Mar?
   g How many Year 8 students were surveyed?
   h What fraction of the Year 8 students surveyed had birthdays in Jan–Mar?
   i How many students surveyed had birthdays in Jul–Dec?
   j How many Year 9 students surveyed had birthdays in Jul–Dec?
   k What fraction of the students with birthdays in Jul–Dec were Year 9 students?

2 Using the table of results for students surveyed in **Q1**, calculate the probability that
   a a student picked at random has a birthday in Jan–Mar
   b a student picked at random is a Year 8 student with a birthday in Jan–Mar
   c a Year 8 student picked at random has a birthday in Jan–Mar
   d a student picked at random has a Jul–Dec birthday
   e a student with a Jul–Dec birthday picked at random is in Year 9
   f a student with a Jul–Dec birthday picked at random is in Year 8
   g a student picked at random is a Year 8 student with a Jul–Dec birthday
   h a Year 9 student picked at random has a birthday in Oct–Dec
   i a student picked at random is in Year 8
   j a student picked at random has a birthday in the first half of the year

Reflect and reason

Tiana says, 'The probability that a Year 9 student picked at random from this survey has a birthday in Apr–Jun is $\frac{21}{120}$.' Explain her mistake and work out the correct probability.

Problem-solving practice

1 The two-way table shows some information about how some Year 8 and Year 9 students travel to school.

	Walk	Car	Bus
Year 8	108	53	39
Year 9	124	37	34

A student from the group is chosen at random.
Work out the probability that the student

a walks to school

b does not walk to school

c is in Year 8 and travels to school by car

d is in Year 9 and travels to school by bus

2 The two-way table gives some information about all of the drinks sold by a café on a Saturday and on a Sunday during one particular weekend.

	Tea	Coffee	Cold drink
Saturday	55	76	49
Sunday	37	43	40

a The owner chooses, at random, a customer who bought a drink on that weekend.
Assuming each customer bought only one drink, what is the probability that she chooses a customer who

i bought a cold drink

ii bought a coffee on Saturday?

b The owner chooses, at random, a customer who bought a drink on the Sunday.
What is the probability that this customer

i bought a cold drink

ii bought a coffee?

c The owner chooses, at random, one customer who bought a drink on each of the two days. Which is more likely:
A: choosing a customer who bought a tea on the Saturday
B: choosing a customer who bought a cold drink on the Sunday?
Show your working.

3 Grace has 40 chickens.
The two-way table shows some information about the chickens.

	Male	Female	Total
Brown		30	32
White	1		8
Total			40

a Copy and complete the two-way table.

b One of Grace's chickens is chosen at random.
Write the probability that this chicken is a brown female.

c One of the white chickens is chosen at random.
Write the probability that this chicken is male.

4 On an activity day, students can play one sport.
Year 9 and Year 10 students can choose to play football, hockey or tennis.
There are 160 Year 9 students. For Year 9, P(football) = $\frac{3}{5}$ and P(hockey) = $\frac{1}{10}$.
There are 150 Year 10 students. For Year 10, P(football) = P(hockey) = P(tennis) = $\frac{1}{3}$.
Use this information to copy and complete the table.

	Football	Hockey	Tennis	Total
Year 9				
Year 10				
Total				

Key points

- A Venn diagram shows sets of data in circles inside a rectangle.
- You write data that is in both sets in the intersection – the part where the circles overlap.

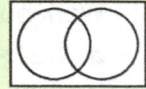

△ Purposeful practice 1

1 a Draw a Venn diagram to show this information on ice creams.

7 people like toffee and chocolate
14 people like chocolate
20 people like toffee
everybody asked likes at least one of the flavours

b How many people are represented in the Venn diagram?

2 a Draw a Venn diagram to show

13 people like mint
8 people like mint and raspberry
18 people like raspberry
everybody asked likes at least one of the flavours

b How many people like raspberry but not mint?

3 a Draw a Venn diagram to show

15 people like vanilla
6 people like banana
5 people like vanilla and banana
everybody asked likes at least one of the flavours

b How many people like vanilla but not banana?

4 a Draw a Venn diagram to show

17 people like strawberry
8 people like lemon
4 people do not like strawberry or lemon
5 people like strawberry and lemon

b How many people are represented in the Venn diagram?

Reflect and reason

For **Q1**, Eric draws this Venn diagram.
Explain his mistakes.

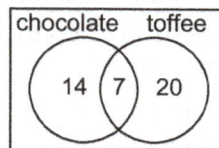

chocolate   toffee
14   7   20

△ Purposeful practice 2

Each Venn diagram shows the types of film people like.

drama   romance
11   4   7

1 What is the probability that a person picked at random likes

a drama
b romance
c romance but not drama?

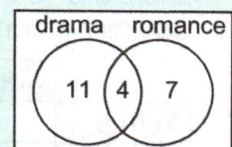

2 What is the probability that a person picked at random likes
   a drama
   b musicals and drama
   c musicals but not drama
   d either musicals or drama but not both?

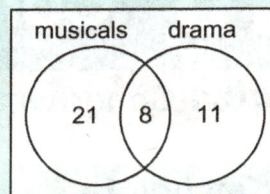
musicals   drama
21 (8) 11

3 What is the probability that a person picked at random
   a likes musicals and romance
   b does not like romance
   c likes musicals but not romance
   d does not like musicals or romance?

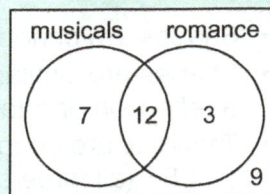
musicals   romance
7 (12) 3
9

Reflect and reason

How can you tell from the Venn diagrams in **Q1** and **Q2** that all the people liked at least one of the types of film?

In a Venn diagram, what does the part outside the two circles represent?

Problem-solving practice

1 An ice cream parlour serves two scoops of ice cream in every cone.
Customers can choose from vanilla and strawberry for each scoop.
From a group of 50 customers,
   35 choose vanilla for at least one of the scoops
   17 choose a scoop of each flavour
   a Show this information in a Venn diagram.
   b What is the probability that a customer chosen from the group at random has
      i one scoop of each flavour   **ii** only vanilla   **iii** only strawberry?

2 A number from 1–9 inclusive is chosen at random.
   a Copy and complete the Venn diagram to show the outcomes for this choice.
   b What is the probability of choosing a number that is
      i a multiple of 3
      ii an even number
      iii a multiple of 3 and an even number
      iv either a multiple of 3 or an even number
      v neither a multiple of 3 nor an even number?

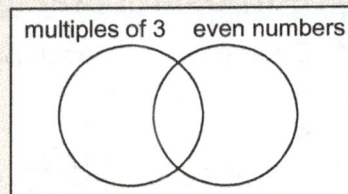
multiples of 3   even numbers

3 A group of students took a survey about their pets. They were asked to tick 'yes' next to each of 'cats', 'dogs' or 'rabbits' if their household contained one of more of each of those animals. The Venn diagram shows the results.
   a How many students are in the group?
   A student from the group is chosen at random.
   b What is the probability that this student ticked 'yes' for
      i rabbits   **ii** rabbits, cats and dogs
      iii cats and dogs   **iv** cats and dogs, but not rabbits
      v only cats or only rabbits   **vi** only dogs
      vii none of the three   **viii** just one of the three?

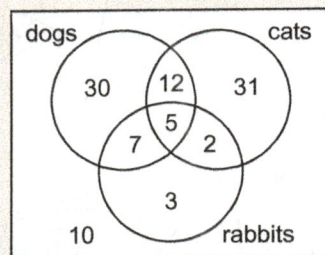
dogs   cats
30   12   31
   7   5   2
      3
10   rabbits

10 Comparing shapes

10.1 Congruent and similar shapes

> ### Key points
>
> - Shapes are congruent if they are the same shape and size.
> - Shapes are similar if one is an enlargement of the other. The enlarged image may be a reflection or rotation (or both) of the object.
> - Triangles are congruent if they have equivalent
>   SSS (all three sides)
>   SAS (two sides and the included angle)
>   ASA (two angles and the included side)
>   AAS (two angles and another side)

△ Purposeful practice 1

Which shapes are

1 congruent to shape X

2 similar to shape X

3 neither congruent nor similar to shape X?

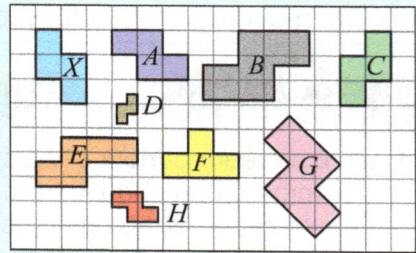

Reflect and reason

Is it possible for shapes to be both congruent and similar to each other? Explain.

△ Purposeful practice 2

1 Decide whether each pair of triangles is congruent and give a reason if so (SSS, SAS, ASA, AAS).

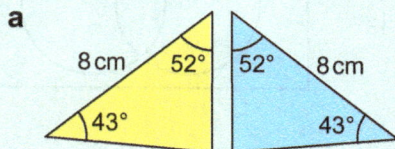

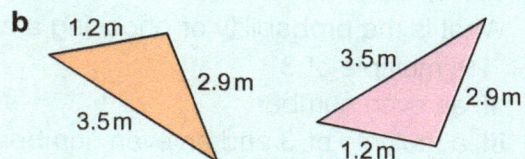

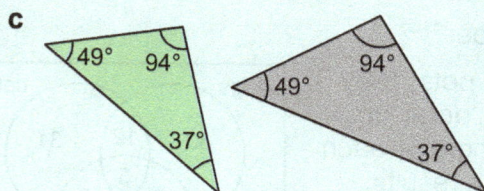

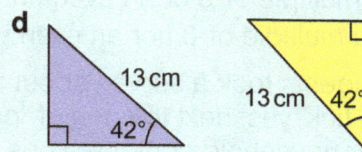

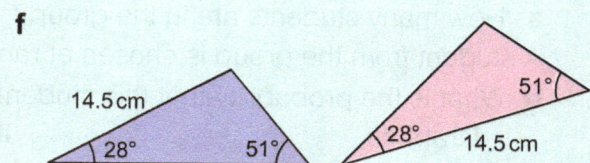

a

8 cm   52°   52°   8 cm

43°   43°

b

1.2 m   3.5 m

2.9 m

3.5 m   2.9 m

1.2 m

c

49°   94°   94°

49°

37°   37°

d

13 cm   13 cm   42°

42°

e

f

14.5 cm   51°

28°   51°   28°   14.5 cm

2 These triangles are all congruent. Work out the missing sides and angles.

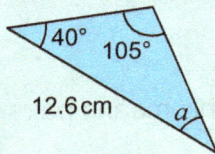

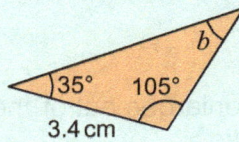

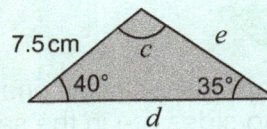

Reflect and reason

A pair of triangles have the same size angles (AAA). Why can't you use this fact to show they are congruent?

⊠ Problem-solving practice

1 Sanjit is asked if triangle A is congruent to triangle B.

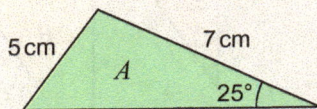

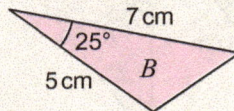

He says, 'Yes, triangle A is congruent to triangle B because both triangles have an angle of 25° and sides 5 cm and 7 cm.'
Is Sanjit correct? Explain.

2 Which of these triangles are congruent to triangle A?
Give reasons for your answers.

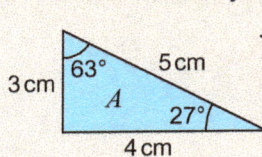

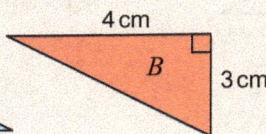

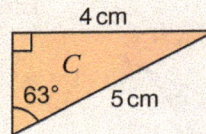

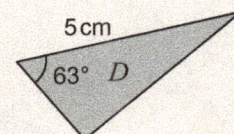

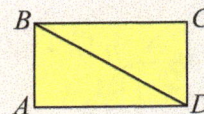

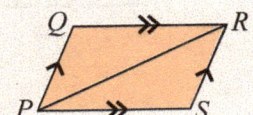

3 Write true or false for each statement.
Give reasons for your answers.
  a Two triangles, both with sides 4 cm, 5 cm and 6 cm, are always congruent.
  b Two right-angled triangles, each with one side 9 cm and another 10 cm, are always congruent.
  c Two triangles, both with sides 5 cm and 8 cm and an angle of 40°, are always congruent.
  d Two triangles, both with angles of 30°, 70° and 80°, are always congruent.

4 AB and CD are parallel lines.
  a Work out the size of all the angles. Give reasons for your answers.
  b Show that triangle ABE and triangle CDE are congruent.

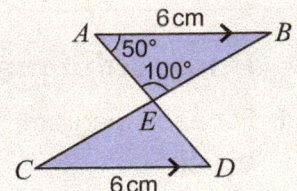

5 $ABCD$ is a rectangle.
Is triangle ABD congruent to triangle CDB?
Give reasons for your answer.

6 $PQRS$ is a parallelogram.
Is triangle PQR congruent to triangle PSR?
Give reasons for your answer.

Key points

- When two shapes are similar, one is an enlargement of the other. This means pairs of corresponding sides are in the same ratio.
- When two shapes are similar, their corresponding angles are equal.
  Triangles with equal corresponding angles are always similar. Other shapes with equal corresponding angles are not necessarily similar.

△ Purposeful practice 1

Each pair of triangles is similar. Work out the missing lengths in each pair.

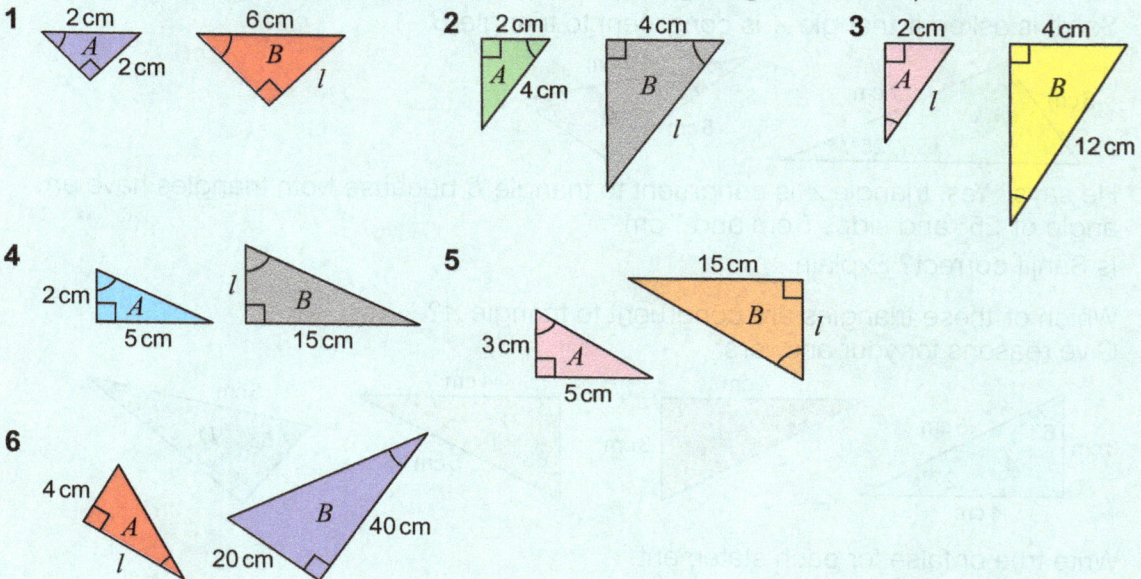

1 2 cm · 2 cm · *A* · 6 cm · *B* · *l*

2 2 cm · 4 cm · *A* · 4 cm · *B* · *l*

3 2 cm · 4 cm · *A* · *l* · *B* · 12 cm

4 2 cm · 5 cm · *A* · *l* · *B* · 15 cm

5 15 cm · *B* · *l* · 3 cm · *A* · 5 cm

6 4 cm · *A* · *l* · 20 cm · *B* · 40 cm

Reflect and reason

Andy works out **Q6** like this:
A : *B*
4 : 40
l : 20
What mistake has Andy made?

△ Purposeful practice 2

1 For each diagram, show that triangles *ABE* and *ACD* are similar.

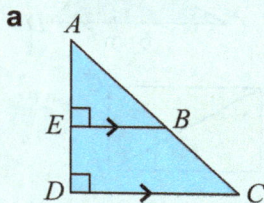

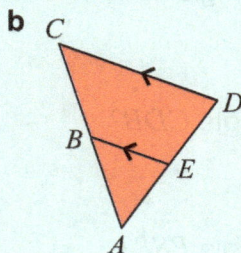

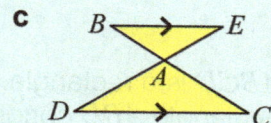

a *A* · *E* · *B* · *D* · *C*

b *C* · *D* · *B* · *E* · *A*

c *B* · *E* · *A* · *D* · *C*

2 For each diagram,
   i show that triangles PQT and PRS are similar   **ii** find the missing length x

a

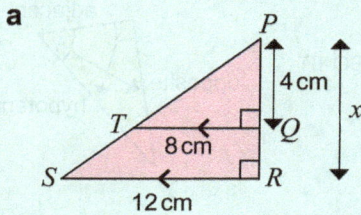

4 cm
x
T 8 cm Q
S 12 cm R
P

b

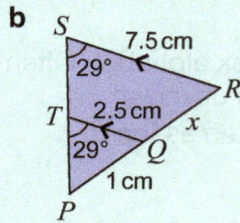

S 7.5 cm
29°
R
T 2.5 cm
29° x
Q
1 cm
P

c

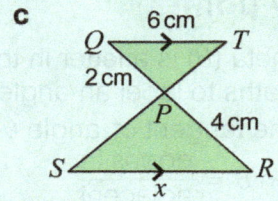

6 cm
Q T
2 cm
P
S 4 cm
x
R

Reflect and reason

Why is it not possible to use this diagram to show that triangles XWY and XVZ are similar?

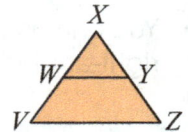

X
W Y
V Z

⊠ Problem-solving practice

1 The two triangular frames are similar triangles.
Dean enlarges the small frame to make the large frame.
Work out the length x of the large frame.

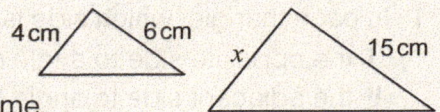

4 cm 6 cm
x 15 cm

2 Show that these two triangles are similar.

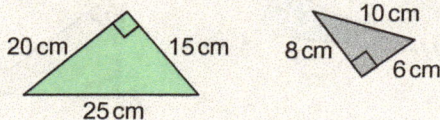

20 cm 15 cm
25 cm
10 cm
8 cm 6 cm

3 Calculate the length of TS.

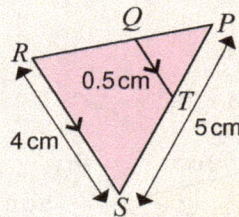

R Q P
0.5 cm
T
4 cm 5 cm
S

4 $ABCD$ and $EFGH$ are two rectangles that are both split exactly in half to make triangles.
There is a space 5 cm wide between rectangle $ABCD$ and rectangle $EFGH$.
Are triangles ABC and FGH similar?
You must show how you get your answer.

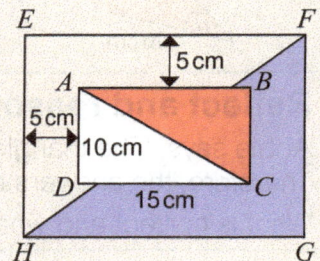

E F
5 cm
A B
5 cm
10 cm
D 15 cm C
H G

5 XYZ is a triangle.
VW is parallel to YZ.
Calculate the perimeter of the trapezium $VYZW$.

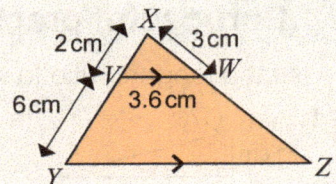

2 cm X 3 cm
V W
6 cm 3.6 cm
Y Z

6 The two triangles in the diagram are similar.
There are two possible values of x.
Work out each of these values.
Note, the triangles are not drawn accurately.

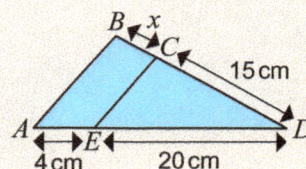

B x C
15 cm
A E D
4 cm 20 cm

Key points

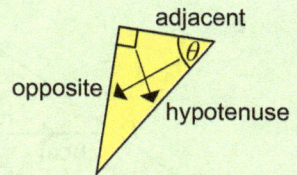

- Theta (θ) is a letter in the Greek alphabet. Often it is used in maths to label an angle that is unknown.
  The tangent of angle θ is written as tan θ.
  $$\tan \theta = \frac{\text{opposite}}{\text{adjacent}}$$

- You can use the $\boxed{\tan}$ key on a calculator to find the tangent of an angle.

- You can use the tangent ratio to find the length of one of the shorter sides in a right-angled triangle.

△ Purposeful practice 1

1 In each triangle, which side is
   i the opposite side to angle θ
   ii the adjacent side to angle θ
   iii the hypotenuse?

a 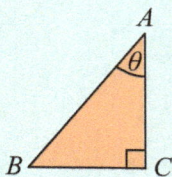 b 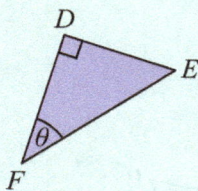 c 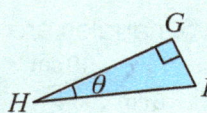 d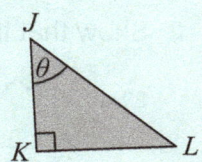

2 Write $\tan \theta$ as $\dfrac{\text{opposite}}{\text{adjacent}}$ for each triangle.

a 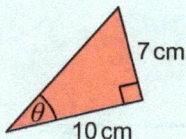 b 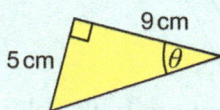 c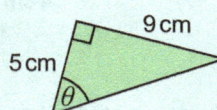

Reflect and reason

Abbie says, 'The triangles in **Q2** parts **b** and **c** have the same size sides and angles. Therefore, the answers to **Q2** parts **b** and **c** are the same.'
What is correct and what is incorrect about Abbie's statement?

△ Purposeful practice 2

Use the tangent ratio to work out x for each triangle, correct to 1 decimal place.

1 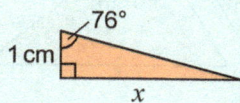   2 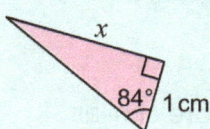   3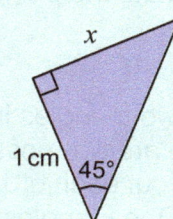

4

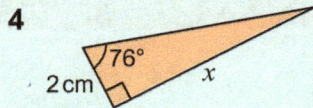
76°
2 cm
x

5

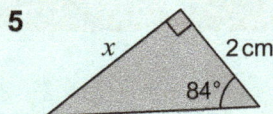
x   2 cm
84°

6

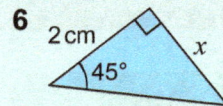
2 cm
45°
x

Reflect and reason

What do you notice about the triangles and your answers to **Q4–6** compared to **Q1–3**?
Explain why this happens.

Predict the opposite length x in a triangle with angle 76° and an adjacent side of 3 cm.

Purposeful practice 3

Use the tangent ratio to work out l for each triangle, correct to 1 decimal place.

1

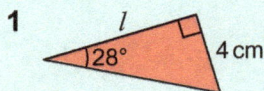
l
28°
4 cm

2

42°
l
5 m

3

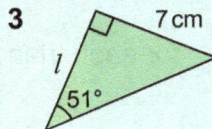
7 cm
l
51°

4

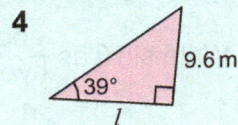
9.6 m
39°
l

Reflect and reason

Chris works out length l in **Q1** as 2.1 cm.
Sophie works out length l in **Q1** as 7.5 cm.

Who is correct? What mistake has the other student made?

Problem-solving practice

1 Work out the length of the rectangle.
Give your answer correct to 1 decimal place.

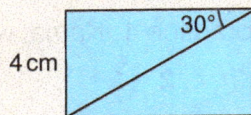
30°
4 cm

2 Emilio says, 'Triangles A and B have exactly the same height.'
Is he correct? Show your working to explain why.

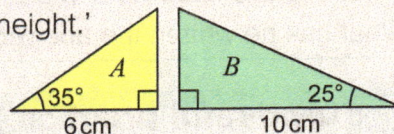
A B
35°   25°
6 cm   10 cm

3 **a** Calculate the height, h, of the equilateral triangle.

   b Calculate the area of the triangle.

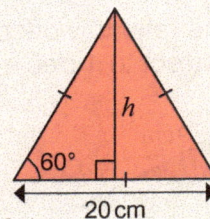
h
60°
20 cm

4 Jamie, Katja and Leo are asked to work out the length of the side labelled x.

Jamie writes
$$\tan 40° = \frac{8}{x}$$
$$x = \frac{\tan 40°}{8}$$

Katja writes
$$\tan 40° = \frac{8}{x}$$
$$x = \frac{8}{\tan 40°}$$

Leo writes
$$\tan 40° = \frac{x}{8}$$
$$x = 8 \tan 40°$$

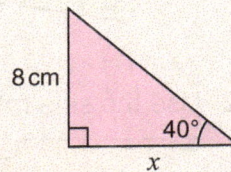
8 cm
40°
x

Who has the correct working? Explain why the others are incorrect.

5 The diagram shows the positions of three phone masts X, Y and Z.
X is 18 miles due north of Y. Z lies due west of Y.
Z is on a bearing of 230° from X.
Calculate the distance of Z from Y.
Give your answer correct to 3 significant figures.

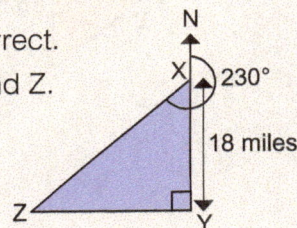
N
X   230°
18 miles
Z   Y

Key points

- The sine of angle θ is written as $\sin\theta$.

  $\sin\theta = \dfrac{\text{opposite}}{\text{hypotenuse}}$

- You can use the $\boxed{\text{sin}}$ key on a calculator to find the sine of an angle.

- You can use the sine ratio to find the length of the opposite side or hypotenuse in a right-angled triangle.

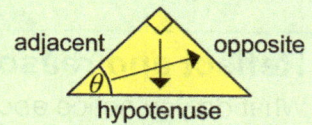

adjacent opposite
θ
hypotenuse

Purposeful practice 1

Write $\sin\theta$ as $\dfrac{\text{opposite}}{\text{hypotenuse}}$ for each triangle.

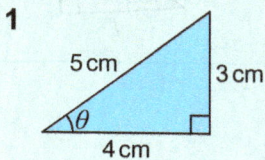

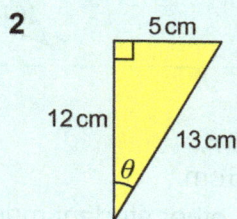

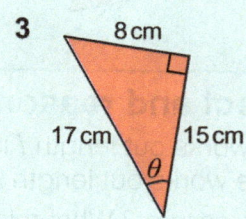

1
5 cm
3 cm
θ
4 cm

2
5 cm
12 cm
13 cm
θ

3
8 cm
17 cm
15 cm
θ

Reflect and reason

For Purposeful practice 1, Kamal writes the answers

1 $\dfrac{3}{4}$ **2** $\dfrac{5}{12}$ **3** $\dfrac{8}{15}$

What mistake has Kamal made?

What has he written the answers to?

Purposeful practice 2

1 Use the sine ratio to work out the opposite side, x, to the angle shown for each triangle, correct to 1 decimal place.

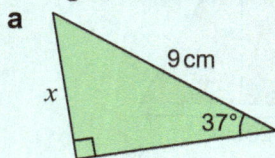

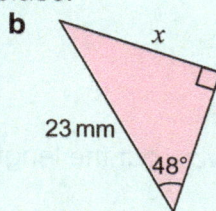

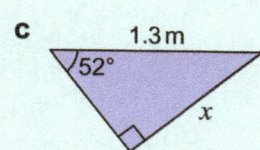

a
9 cm
x
37°

b
x
23 mm
48°

c
1.3 m
52°
x

2 Use the sine ratio to work out the hypotenuse, y, correct to 1 decimal place.

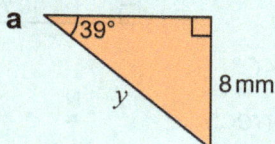

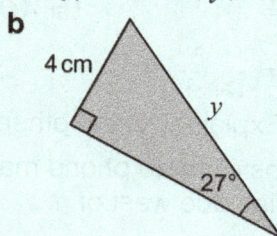

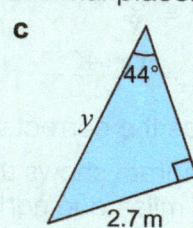

a
39°
y
8 mm

b
4 cm
y
27°

c
44°
y
2.7 m

3 Use the sine ratio to work out z for each triangle, correct to 1 decimal place.

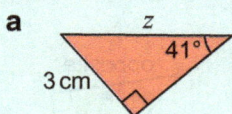

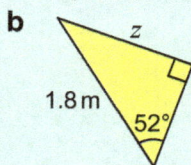

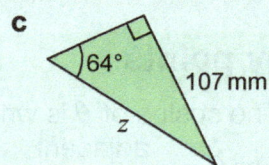

a

z
41°
3 cm

b

z
1.8 m
52°

c

64°
107 mm
z

Reflect and reason

Harry says, 'sin θ can never be greater than 1.'

Is Harry correct? Explain.

Problem-solving practice

1 Work out the vertical height of triangle ABC.
Give your answer correct to 3 significant figures.

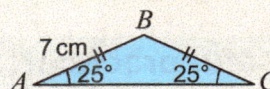

B
7 cm 25° 25° C
A

2 Work out the perimeter of the triangle.
Give your answer correct to 3 significant figures.

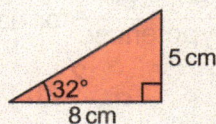

5 cm
32°
8 cm

3 A rectangular frame has a diagonal support, as shown in the diagram.

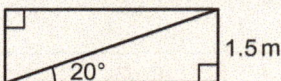

1.5 m
20°

How long is the diagonal support?
Give your answer correct to 2 decimal places.

4 A square has sides 10 cm.
Work out the length of the diagonal.
Give your answer correct to 3 significant figures.

5 A tent in the shape of a triangular prism is pegged down
from the top with a 2.5 m long rope.
The rope makes an angle of 45° with the ground.

a Work out the height of the tent.
Give your answer correct to 3 significant figures.

b Work out the length x.
Give your answer correct to 3 significant figures.

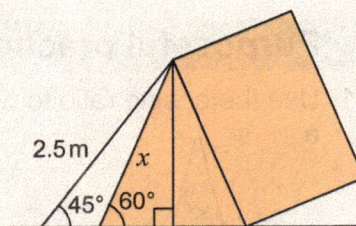

2.5 m
x
45° 60°

6 Calculate the area of the parallelogram.

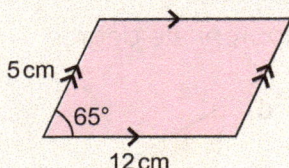

5 cm
65°
12 cm

7 Work out the value of x.
Give your answer correct to 2 decimal places.

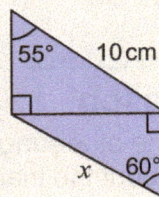

55° 10 cm
x 60°

Key points

- The cosine of θ is written as $\cos\theta$.
  $$\cos\theta = \frac{\text{adjacent}}{\text{hypotenuse}}$$

- You can use the $\boxed{\cos}$ key on a calculator to find the cosine of an angle.

- You can use the cosine ratio to find the length of the adjacent side or hypotenuse in a right-angled triangle.

- $\tan\theta$, $\sin\theta$ and $\cos\theta$ are called trigonometric ratios. They are part of a maths topic called trigonometry.

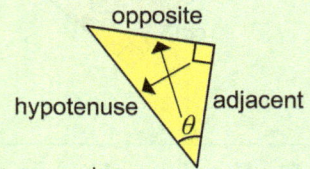

Purposeful practice 1

Write $\cos\theta$ as $\dfrac{\text{adjacent}}{\text{hypotenuse}}$ for each triangle.

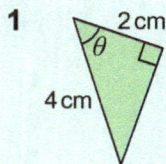

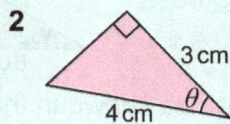

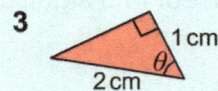

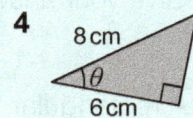

1 2 cm, 4 cm, θ

2 3 cm, 4 cm, θ

3 1 cm, 2 cm, θ

4 8 cm, 6 cm, θ

Reflect and reason

What do you notice about your answers to **Q1** and **Q3** and then **Q2** and **Q4**?

How can you describe these pairs of triangles?

Copy and complete this sentence:

Corresponding angles in _____ triangles have the same cosine ratio.

Is the same true for tangent and sine ratios?

Purposeful practice 2

1 Use the cosine ratio to work out side x for each triangle, correct to 1 decimal place.

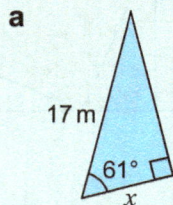

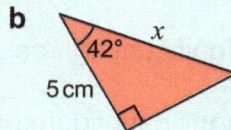

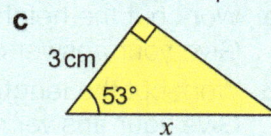

a 17 m, 61°, x

b 42°, x, 5 cm

c 3 cm, 53°, x

2 Use the correct trigonometric ratio to work out side x, to an appropriate degree of accuracy.

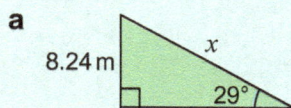

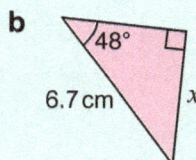

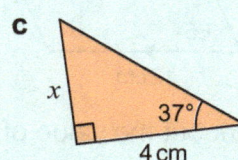

a 8.24 m, x, 29°

b 48°, 6.7 cm, x

c x, 37°, 4 cm

Reflect and reason

Work out some of the other angles and/or sides in each triangle in **Q1** and **Q2**.

What can you say about the triangles in **Q1a** and **Q2a**, **Q1b** and **Q2b**, and **Q1c** and **Q2c**?

Explain your answer.

1 A lighthouse (L) is 20 km due north from a ship.
   The ship (S) is sailing on a bearing of 050° towards a buoy (B).
   The buoy lies due east of the lighthouse.
   Work out how far the ship is from the buoy.
   Give your answer correct to 1 decimal place.

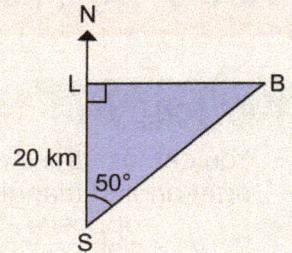

2 Work out the vertical height of triangle *XYZ*.

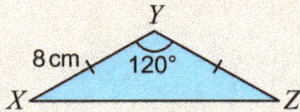

3 Ewan is making a ramp from the ground to a step.
   He starts the ramp 2.25 m from the step.
   The ramp is to make a 10° angle with the ground.
   What is the length of the ramp?
   Give your answer correct to 3 decimal places.

4 *ABCD* is a rectangle.

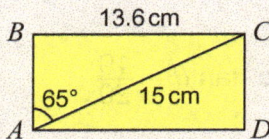

   Calculate the area of the rectangle.
   Give your answer correct to 3 significant figures.

5 *ABC* is an equilateral triangle.
   Work out the area of the triangle.
   Give your answer correct to 3 significant figures.

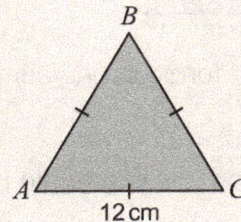

6 *ABC* is a right-angled triangle.
   D is a point on *AB*.
   Work out the perimeter of triangle *ACD*.
   Give your answer correct to 1 decimal place.

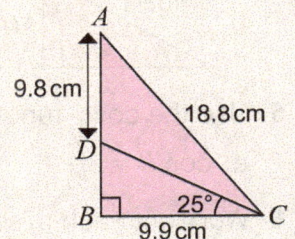

7 *ABD* and *BCD* are both right-angled triangles.
   Work out the length *CD*.

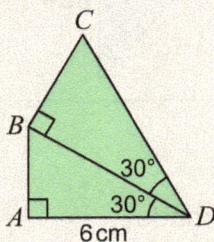

10.6 Using trigonometry to find angles

Key points

- You can use the inverse trigonometric functions to work out unknown angles in a right-angled triangle.

$$\tan\theta = \frac{\text{opposite}}{\text{adjacent}} \qquad \theta = \tan^{-1}\frac{\text{opposite}}{\text{adjacent}}$$

$$\sin\theta = \frac{\text{opposite}}{\text{hypotenuse}} \qquad \theta = \sin^{-1}\frac{\text{opposite}}{\text{hypotenuse}}$$

$$\cos\theta = \frac{\text{adjacent}}{\text{hypotenuse}} \qquad \theta = \cos^{-1}\frac{\text{adjacent}}{\text{hypotenuse}}$$

- You can usually find the inverse trigonometric function on a calculator by pressing [INV] [SHIFT] or [2nd] and looking for [tan⁻¹] [sin⁻¹] and [cos⁻¹]

Purposeful practice 1

Give all answers in Purposeful practice 1 to 1 decimal place.

1 Use the $\tan^{-1}$ function on your calculator to find θ.

  a $\tan\theta = \frac{7}{20}$ **b** $\tan\theta = \frac{11}{20}$ **c** $\tan\theta = \frac{19}{20}$

2 Work out each missing angle by using the tangent ratio.

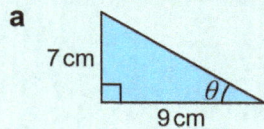

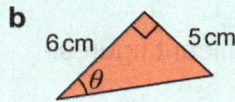

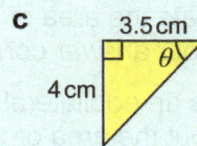

  a   7 cm, 9 cm, θ
  b   6 cm, 5 cm, θ
  c   3.5 cm, 4 cm, θ

3 Use the $\sin^{-1}$ function on your calculator to find θ.

  a $\sin\theta = \frac{7}{20}$ **b** $\sin\theta = \frac{11}{20}$ **c** $\sin\theta = \frac{19}{20}$

4 Work out each missing angle by using the sine ratio.

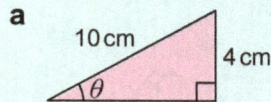

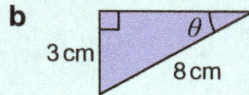

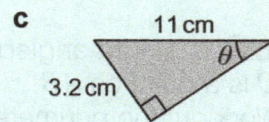

  a   10 cm, 4 cm, θ
  b   3 cm, 8 cm, θ
  c   11 cm, 3.2 cm, θ

5 Use the $\cos^{-1}$ function on your calculator to find θ.

  a $\cos\theta = \frac{7}{20}$ **b** $\cos\theta = \frac{11}{20}$ **c** $\cos\theta = \frac{19}{20}$

6 Work out each missing angle by using the cosine ratio.

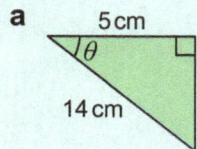

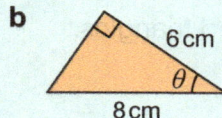

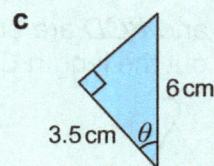

  a   5 cm, 14 cm, θ
  b   6 cm, 8 cm, θ
  c   6 cm, 3.5 cm, θ

Reflect and reason

Miko works out **Q6c** and gets the answer 0.6.

How can you tell that he is likely to be wrong? What mistake has he made?

Sketch each triangle and label the sides: opposite, adjacent or hypotenuse.
Then use the correct inverse trigonometric function to work out the unknown angle.

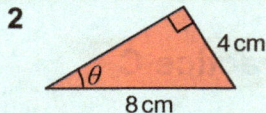

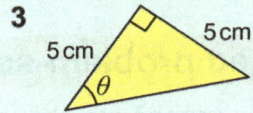

1 3 cm, 6 cm, θ

2 4 cm, 8 cm, θ

3 5 cm, 5 cm, θ

Reflect and reason

Write three trigonometric ratios that you can work out without using a calculator.
Instead of using a calculator, you can memorise them.

⊠ Problem-solving practice

1 *ABCD* is a rectangle.
Work out the angle that the diagonal makes with side *AB*.
Round your answer to an appropriate degree of accuracy.

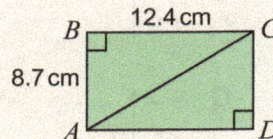

B 12.4 cm *C*
8.7 cm
A *D*

2 Mrs Summer asks her class to work out the size of angle *a*.
When she marks the work, she records the most common errors in the table.

Error 1	Error 2	Error 3	Error 4
$a = \sin \dfrac{15}{20}$	$a = \cos^{-1} \dfrac{15}{20}$	$a = \sin^{-1} \dfrac{20}{15}$	$a = \tan^{-1} \dfrac{15}{20}$

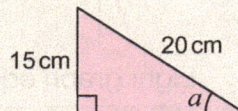

15 cm 20 cm *a*

  a Describe the error in each calculation.

  b Calculate the correct size of angle *a*.
     Give your answer correct to 1 decimal place.

3 A ladder is leaning against a vertical wall. The ladder is 5 m long.
The bottom of the ladder is 2 m from the bottom of the wall.
A ladder is only safe to use when the angle between the ladder and the ground
is 75°.
Is this ladder safe to use? You must show all your working.

4 Three schools, A, B and C, are positioned as described:

    School A is 9 miles due north of school B.
    School C is 7 miles due west of school B.

Calculate the bearing of school A from school C.
Give your answer correct to the nearest degree.

5 *ABCD* is a kite made by joining two congruent right-angled triangles.
Calculate the size of angle *ABC*.
Round your answer to an appropriate degree of accuracy.

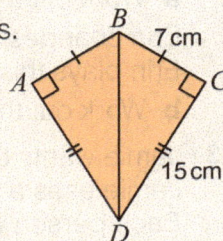

B 7 cm
A *C*
15 cm
D

6 The diagram shows a line segment that intersects the *x*-axis.
Work out the acute angle between the line segment and
the *x*-axis.
Round your answer to an appropriate degree of accuracy.

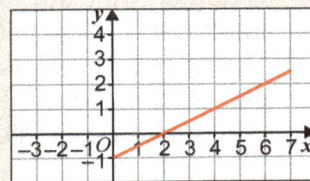

Mixed exercises C

Mixed problem-solving practice C

1 Six graphs are shown.

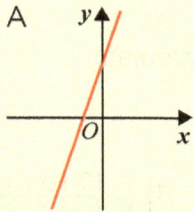

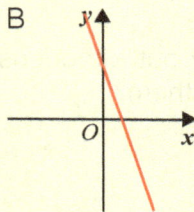

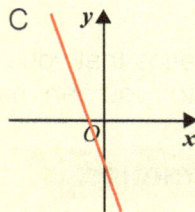

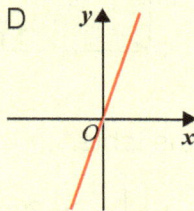

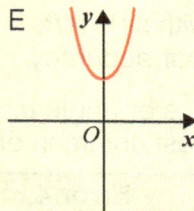

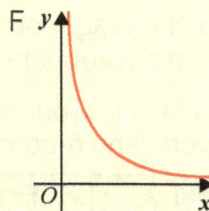

Eight graph equations are shown.

G: $y = x^2 + 3$ H: $y = 3x$ I: $y = x^2 - 3$ J: $y = \dfrac{3}{x}$

K: $y - 3x = -3$ L: $y - 3x = 3$ M: $y + 3x = -3$ N: $y + 3x = 3$

a Match each graph A–F to the correct equation G–N.

b Draw the graphs for the equations not used in part **a**.

c Which two of the equations have simultaneous solutions $x = 1$ and $y = 0$?

2 Erin plays a game where she throws a hoop at a target.
The table shows information about the probability of each possible score.

Score	0	1	2	3	5	10
Probability	0.07	0.30	x	$3x$	0.21	0.10

Erin is three times as likely to score 3 points as she is to score 2 points.

a Work out the value of x.

Erin changes the target so that the probability of each score is $\frac{1}{6}$.
Erin plays this game twice.

b Work out the probability that Erin scores a total of 10 for the two games.

3 Jamie wants to raise money for charity so he designs a game.
Jamie uses a fair 12-sided dice numbered from 1 to 12 for the game.
Each person will roll the dice once.
A person wins the game if the dice lands on a multiple of 5.
Each person pays 50p to play the game once.
The prize for a win is £1.
Jamie thinks that the game will be played 150 times.
Work out an estimate for how much money Jamie will raise for charity.

4 Triangles *ABC* and *DEF* are right-angled triangles.
Are triangles *ABC* and *DEF* congruent?
You must show your working.

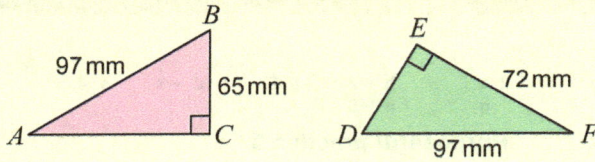

5 *D* is the midpoint of *BC*.
Work out the area of trapezium *ABDE*.

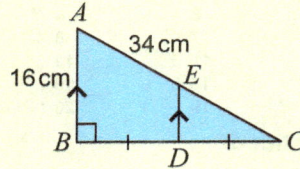

6 130 Year 9 students and 110 Year 10 students are asked for their favourite type of film from action, comedy and science fiction.
A total of 85 students prefer science fiction, and 40 of these students are in Year 9.
65 Year 9 students prefer comedy.
30 of the students who prefer action are in Year 10.
A Year 9 student is chosen at random.
Work out the probability that this student prefers action films.

7 100 students are asked if they own a phone and/or a tablet.
All students surveyed own at least a phone or a tablet.
39 students own both a phone and a tablet.
99 students own a phone.
A student is chosen at random.
What is the probability that this student owns

  a only a phone   **b** only a phone or only a tablet?

8 The diagram shows a quadrilateral *ABCD*.
Calculate the length of *CD*.
Give your answer correct to 3 significant figures.

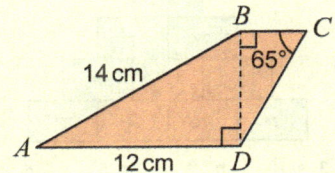

9 Work out the size of angle *BAD*.
Give your answer correct to 1 decimal place.

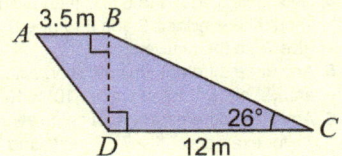

10 **a** Draw the graph of $y = x^2 - 5$.
   b Use your graph to find estimates for the solutions of
     i $x^2 - 5 = 0$ **ii** $x^2 - 5 = 2$

11 A café sells tea and coffee.
5 teas and 2 coffees cost a total of £15.00.
2 teas and 5 coffees cost a total of £16.50.
Draw a graph to work out the cost of one tea and the cost of one coffee.

12 *ABCD* is a trapezium.
Work out the size of angle *CDA*.
Give your answer correct to 1 decimal place.

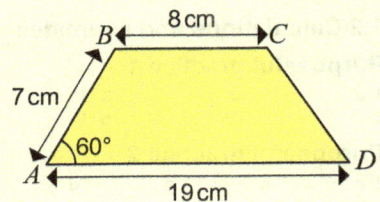

Answers

1 Indices and standard form

1.1 Indices

Purposeful practice 1

1 4^3	2 4^4	3 4^5	4 4^6
5 4^7	6 4^8	7 4^9	8 4^{11}
9 4^{13}	10 4^{17}	11 3^9	12 3^{12}
13 3^{15}	14 3^{18}	15 5^5	16 6^5
17 $(-6)^5$	18 $(-7)^5$	19 $(-7)^9$	20 $(-11)^9$

Purposeful practice 2

1 4^4	2 4^3	3 4^4	4 4^3
5 4^4	6 4^3	7 3^3	8 3^4
9 2^4	10 2^8	11 3^8	12 3^4
13 3^{10}	14 3^8	15 5^5	16 6^5
17 $(-6)^5$	18 $(-6)^7$	19 $(-1)^7$	20 $(-1)^6$

Purposeful practice 3

1 2^5	2 2^6	3 2^7	4 2^8	5 2^9	6 2^{10}
7 2^7	8 2^8	9 2^9	10 2^1	11 2^3	12 2^2
13 5^6	14 5^7	15 5^8	16 5^6	17 5^1	18 5^2

Problem-solving practice

1

×	5^2	5^6	5^4	5^8	5^5
5^3	5^5	5^9	5^7	5^{11}	5^8
5^2	5^4	5^8	5^6	5^{10}	5^7
5^6	5^8	5^{12}	5^{10}	5^{14}	5^{11}
5^7	5^9	5^{13}	5^{11}	5^{15}	5^{12}
5^9	5^{11}	5^{15}	5^{13}	5^{17}	5^{14}

2

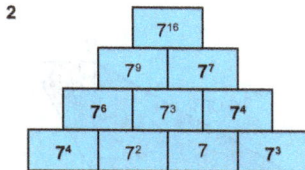

Pyramid:
- 7^{16}
- 7^9, 7^7
- 7^6, 7^3, 7^4
- 7^4, 7^2, 7, 7^3

3 a 2^5 b 2^3 c 5^8 d 2^6 e 3^5 f 5^7

4 Felix multiplied 3 and 6 and then divided by 2. Instead, he should have added 3 and 6 to give 9 and then subtracted 2 to give 7, so the answer is 3^7.

5 Any three different multiplication calculations that have an answer of 10^{12}, for example, $10^2 \times 10^{10}$, $10^3 \times 10^9$ and $10^4 \times 10^8$.

6 Any three different division calculations that have an answer of 7^4, for example, $7^{10} \div 7^6$, $7^6 \div 7^2$ and $7^{25} \div 7^{21}$.

7 Any three different calculations using multiplication and division that have an answer of 13^5, for example, $13^2 \times 13^6 \div 13^3$, $13^{10} \times 13^3 \div 13^8$ and $13^1 \times 13^6 \div 13^2$.

8 $x = 6$

9 a 9 b 2 c 8

10 Two values for a and b that total 14 but are not 7, for example $a = 1$ and $b = 13$.

11 $3^{15} \div 3^5$, $3^{20} \div 3^9$, $3^8 \div 3^5 \times 3^9$, $3^4 \times 3^9$

1.2 Calculations and estimates

Purposeful practice 1

1 3	2 3	3 4	4 4	5 7
6 7	7 10	8 10	9 12	10 12

Purposeful practice 2

1 a -1 b -2 c -3 d -10 e -20 f -30

2 a 2 b -2 c 3 d -3 e 4 f -4
  g 5 h -5

Purposeful practice 3

Students' own answers based on the level of rounding used, for example:

1 10	2 480	3 5	4 4
5 6	6 300	7 8	8 6

Problem-solving practice

1 28 cm

2 a A and G, B and E, C and H, D and F
  b E = 3, F = 5, G = 4, H = 3

3 Students' own estimates, for example:
  a 10 b 9 c 7 d 10 e 4 f -1

4 Students' own answers, for example, Ethan used a better method, as he also rounded 38.5 to the nearest number that is divisible by 5.

5 Dana, because estimating the answer by replacing the calculation with $\frac{4 + 6^2}{\sqrt{64}}$ gives an answer of 5, which is much closer to Dana's answer.

6 Students' answers will vary depending on the level of rounding used, for example, A, B and C.

7 $\sqrt{20}$ is closer to $\sqrt{16}$ than $\sqrt{25}$, and Shey has only divided 5 by 2 rather than dividing the whole numerator by 2.

1.3 More indices

Purposeful practice 1

1 4^2	2 2^4	3 4^4	4 2^8	5 4^6
6 2^{12}	7 3^3	8 3^8	9 3^9	10 3^{12}

Purposeful practice 2

1 a 2^0 b 1 c 1
2 a 3^0 b 1 c 1
3 a 1 b 1 c 1 d 1

Purposeful practice 3

1 a $3^{-1} = \frac{1}{3^1} = \frac{1}{3}$ b $3^{-2} = \frac{1}{3^2} = \frac{1}{9}$ c $3^{-3} = \frac{1}{3^3} = \frac{1}{27}$

  d $5^{-1} = \frac{1}{5^1} = \frac{1}{5}$ e $5^{-2} = \frac{1}{5^2} = \frac{1}{25}$ f $5^{-3} = \frac{1}{5^3} = \frac{1}{125}$

2 a $\frac{1}{16}$ b $\frac{1}{81}$ c $\frac{1}{49}$ d $\frac{1}{4}$

  e $\frac{1}{8}$ f $\frac{1}{16}$ g $\frac{1}{10\,000}$ h $\frac{1}{1\,000\,000}$

3 a i 2^{-4} ii $\frac{1}{16}$ b i 2^{-3} ii $\frac{1}{8}$

  c i 2^0 ii 1 d i 2^{-3} ii $\frac{1}{8}$

  e i 3^{-3} ii $\frac{1}{27}$ f i 3^{-2} ii $\frac{1}{9}$

  g i 5^0 ii 1 h i 10^{-3} ii $\frac{1}{1000}$

  i i 2^0 ii 1 j i 2^{-3} ii $\frac{1}{8}$

  k i 2^{-3} ii $\frac{1}{8}$ l i 2^2 ii 4

  m i 3^0 ii 1 n i 3^2 ii 9

  o i 5^{-2} ii $\frac{1}{25}$ p i 5^2 ii 25

Problem-solving practice

1 Kyle has used the power for the top of the fraction instead of using 1 at the top of the fraction to give $\frac{1}{7^2} = \frac{1}{49}$.

Mia has ignored the negative sign so she should have written $\frac{1}{7^2} = \frac{1}{49}$.

2

×	2^{-2}	2^{-3}	2^{-5}
2^2	1	$\frac{1}{2}$	$\frac{1}{8}$
2^{-1}	$\frac{1}{8}$	$\frac{1}{16}$	$\frac{1}{64}$
2^1	$\frac{1}{2}$	$\frac{1}{4}$	$\frac{1}{16}$

3 a 2^{-3} **b** 2^2

4 3^{-1}

5 5^{-6}

6 Any three different multiplication calculations that have an answer of 7^{-3}, for example, $7^3 \times 7^{-8}$, $7^2 \times 7^{-5}$ and $7^{25} \times 7^{-28}$.

7 Any three different division calculations that have an answer of $\frac{1}{100\,000}$, for example, $10^{10} \div 10^{15}$, $10^{-8} \div 10^{-3}$ and $10^{18} \div 10^{23}$.

8 No. $\frac{1}{64} = 2^{-6}$ and $0.5 = 2^{-1}$ so Evie has written $\frac{1}{64}$ in the wrong place, it should have been first.

9 a 7   **b** 3   **c** −2

1.4 Standard form

Purposeful practice 1

1 Yes   **2** No   **3** No   **4** Yes
5 No   **6** Yes   **7** No   **8** No

Purposeful practice 2

1 8.3×10^4 **2** 8.3×10^6 **3** 8.35×10^6 **4** 1.35×10^6
5 9.2×10^7 **6** 9.2×10^5 **7** 1.23×10^5 **8** 1.23×10^8

Purposeful practice 3

1 26 000   **2** 2 600 000   **3** 2 610 000   **4** 2 000 000
5 2100   **6** 21.4   **7** 21 700 000   **8** 2.7

Purposeful practice 4

1 8.3×10^{-5} **2** 8.3×10^{-3} **3** 8.3×10^{-4} **4** 1.25×10^{-4}
5 1.25×10^{-6} **6** 5×10^{-6} **7** 5.9×10^{-7} **8** 5.9×10^{-9}

Purposeful practice 5

1 0.000 26
2 0.000 002 6
3 0.000 000 261
4 0.000 002
5 0.0021
6 0.21
7 0.000 000 217
8 0.000 000 002 7

Problem-solving practice

1 a 4 900 000, 12 000 000, 13 000 000, 6 800 000, 140 000 000, 120 000 000, 51 000 000 and 49 000 000
   b Mercury, Mars, Venus, Earth, Neptune, Uranus, Saturn, Jupiter
2 Jess has included 5 zeros instead of multiplying 7.48 by 100 000 to give 748 000.
3 Yuri has not worked out the power of 10 correctly. The correct answer should be 3.8×10^{-5}.
Emily has not started with a number between 1 and 10; 0.38 is less than 1.
4 a Everything except the nucleus of an atom.
   b Nucleus of an atom, oxygen molecule, carbon atom, protein molecule and strand of hair
5 Earth and Mars are closer as 7.834×10^7 is smaller than 6.5×10^8.
6 390, 3100, 3.4×10^3, 3×10^4
7 0.000 000 42, 4.6×10^{-7}, 4.5×10^{-6}, 4.55×10^{-6}

2 Expressions and formulae

2.1 Solving equations

Purposeful practice 1

1 a $a = 8$ **b** $b = 50$ **c** $c = \frac{100}{3}$

2 a $d = 6$ **b** $e = 12$ **c** $h = 20$
3 $x = 10$

Purposeful practice 2

1 a $x = 12$ **b** $x = 18$ **c** $x = 15$
   d $x = 20$ **e** $x = -20$ **f** $x = -14$
2 a $x = 14$ **b** $x = 16$ **c** $x = 27$
   d $x = 8$ **e** $x = 1$ **f** $x = 10$

Problem-solving practice

1 a $\frac{2n}{5} = 20$ **b** 50
2 a $\frac{n}{4} - 3 = 7$ **b** 40
3

$$\frac{x}{5} + 11 = 7$$
$$-11 \quad\quad -11$$
$$\frac{x}{5} = -4$$
$$\times 5 \quad\quad \times 5$$
$$x = -20$$

4 Ava subtracted 3 first, instead of multiplying by 5 first.
5 a–h are all $a = 24$; this is because the working for each equation results in 12×2.
No, as $\frac{a}{3} - 5 = 7$ will result in $12 \times 3 = 36$.
6 a $\frac{2n}{5} = 10$ because $n = 25$ **b** $\frac{n}{5} - 4 = 10$ because $n = 70$

2.2 Substituting into expressions

Purposeful practice 1

1 a 1   **b** 2   **c** 4   **d** 9
2 a 8   **b** 16   **c** 36   **d** 12
3 a 81   **b** 27   **c** 36   **d** 144
4 a 4   **b** 8   **c** 16   **d** 36
5 a 36   **b** 18   **c** 36   **d** 144
6 a 0   **b** 0   **c** 0   **d** 0

Purposeful practice 2

1 a i 64   **ii** 36   **iii** 4   **iv** 49
   b i 34   **ii** 20   **iii** 10   **iv** 29
   c i 4   **ii** 4   **iii** 16   **iv** 9
   d i −16   **ii** 12   **iii** −8   **iv** −21
2 a i 27   **ii** 64   **iii** −1   **iv** −8
   b i 152   **ii** 72   **iii** 26   **iv** −133
   c i −8   **ii** 8   **iii** −64   **iv** 27
   d i −98   **ii** 56   **iii** −28   **iv** 117
3 a $\frac{1}{9}$ **b** $\frac{1}{4}$ **c** $\frac{5}{36}$ **d** $\frac{1}{7}$

Problem-solving practice

1 a E
   b i 100   **ii** 256   **iii** 400
2 a Ewan squared −3 and then multiplied it by 2 instead of multiplying by 2 and then squaring.
   b Zach didn't square −6 correctly; it should be 36, not −36.
3 Student D. Student A hasn't squared correctly (they've doubled instead). Student B hasn't multiplied inside the brackets. Student C hasn't squared −10 correctly.
4 $t^2 - u^2$
5 $p^2 - q^2$
6 a ab **b** b^2
7 Students' own answers where $x = y$, for example $x = 4$ and $y = 4$, or $x = -y$, for example $x = 4$ and $y = -4$.
8 $a = 0$ or $a = 2$

2.3 Writing and using formulae

Purposeful practice 1

1 a 60   **b** $12n$ **c** nx
   d $nx + 20$ **e** $nx + 30$ **f** $nx + y$
2 a $P = ny + z$ **b** $T = hm + k$ **c** $E = tx - w$
3 a $T = 3y$ **b** $T = 5x$ **c** $T = 3y + 5x$
   d $T = ay + 5x$ **e** $T = ay + bx$

Purposeful practice 2

Plumber	Call-out fee	Hourly rate (cost per hour)	Formula
A	£50	£50	$P = £(50h + 50)$
B	£20	£50	$P = £(50h + 20)$
C	£50	£30	$P = £(30h + 50)$

Problem-solving practice

1 Emily is wrong because she added instead of multiplying. It should be $C = 21A$

2 a £70   **b** £160   **c** £40
   d $C = 30d + 40$ **e** £400

3 a $C = 20h + 30$ **b** £330

4 a $T = 45w + 20$ **b** 200 minutes or 3 hours and 20 minutes

2.4 Using and rearranging formulae

Purposeful practice 1

1 a $x = y - 2$ **b** $x = y - 5$ **c** $x = y - 2$ **d** $x = w - z$
   e $x = a - z$ **f** $x = a - b$ **g** $x = a - b$ **h** $x = c - b$

2 a $y = \frac{x}{z}$ **b** $y = \frac{x}{a}$ **c** $y = \frac{x}{z}$ **d** $y = \frac{a}{z}$
   e $y = \frac{a}{b}$ **f** $y = \frac{a}{2}$ **g** $y = \frac{a}{5}$ **h** $y = \frac{x}{5}$

3 a $P = 2N$ **b** $P = NT$ **c** $P = \frac{2}{N}$ **d** $P = \frac{2}{a}$
   e $P = \frac{x}{a}$ **f** $P = \frac{y}{a}$ **g** $P = \frac{y}{x}$ **h** $P = \frac{a}{x}$

4 a $V = \frac{M}{D}$ **b** $D = \frac{M}{V}$ **c** $b = a - c$ **d** $c = a - b$
   e $q = p + t$ **f** $t = p - q$ **g** $M = LN$ **h** $N = \frac{M}{L}$

Purposeful practice 2

1 a $a = y - 2b$ **b** $a = y - 5b$ **c** $a = y - 5b$
   d $a = y - bc$ **e** $a = p + 4c$ **f** $a = p + 9u$
   g $a = p + xy$ **h** $a = c + tx$

2 a $x = \frac{p}{2}$ **b** $x = \frac{p + a}{2}$ **c** $x = \frac{p - b}{2}$
   d $x = \frac{p - 3b}{2}$ **e** $x = \frac{p + 5b}{2}$ **f** $x = \frac{p + 5}{m}$
   g $x = \frac{p - 4}{m}$ **h** $x = \frac{y - c}{m}$

Problem-solving practice

1 Sophie has divided by 3 before subtracting 5; she should have done it the other way round.
Jordan has only divided the 5 by 3; he should have divided all of $y - 5$ by 3.

2 $s = \frac{d}{t}$

3 $u = v - at$

4 $V = \frac{m}{D}$ and $m = DV$

5 $y = 2x + 7$ and $x = \frac{y - 7}{2}$

2.5 Index laws and brackets

Purposeful practice 1

1 a x^2 **b** x^3 **c** x^4 **d** x^5 **e** $2x^3$ **f** $2x^3$
   g $3x^5$ **h** $15x^2$ **i** $15x^3$ **j** $15x^5$ **k** $12x^3$ **l** $12x^4$

2 a n **b** n^4 **c** n^3 **d** n^4 **e** $2n^2$ **f** n^3
   g n^2 **h** n **i** n^4 **j** $6n^3$ **k** n^3 **l** n^2
   m $3n^2$ **n** $\frac{1}{2}n^2$ **o** $2n^4$ **p** $\frac{1}{2}n^4$ **q** $\frac{n^2}{3}$ **r** 3

Purposeful practice 2

1 a $x^3 + 3x$ **b** $x^4 + 3x^2$ **c** $x^4 + 3x^3$
   d $5x^4 + 15x^3$ **e** $10x^4 + 15x^3$ **f** $10x^5 + 15x^4$

2 a $y^4 - y^3$ **b** $2y^4 - y^3$ **c** $2y^4 - 3y^3$
   d $8y^4 - 12y^3$ **e** $10y^4 - 12y^3$ **f** $-y^3 + 2y$
   g $-3y^3 + 2y^2$ **h** $-12y^3 + 8y^2$

3 a $n(n^2 + 1)$ **b** $n(n^2 + 5)$ **c** $n^2(n + 5)$
   d $5n^2(n + 1)$ **e** $5n^2(2n + 1)$ **f** $5n^2(n + 2)$
   g $2n^2(n + 5)$ **h** $2n^2(2n + 5)$

4 a $m^3(m^2 - 1)$ **b** $m^3(1 - m^2 + 1)$ **c** $m^3(3m^2 - 1)$
   d $3m^3(m^2 - 1)$ **e** $3m^3(3m^2 - 1)$ **f** $2m(4m - 1)$
   g $2m^2(m^3 - 4)$ **h** $2m^2(3m^3 - 4)$

Problem-solving practice

1

×	$2x$	x^2	$4x^3$
$3x$	$6x^2$	$3x^3$	$12x^4$
$3x^2$	$6x^3$	$3x^4$	$12x^5$
$2x^3$	$4x^4$	$2x^5$	$8x^6$

2

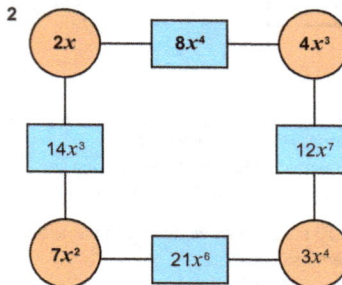

3 a $3x^3$ **b** $4y^2$ **c** $25z^8$

4 Students' own answers with product $20x^5$, for example, $x^2 \times 20x^2$, $2x \times 10x^3$ and $4x^3 \times 5x$.

5 Students' own answers, for example, $\frac{3x^3}{x}$, $\frac{6x^4}{2x^2}$ and $\frac{30x^9}{10x^7}$.

6 a $2x^2(x^2 + 3) = 2x^4 + 6x^2$
   b $5y^3(4y^4 - 5) = 20y^7 - 25y^3$

7 a Alesha has added the digits and not multiplied them.
   b Ryan hasn't multiplied the second term in the brackets by $2x^3$.
   c $8x^4 - 10x^3$

8 $24p^5 + 8p^3 = 8p^3(3p^2 + 1)$
$24p^5 + 16p^3 = 8p^3(3p^2 + 2)$
$24p^6 + 12p^3 = 12p^3(2p^3 + 1)$
$24p^5 + 12p^3 = 12p^3(2p^2 + 1)$
$24p^6 + 8p^3 = 8p^3(3p^3 + 1)$
$24p^6 + 16p^3 = 8p^3(3p^3 + 2)$

9 4 isn't the largest factor of 24 and 36; the largest factor is 12. x^2 isn't the largest factor of x^6 and x^5; the largest factor is x^5.
Sameer's answer should be $12x^5(2x^3 - 3)$

10 Yes, as $15a^3 - 25a^2 = 5a^2(3a - 5)$ and $18a^6 - 30a^5 = 6a^5(3a - 5)$.

2.6 Expanding double brackets

Purposeful practice 1

1 a i $x^2, 3x, 2x, 6$ **ii** $x^2 + 5x + 6$
   b i $x^2, 4x, 2x, 8$ **ii** $x^2 + 6x + 8$
   c i $x^2, 4x, 3x, 12$ **ii** $x^2 + 7x + 12$
   d i $x^2, 4x, 4x, 16$ **ii** $x^2 + 8x + 16$
   e i $x^2, 5x, 4x, 20$ **ii** $x^2 + 9x + 20$
   f i $x^2, 7x, 4x, 28$ **ii** $x^2 + 11x + 28$

2 a $x^2 + 8x + 15$ **b** $x^2 + 9x + 18$ **c** $x^2 + 10x + 24$
   d $x^2 + 11x + 30$ **e** $x^2 + 13x + 42$ **f** $x^2 + 15x + 56$

Purposeful practice 2

1 $x^2 + x - 6$
2 $x^2 + 3x - 10$
3 $x^2 + 6x - 16$
4 $x^2 + 5x - 24$
5 $x^2 + 3x - 40$
6 $x^2 + x - 56$
7 $x^2 - 6x - 7$
8 $x^2 - 4x - 21$
9 $x^2 - x - 42$
10 $x^2 + 4x - 12$
11 $x^2 + 3x - 18$
12 $x^2 + x - 12$
13 $x^2 - 7x + 12$
14 $x^2 - 8x + 15$
15 $x^2 - 10x + 21$

Problem-solving practice

1 Maisy's mistake is she has missed out the terms $9x$ and $-4x$.
Alfie's mistake is he has written $-5x$ instead of $+5x$.

2 $(n + 7)(n + 4) = n^2 + 4n + 7n + 28 = n^2 + 11n + 28$

3 Abdul:
$(n - 2)(n + 5) = n^2 + 5n - 2n - 10$
$\qquad\qquad = n^2 + 3n - 10$
$(n + 5)(n - 2) = n^2 - 2n + 5n - 10$
$\qquad\qquad = n^2 + 3n - 10$
So Abdul is correct.
Ben:
$(n - 2)(n + 5) = n^2 + 5n - 2n - 10$
$\qquad\qquad = n^2 + 3n - 10$
$(n - 5)(n + 2) = n^2 + 2n - 5n - 10$
$\qquad\qquad = n^2 - 3n - 10$
So Ben is not correct.

4 a $(x + 5)(x - 5) = x^2 - 5x + 5x - 25 = x^2 - 25$
  b Yes, $x^2 - 25$ is a quadratic expression as it contains an x^2 term and no higher powers of x.
5 Left-hand side $= n^2 - 3n + 2n - 6 = n^2 - n - 6$
  Right-hand side $= n^2 - 3n + 2n - 6 = n^2 - n - 6$
6 Area $= (x + 12)(x + 8) - (x + 5)(x + 3)$
  $= (x^2 + 8x + 12x + 96) - (x^2 + 3x + 5x + 15)$
  $= (x^2 + 20x + 96) - (x^2 + 8x + 15)$
  $= 12x + 81$
7 Area $= (x + 11)(x + 11) - (x + 6)(x + 6)$
  $= (x^2 + 11x + 11x + 121) - (x^2 + 6x + 6x + 36)$
  $= (x^2 + 22x + 121) - (x^2 + 12x + 36)$
  $= 10x + 85$
8 $(x + 21)(x - 3) = x^2 - 3x + 21x - 63$
  $\qquad\qquad\quad = x^2 + 18x - 63$

3 Dealing with data

3.1 Planning a survey

Purposeful practice 1

1 B
2 All the insects in the pond.
3 All the chocolate bars produced in that factory on that Friday.
4 All the people in the country who will be able to vote at the next election.

Purposeful practice 2

1 A, D
2 C, D
3 A
4 C, with students' own reasons, for example: this would give her a good idea of how opinions vary across different age groups. Knowing the person's name or name of tutor group isn't very useful, and people may not be fully honest if she knows who they are.

Problem-solving practice

1 Freya is correct as this is all students at the school. Kelly's may include children who go to a different school and Anish may include staff and exclude anyone who is absent.
2 a Students on the school register.
  b Year group and mode of transport to school.
3 a The teenagers in his town.
  b Time spent playing games on consoles.
4 Students' own answers showing that the manager is investigating time spent using each facility, for example, is the gym used more than the swimming pool and fitness classes?
5 Students' own answer, for example, what sports different age groups watch or what sports different age groups take part in/enjoy.
6 This is a biased sample as Ava only asks her friends. Ava should ask a random sample of students from across the school.
7 a Too many people to survey if she asks everyone in the town.
  b Method D as this is random.

3.2 Collecting data

Purposeful practice 1

1 a 1–5, 6–10, 11–15, 16–20, 21–25
  b 1–10, 11–20, 21–30, 31–40, 41–50
  c 1–20, 21–40, 41–60, 61–80, 81–100

2 a 1–5, 6–10, 11–15, 16–20
  b 1–10, 11–20, 21–30, 31–40
  c 1–25, 26–50, 51–75, 76–100
3 a $0 \leq x < 5$, $5 \leq x < 10$, $10 \leq x < 15$, $15 \leq x < 20$, $20 \leq x < 25$
  b $0 \leq x < 8$, $8 \leq x < 16$, $16 \leq x < 24$, $24 \leq x < 32$, $32 \leq x < 40$
  c $0 \leq x < 15$, $15 \leq x < 30$, $30 \leq x < 45$, $45 \leq x < 60$, $60 \leq x < 75$
4 a Discrete
  b 101–140, 141–180, 181–220, 221–260, 261–300
5 a Continuous
  b $300 \leq x < 330$, $330 \leq x < 360$, $360 \leq x < 390$, $390 \leq x < 420$, $420 \leq x < 450$
  c $300 \leq x < 337.5$, $337.5 \leq x < 375$, $375 \leq x < 412.5$, $412.5 \leq x < 450$

Purposeful practice 2

1 Students' own answers with 3–5 suitable groups, for example, 0–25, 26–50, 51–75, over 75.
2 Students' own answers with 3–5 suitable groups, for example, $0 \leq h < 2$, $2 \leq h < 4$, $4 \leq h < 6$, $6 \leq h < 8$, 8 or more.
3 Students' own answers, for example

Screen time in hours	Age			
	0–25	26–50	51–75	Over 75
$0 \leq h < 4$				
$4 \leq h < 8$				
$h \geq 8$				

Problem-solving practice

1 a

Test results	Tally	Frequency
1–10	I	1
11–20	II	2
21–30	ЖЖ	5
31–40	ЖЖ ЖЖ	10
41–50	II	2

  b 20
  c 31–40
2 a Students' own answers, for example

Height (cm)	Tally	Frequency
$0 < h \leq 5$	I	1
$5 < h \leq 10$	III	3
$10 < h \leq 15$	ЖЖ II	7
$15 < h \leq 20$	IIII	4

  b 15
  c $10 < h \leq 15$
3 a 40 and 50 are in 2 classes. Height is continuous data so intervals should be written $30 < h \leq 40$, etc.
  b The class widths aren't equal; the first class is 5, then 3 then 4. They should be $0 < m \leq 4$, $4 < m \leq 8$ and $8 < m \leq 12$.
  c Number of children is discrete data so intervals should be written 0–19, etc.
  d Both inequality signs are the same but there should be one including 'or equal to', for example $0 < t \leq 2$, etc.

3.3 Calculating averages

Purposeful practice 1

1 a 2
  b

Value	Frequency
0	2
1	3
2	2
3	4

  c 2

2 a 0, 0, 0, 0, 1, 1, 1, 1, 1, 1, 2, 2, 2, 2, 2, 2, 2, 2, 2, 3
  b 2
  c 2
3 0–6 years
4 $30 < m \leqslant 40$

Purposeful practice 2

1 Q1 1.7, **Q2** 1.4 children
2 Q3 6.6 years, **Q4** 33.8 g

Problem-solving practice

1 a Tia is correct. Ryan has only found the middle class, not the median. Seth has correctly worked out that the median is the 14th number but this is not the median; he then needs to work out what the 14th number is.
  b 1.5 pets
2 a The director has divided the total of the frequency by how many groups there are. She should have worked out the total of the midpoints multiplied by the frequency and then divided this total by the total of the frequency.
  b 9 hours
  c $5 \leqslant h < 10$
3 a 3
  b 25 cm
  c $20 \leqslant l < 30$

3.4 Displaying and analysing data

Purposeful practice 1

1 a A 54, B 58
  b A 28, B 27
  c A 32, B 34
  d A 70, B 65

Purposeful practice 2

1 a, b

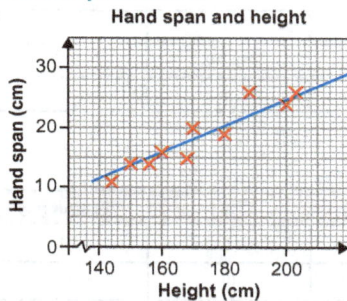

Hand span and height

  c i Between 16 and 20 cm   **ii** Between 180 and 188 cm

Problem-solving practice

1 165 to 169 cm
2 a

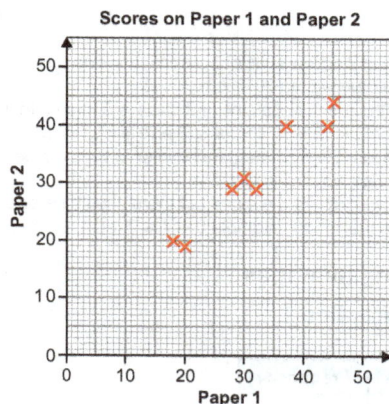

Scores on Paper 1 and Paper 2

  b 24 to 26
3 Students' own answers, for example, 95 grams is over 5 grams lower than the value suggested by the line of best fit.
4 Students should draw the scatter graph and the line of best fit and then say, 'No, as the measurements for this leaf are too far away from the line of best fit.'

3.5 Presenting and comparing data

Purposeful practice 1

1

Typing speed before course		Typing speed after course
9 7	1	
9 6 6 5 1	2	1 2 4
8 8 6 5 5 2 0	3	5 7 7 9
7 5 4 2 1 1	4	0 2 2 6 8
	5	1 1 2 4 4 5 7
	6	3

Key: Key:
7|1 means 17   2|1 means 21

Purposeful practice 2

1

Type A		Type B
6	12	
7 6 4	13	
9 3 1 0	14	
9 7	15	
5 3	16	1 2 4
	17	6
	18	2 4 6 9
	19	2 3 5 8

Key: Key:
6|12 means 12.6   16|1 means 16.1

2

Diameter (cm)	Type A	Type B
$12 < d \leqslant 14$	5	0
$14 < d \leqslant 16$	5	0
$16 < d \leqslant 18$	2	4
$18 < d \leqslant 20$	0	8

3

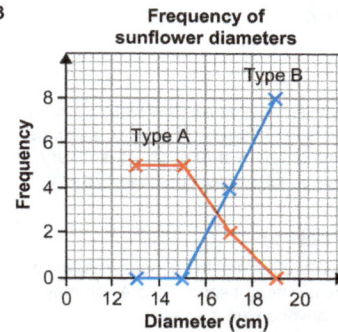

Frequency of sunflower diameters

4 Type A: mean 14.6 cm, median 14.2 cm, range 3.9 cm
  Type B: mean 18.2 cm, median 18.5 cm, range 3.7 cm
5 Type A: 14.5 cm, Type B: 18.3 cm
6 Students' own answer, for example, Type B diameters are larger on average, as Type B mean is 18.2 cm compared to Type A mean of 14.6 cm. There is a slightly greater spread in the Type A diameters than Type B, as the Type A range is 3.9 cm compared to Type B range of 3.7 cm.

Problem-solving practice

1 a

Time on dry day		Time on rainy day
9 8 6 6 5 5 4 4 4 3 3	0	4 5 6 6 7 9 9
8 4 3 1 1 0 0 0	1	0 0 1 2 5 7 9 9
	2	2 5 7 8
	3	1

Key: Key:
3|0 means 3   0|4 means 4

b The median for the dry day (8.5 minutes) is lower than the median for the rainy day (11.5 minutes), so on average the students take less time on a dry day.

c The range for the dry day (18 minutes) is lower than the range for the rainy day (27 minutes) so the times are more spread out on a rainy day.

2 On average, the Year 11 students (median 171 cm) are taller than Year 9 students (median 166 cm). The heights of the Y9 students (range 31 cm) are slightly more spread out than the heights of the Year 11 students (range 29 cm).

3 Students' own answers, for example:
An estimate of mean height with fertiliser is 53.1 cm, which is taller than an estimate of mean height without fertiliser, 47.5 cm. The data suggests that plants grow taller with fertiliser, so the biologist is correct.

4 Students' own answers, for example:
On average, Anya (estimate of mean 28.8 minutes to 1 d.p.) runs 3 km faster than Dina (estimate of mean 30.2 minutes to 1 d.p.). The data shows that, on average, Anya runs races in a shorter time than Dina, so Anya is not correct.

Mixed exercises A

Mixed problem-solving practice A

1 Students' own answers, for example: the age of the males is more spread out (as the range for the males is 45 but the range for the females is 34). On average, the females are younger than the males (as the mean for the females is 30.8 and the mean for the males is 36.77).

2 No, as BMI $= \dfrac{86}{1.85^2} = \dfrac{86}{3.4225} = 25.1278...$, so it is above the healthy range.

3 5.76×10^{15} (approx)

4 $x = 72°$

5 a $10 < m \leqslant 20$

b 17.6 kg

c Students' own answers, for example, the estimate of the mean for flight B is 26 kg, so on average the suitcases for flight B are heavier.

6 a $1000^x = 10^{3x} = 10^4$, so $A = 3x$

b $x = \dfrac{A}{3}$

7 a A and Y, E and X, F and Z

b X: 121 cm², Y: 176 cm², Z: 256 cm²

8 a $(4.7 \times 10^5)^7$

b $(3.5 \times 10^7)^{-8}$

9 a 19

b 4

c Without revision list: $S = 4h + 8$, with revision list: $S = 12h + 4$

d Students' own answer, for example, as long as they revised for at least half an hour, students who used the revision list achieved a higher score than those who didn't. For every extra hour that students revise with the list they score 12 more marks, and without the list they score 4 more marks.

10 a Area $= x^2 + 15x + 36$

b Yes, as $(x + 12)(x + 3) = x^2 + 15x + 36$, which is the same expression as shape A.

4 Multiplicative reasoning

4.1 Enlargement

Purposeful practice 1

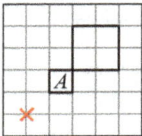

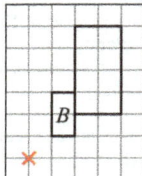

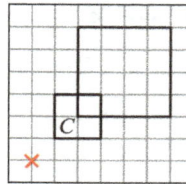

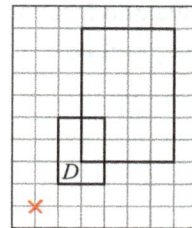

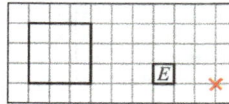

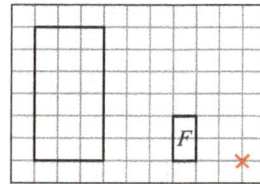

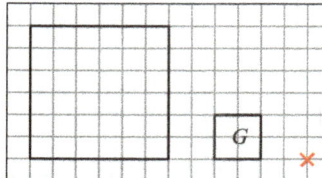

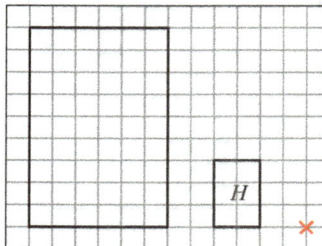

Purposeful practice 2

1 Enlargement by scale factor 4, with centre of enlargement (0, 1).

2 Enlargement by scale factor 2, with centre of enlargement (2, 4).

3 Enlargement by scale factor 3, with centre of enlargement (0, 3).

Purposeful practice 3

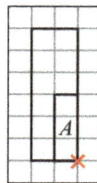

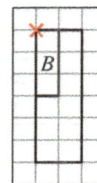

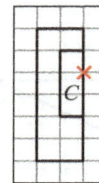

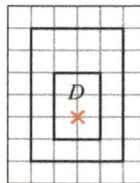

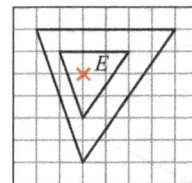

Problem-solving practice

1 a F   **b** E   **c** D

2 a Shape W is an enlargement of shape Y by scale factor 3 and centre of enlargement (4, −5).

b Shape S is an enlargement of shape T by scale factor 3 and centre of enlargement (3, 1).

c Shape W is an enlargement of shape X by scale factor 3 and centre of enlargement (4, −2).

3 No, shape B is the correct shape and size but it is not in the correct position. It needs to be translated 3 squares in the positive x-direction.

4.2 Negative and fractional scale factors

Purposeful practice 1

1
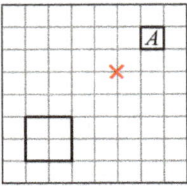
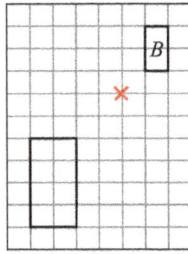
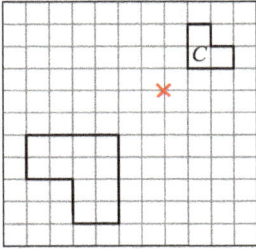

2
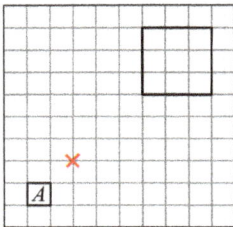
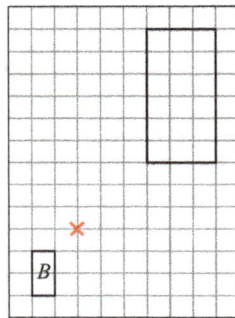
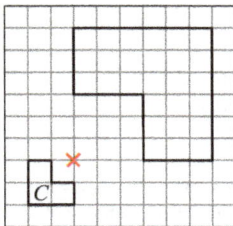
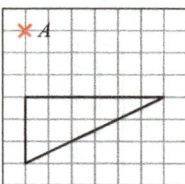
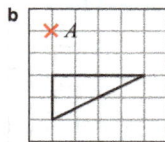
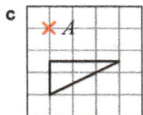

Purposeful practice 2

1 a 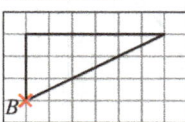   b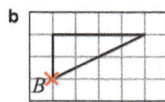

c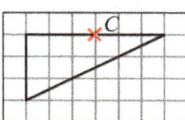

2 a 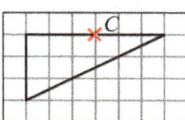   b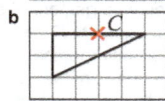

c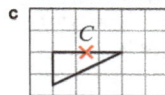

3 a 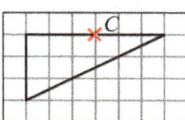   b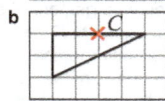

c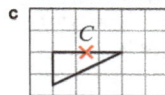

Problem-solving practice

1 S
2 a $\frac{1}{3}$, (−5, −5)   b −2, (0, 0)
3 The triangle is the right size but in the wrong position; the top vertex should be at (1, 2).
4 The scale factor should be $-\frac{1}{2}$ and the centre of enlargement should be (0, 2).

4.3 Percentage change

Purposeful practice 1

1 Coat: £100, Jeans: £60, T-shirt: £4
2 Coat: £112.50, Jeans: £67.50, T-shirt: £4.50
3 Coat: £150, Jeans: £90, T-shirt: £6
4 Coat: £200, Jeans: £120, T-shirt: £8

Purposeful practice 2

1 442 000
2 800 100
3 667 325
4 396 700
5 276 500
6 672 000

Purposeful practice 3

1 a 35%   b 25%
2 a 50%   b 40%
3 a 75%   b 30%
4 a 12.5%   b 5%

Problem-solving practice

1 a D   b £18 600
2 £9.60
3 a £560   b Chris by £5
4 Town A
5 71.4%
6 $\frac{120}{380} \times 100 = 31.6\%$ (1 d.p.) which is more than 30%
7 a Sanjit should have used the actual profit of 59 as the numerator and the original cost of 236 as the denominator.
   b 25%

4.4 Compound measures

Purposeful practice 1

1 a 1200 m/min   b 72 000 m/hour
  c 72 km/h   d 45 mph
2 a 115.2 km/h   b 115 200 m/hour
  c 1920 m/min   d 32 m/s
3 a 120 km/h   b 60 km/h
  c 15 km/h   d 960 km/h
4 a 90 km   b 180 km
  c 720 km   d 11.25 km
5 a 1 hour   b 2 hours
  c $2\frac{1}{2}$ hours   d $\frac{1}{2}$ hour

Purposeful practice 2

1 a 7.3 g/cm³   b 7.13 g/cm³   c 8.75 g/cm³   d 8.89 g/cm³
2 a 14.4 g   b 22.66 g   c 17.6 g   d 17.88 g
3 a 4 cm³   b 3 cm³
4 a 5 N/m²   b 9 N/m²   c 13 N/m²   d 30 N/m²
5 a 42 N   b 72 N   c 90 N   d 126 N

Problem-solving practice

1 105 m/s, as 360 km/h = 100 m/s
2 Platinum, as density of gold = 19.32 g/cm³ and density of platinum = 21.45 g/cm³
3 Javid's piece of silver is heavier. Moira's piece has mass 10.49 × 3.5 = 36.715 g.
4 1574 g
5 a Will divided by minutes so his answer is in km/min, and Silas divided 5000 m by half an hour, not 5 km, so his answer is in m/h
  b 10 km/h
6 Clare arrives first. Her journey takes
   36 ÷ 45 = 0.8 hours = 48 minutes, so she arrives at 8.48 am.
   Darren's journey takes 20 ÷ 30 = 0.66... hours = 40 minutes so he arrives at 8.55 am.

7 58 mph
8 1 hour

4.5 Direct and inverse proportion

Purposeful practice 1

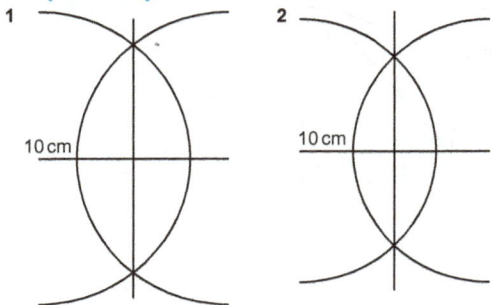

1 a 28p   **b** 24p   **c** 30p   **d** 21p   **e** 22p
2 a Pack D   **b** Pack C

Purposeful practice 2

1 a £1.80   **b** £2.20   **c** £1.30
2 a 60p   **b** 55p   **c** 65p
3 a Pack B   **b** Pack C

Purposeful practice 3

1 a 8 days   **b** 2 days   **c** 1 day
2 a i 12 days   **ii** 3 days   **iii** 4 days
   b i 9 days   **ii** 18 days   **iii** 12 days

Problem-solving practice

1 6 pints, as £0.80 ÷ 2 pints = 40p per pint,
£1.12 ÷ 4 pints = 28p per pint,
£1.50 ÷ 6 pints = 25p per pint.
2 1000 as 9.99 ÷ 5 = 1.998. This rounds to £2.00, which is less than £2.71.
3 The 2.9 kg size box, as £2.40 ÷ 1.5 kg = £1.60 per kg,
£3.77 ÷ 2.9 kg = £1.30 per kg,
£5.94 ÷ 4.5 kg = £1.32 per kg.
4 80 tea bags as these cost 33p per 10 tea bags. The 30 bag box costs 40p per 10 bags and the 240 bag box costs 34p per 10 bags.
5 Bottles as the bottles cost £2.60 ÷ 8 litres = £0.33 per litre (to 2 d.p.) and the cans cost £1.65 ÷ 1.98 litres = £0.83 per litre (to 2 d.p.)
6 No, as the number of people doubles so he should have halved the number of hours, giving 3 hours.
7 12 minutes

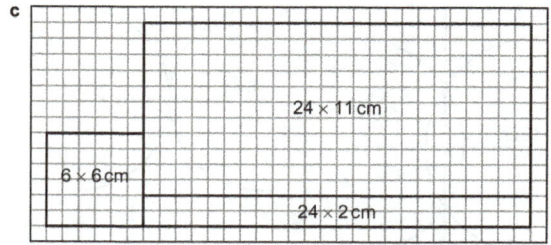

5 Constructions

5.1 Using scales

Purposeful practice 1

1 a

6 × 2.5 cm

b 3 × 1.25 cm

c 12 × 5 cm

2 a

12 × 5.5 cm
3 × 3 cm
12 × 1 cm

b 1.5 × 1.5 cm
6 × 2.75 cm
6 × 0.5 cm

c

24 × 11 cm
6 × 6 cm
24 × 2 cm

Purposeful practice 2

1 Map		Real life
1	:	10 000
1 cm		**10 000** cm = **100** m
3 cm		**300** m
5 cm		1 km
2 Map		Real life
1	:	20 000
1 cm		**20 000** cm = **200** m
3 cm		**600** cm
5 cm		1000 m = 1 km
3 Map		Real life
1	:	50 000
1 cm		**50 000** cm = **500** m = **0.5** km
3 cm		**1.5** km
2 cm		1 km
4 Map		Real life
1	:	100 000
1 cm		**100 000** cm = **1000** m = **1** km
3 cm		**3** km
5 cm		5 km

Problem-solving practice

1 8 cm
2 a The diagram is drawn using a scale of 1 : 100, not 1 : 50.
   b

Hall 3 × 6 cm	Kitchen 7 × 6 cm

Living room
10 × 9 cm

Scale 1 : 50

3 52 km
4 a 910 m (approx)   **b** 2.25 km (approx)   **c** 3.45 km (approx)

5.2 Basic constructions

Purposeful practice 1

1

10 cm

2

10 cm

3

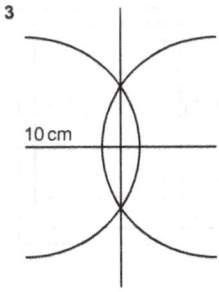

10 cm

4

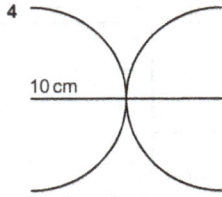

10 cm

5

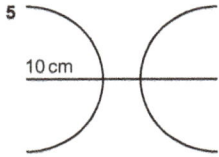

10 cm

Purposeful practice 2

1 a

b

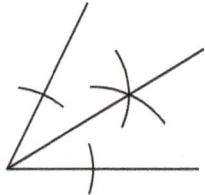

c

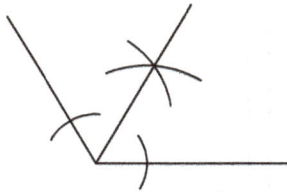

d

2 a, b

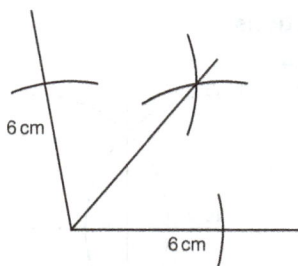

6 cm

6 cm

3 a, b

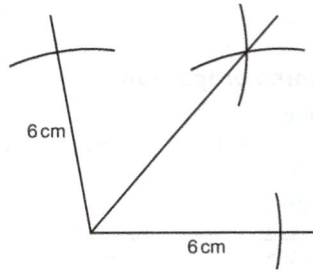

6 cm

6 cm

4 a, b

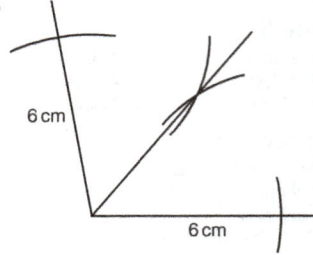

6 cm

6 cm

5 a, b Students' own construction, for example,

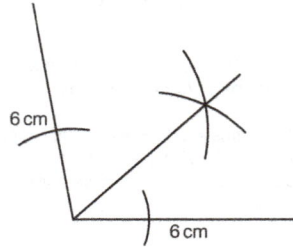

6 cm

6 cm

Problem-solving practice

1 a No, Sara has not kept her compasses the same distance when drawing the arcs from points A and B.

b No, Felix hasn't set his compasses wide enough when drawing the arcs from points A and B, they need to be set to over half of the length of line AB.

2 The line does not divide the angle equally in half. Eva has drawn the arcs from the end of each line instead of drawing an arc from the vertex first.

3 a–c

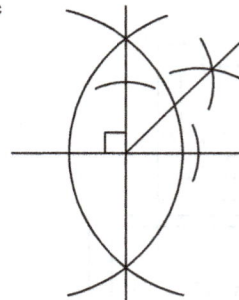

d 45°

4 a, b Students' artworks may vary if diagram copied rather than traced. For example:

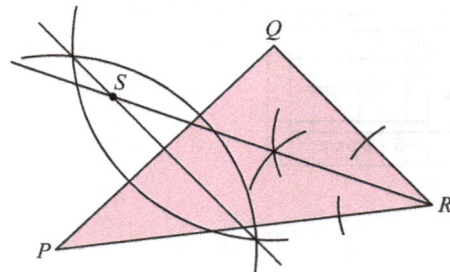

115

5.3 Constructing triangles

Purposeful practice 1

1–4 Students' own construction.

Purposeful practice 2

Diagrams in this exercise are not drawn to scale.

1

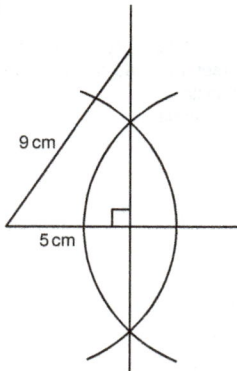

2

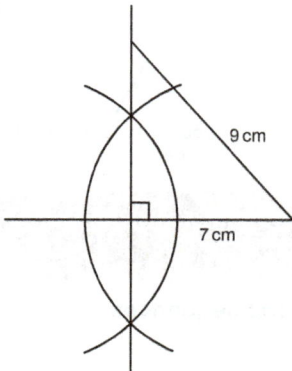

3

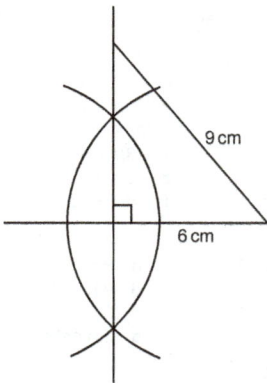

4

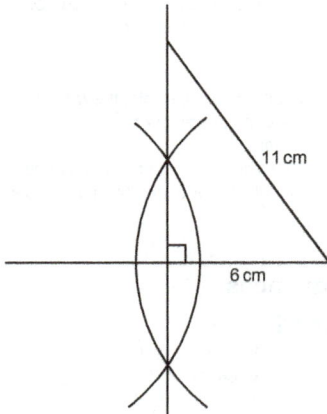

Problem-solving practice

1–3 Students' own construction.

4 No, Sofia can draw the first line using her ruler and then she only needs to set her compasses up twice to the distances for the other two lines.

5 a The compasses need to be set to 11 cm, not 8 cm.

  b Students' own construction.

6 The length of any side of a triangle must be less than the total of the other two sides. 12 cm > 4 cm + 6 cm, so it is not possible to draw this triangle.

7 a Millie doesn't know how long the other line is so cannot use this method.

  b (Diagram not drawn to scale.)

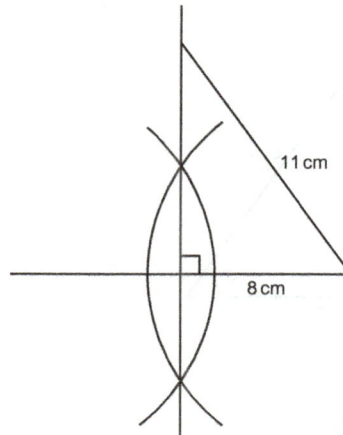

5.4 Using accurate scale diagrams

Purposeful practice 1

1 a

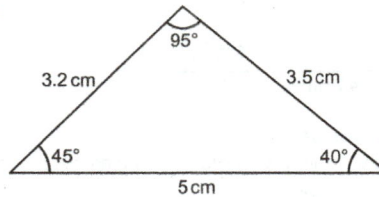

b

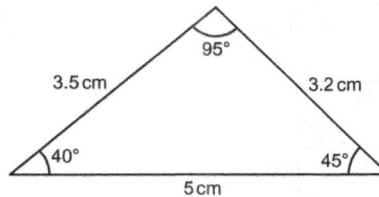

c

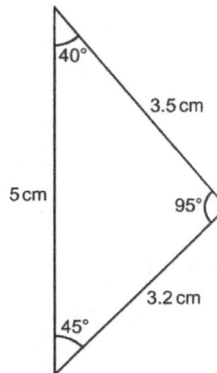

2 a

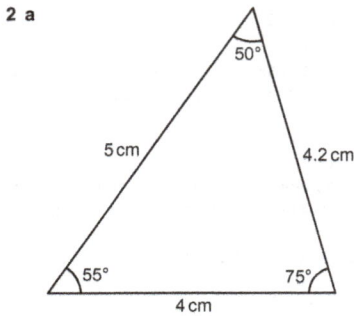

b

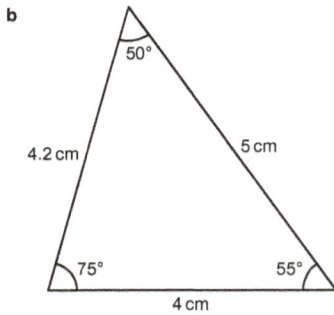

c

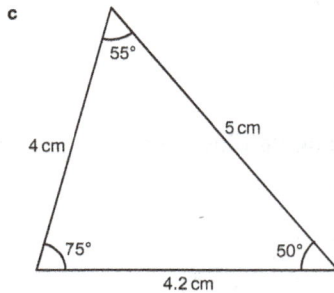

Purposeful practice 2

1 Students' own scale drawings; diagrams shown are not to scale.

a

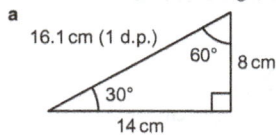

16.1 cm (1 d.p.) 60° 8 cm 30° 14 cm

b

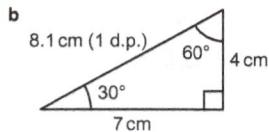

8.1 cm (1 d.p.) 60° 4 cm 30° 7 cm

c

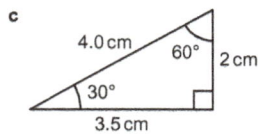

4.0 cm 60° 2 cm 30° 3.5 cm

2 Approximately 81 cm

Problem-solving practice

Diagrams in this exercise are not drawn to scale.

1 a

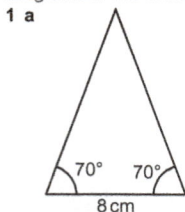

70° 70° 8 cm

b 78.8 cm

2

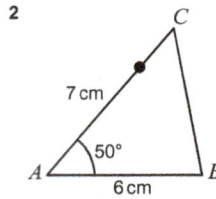

C 7 cm 50° 6 cm A B

3 a Jade has marked an angle of 140°, instead of 40°, as she's used the outside scale on the protractor instead of the inside.

b Triangle with angles as shown in question.

4 a Students' own choice of scale, for example:

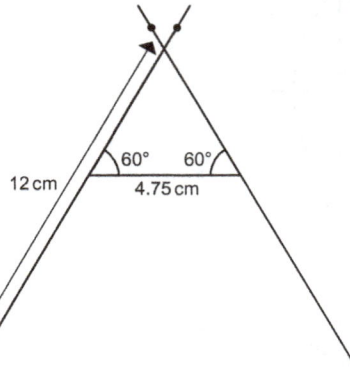

60° 60° 12 cm 4.75 cm

b The two longer sloped sides form an equilateral triangle with the ground, so the feet must be 2.4 m apart.

6 Sequences, inequalities, equations and proportion

6.1 nth term of arithmetic sequences

Purposeful practice 1

1 a 2, 4, 6, 8, 10   **b** $-2, -4, -6, -8, -10$
  c 1, 3, 5, 7, 9   **d** 5, 7, 9, 11, 13
  e 12, 14, 16, 18, 20   **f** $-1, -3, -5, -7, -9$
  g $0, -2, -4, -6, -8$ **h** $5, 3, 1, -1, -3$

2 a $2n + 1$ **b** $2n - 2$ **c** $-2n - 1$
  d $-2n + 4$ **e** $-2n + 8$ **f** $-2n + 7$

3 a $3n$ **b** $-3n$ **c** $3n + 1$
  d $-3n - 1$ **e** $3n - 7$ **f** $-3n + 11$

4 a $5n - 4$ **b** $5n + 4$ **c** $-5n + 2$
  d $-5n + 17$ **e** $5n - 12$ **f** $-5n + 15$

Purposeful practice 2

1 a 3, 5, 7   **b** $2n + 1$ **c** 13   **d** 18th
2 a 1, 3, 5   **b** $2n - 1$ **c** 11   **d** 19th
3 a 1, 5, 9   **b** $4n - 3$ **c** 21   **d** 10th
4 a 4, 7, 10   **b** $3n + 1$ **c** 19   **d** 12th pattern

Problem-solving practice

1 Yes, with students' own reasoning, for example, the number of square tiles is the same as the pattern number.

2 a $3n + 2$ **b** 16

3 a 20   **b** 205

4 No, with students' own reasoning, for example, the nth term is $4n - 1$ and when you solve the equation $4n - 1 = 121$ the solution is not a whole number.

5 a Yes, with students' own reasoning, for example, the number of white squares is given by multiples of 3, and 60 is a multiple of 3.

  b 57

6 $6n + 12$

6.2 Non-linear sequences

Purposeful practice 1

1 a 1, 4, 16, 64   **b** 2, 8, 32, 128
  c 64, 16, 4, 1   **d** 64, 16, 4, 1
  e 64, 32, 16, 8   **f** 64, 32, 16, 8
  g 7, 14, 28, 56   **h** 0, 0, 0, 0

2 a $+5$ **b** $\times 5$ **c** $\times \frac{1}{5}$ **d** -5

e $\times \frac{1}{10}$ **f** -9000 **g** $\times \frac{1}{3}$ **h** $+3$

3 a a, d, f, h **b** b, c, e, g

Purposeful practice 2

1 a $1, -1, 1, -1$ **b** $1, -2, 4, -8$
c $16, -8, 4, -2$ **d** $-16, 8, -4, 2$
e $-1, -5, -25, -125$ **f** $-1, 5, -25, 125$
g $500, -100, 20, -4$ **h** $-500, -100, -20, -4$

2 a i 3 **ii** $\times -1$
b i -7 **ii** $\times -1$
c i 81 **ii** $\times 3$
d i 81 **ii** $\times -3$
e i -81 **ii** $\times -3$
f i -81 **ii** $\times 3$
g i -125 **ii** $\times -\frac{1}{2}$
h i -125 **ii** $\times \frac{1}{2}$
i i 125 **ii** $\times -\frac{1}{2}$
j i 125 **ii** $\times \frac{1}{2}$

Problem-solving practice

1 a The term-to-term rule doesn't work for the other terms, $2 + 1 \neq 4$, etc.
b $\times 2$
2 No, the term-to-term rule is $\times 2$. If it were $\times -2$, the terms would alternate between positive and negative numbers.
3 No, Emily has got the second term correct but she has then incorrectly multiplied by a negative number. The sequence should be $64, -32, 16, -8, 4$.
4 No, with students' own reasoning, for example, all except the first term will have a 5 in the ones column.
5 a -27 **b** 6th
6 1944
7 0.75
8 5th term (625)
9 a $400, 200$ **b** $5, 625$ **c** $-1250, -2$ **d** $3, 192$
10 No; as the term-to-term rule is $\times \frac{1}{2}$ the terms will get smaller but never negative. When the first term is positive, the term-to-term rule for a geometric sequence needs to be multiplied by a negative number to get negative terms.
11 $\times 10$
12 a Students' own answer, for example, first term 5, term-to-term rule $\times 2$.
b Students' own answer, for example, first term 20, term-to-term rule $\times \frac{1}{2}$.
c Students' own answer, for example, first term -2, term-to-term rule $\times -10$.
13 a 7th month **b** £4470

6.3 Inequalities

Purposeful practice 1

1 a $3 < x$ **b** $x < 3$ **c** $x > 3$
d $3 > x$ **e** $3 \leq x$ **f** $x \geq 3$
2 a $-1 < x < 2$ **b** $-1 < x \leq 2$ **c** $-1 \leq x < 2$
d $-1 \leq x < 2$ **e** $-1 < x \leq 2$

Purposeful practice 2

1 a
b
c
d
e
f

2 a
1 and 2
b
1, 2 and 3
c
0, 1, 2 and 3
d
0, 1 and 2
e
-1, 0, 1 and 2
f
1 and 2
g
2 and 3
h
$-2, -1$, 0, 1, 2 and 3
i
$-3, -2, -1$ and 0
j
$-2, -1$, 0 and 1
k
$-2, -1$ and 0
l
-2 and -1

3 a $x \geq -1$ **b** $x < 0$
c $x \leq 2$ **d** $-1 \leq x \leq 2$
e $-1 < x \leq 2$ **f** $-2 \leq x < 2$
g $-3 < x < 2$ **h** $-4 < x \leq -1$

Problem-solving practice

1 a i E **ii** C **iii** No match
iv A **v** D **vi** B
b x is greater than or equal to 2
2 Jess has the signs in the wrong order; it should be $-2 \leq x < 3$, as -2 is included but 3 isn't.
Rashid has written the signs backwards.
3 a $x - 9 < 4$ **b** 12
4 a
b $-2, -1$, 0, 1
5 a D and E
b B, as it is the only one that includes -4; A, C and F have a circle at -4 but don't include -4. The number lines for C, E and F go lower than -4, but the inequalities represented don't use the numbers this low.
c F, as there is no upper limit (it goes to infinity), but the others all stop before then.
6 a A and D
b C, as the inequality includes -5.
c B, as the inequality includes 4.

6.4 Solving equations

Purposeful practice 1

1 **a** $x = 8$ **b** $x = 13$ **c** $x = 13$

   d $x = -8$ **e** $x = -16$ **f** $x = 11$

   g $x = \frac{19}{3}$ or $6\frac{1}{3}$ **h** $x = -1$ **i** $x = -\frac{2}{7}$

2 **a** $x = 1$ **b** $x = \frac{3}{2}$ or $1\frac{1}{2}$ **c** $x = \frac{7}{2}$ or $3\frac{1}{2}$

   d $x = 5$ **e** $x = 2$ **f** $x = -2$

   g $x = -\frac{8}{3}$ or $-2\frac{2}{3}$ **h** $x = \frac{2}{3}$ **i** $x = \frac{7}{18}$

3 **Q1g**: $x = 6.33$, $\frac{3x-5}{7} = 1.998...$; no

   Q1i: $x = -0.29$, $\frac{7x-3}{5} = -1.006$; no

   Q2b: $x = 1.5$, $\frac{2x+3}{4} = \frac{6}{4} = 1.5$; yes

   Q2c: $x = 3.5$, $\frac{2x+3}{4} = \frac{10}{4} = 2.5$; yes

   Q2g: $x = -2.67$, $\frac{4x-1}{5} = -2.336$, $2x + 3 = -2.34$; no

   Q2h: $x = 0.67$, $\frac{4x-1}{5} = 0.336$, $2x - 1 = 0.34$; no

   Q2i: $x = 0.39$, $\frac{2x-1}{4} = -0.055$, $5x - 2 = -0.05$; no

Purposeful practice 2

1 11 or −11

2 $x = 13\,\text{cm}$

3 1.68 m

Problem-solving practice

1 **a** She should not have added 4 first; she should have multiplied by 2 to give $3x - 4 = 10$, then added 4 to give $3x = 14$, then divided by 3.

   b $x = \frac{14}{3}$ or $4\frac{2}{3}$

2 **a** $\frac{5x+8}{3} = 2x$ then multiply both sides by 3 to give $5x + 8 = 6x$

   b $x = 8$

   c 16 cm

3 11

4 **a** 9 cm

   b 30 cm

5 40°, 70°, 70°

6 Taylor should have square rooted 64 to give 8, not divided by 2.

7 18 cm

6.5 Proportion

Purposeful practice

1 **a i** 21, 35; × 7   **ii** $y = 7x$

   b i × 1.5, × 1.5; 10, 14; × 2   **ii** $y = 2x$

2 **a i** $y = 10, 6; xy = 30$ **ii** $y = \frac{30}{x}$

   b i $y = 8, 3.2, 2; xy = 32$ **ii** $y = \frac{32}{x}$

   c i 1.5; $y = 7, 4.2, 3; xy = 21$ **ii** $y = \frac{21}{x}$

Problem-solving practice

1 **a** $2 + 3 = 5$, but this doesn't work for the other values in the table.

   b $y = 2.5x$

2 **a** $y = 40x$

   b $y = 2800$

3 $y = 51.2$

4 **a** $P = 1.85m$

   b £4.07

5 **a** $b = \frac{84}{d}$ or $d = \frac{84}{b}$ or $bd = 84$

   b 10.5 days

6 $y = 22.5$

7 Circles, Pythagoras and prisms

7.1 Circumference of a circle

Purposeful practice 1

1 **a** 6 cm   **b** 7 cm   **c** 6.6 cm   **d** 60 cm

2 **a** 4 cm   **b** 4.5 cm   **c** 4.9 cm   **d** 445 cm

Purposeful practice 2

1 Students' answers may vary but should be close to the values shown.

   a 30 cm   **b** 60 cm   **c** 36 cm   **d** 72 cm

2 **a** $10\pi\,\text{cm}$ **b** $20\pi\,\text{cm}$ **c** $12.2\pi\,\text{cm}$ **d** $24.4\pi\,\text{cm}$

3 **a** 31.42 cm   **b** 62.83 cm   **c** 38.33 cm   **d** 76.65 cm

4 **a** 18 cm   **b** 21 cm

Purposeful practice 3

1 **a** 8.6 cm   **b** 0.86 m   **c** 86 mm

2 **a** 6.0 cm   **b** 0.60 m   **c** 60 mm

Problem-solving practice

1 Zara as she has correctly multiplied the diameter by π, but Mark has multiplied the radius by π.

2 C as this circle has the largest diameter of 11 cm; the diameter of A is only 8 cm and the diameter of B is 10 cm.

3 £3.54

4 23

5 20.4 cm

6 117.8 m

7 71.1 cm

8 22.0 cm

7.2 Area of a circle

Purposeful practice 1

1 **a** $4\pi\,\text{cm}^2$ **b** $9\pi\,\text{cm}^2$ **c** $25\pi\,\text{cm}^2$ **d** $100\pi\,\text{cm}^2$

   e $\pi\,\text{cm}^2$ **f** $25\pi\,\text{cm}^2$ **g** $100\pi\,\text{cm}^2$ **h** $2500\pi\,\text{cm}^2$

2 Students' answers may vary but should be close to the values shown.

   a $12\,\text{cm}^2$ **b** $27\,\text{cm}^2$ **c** $75\,\text{cm}^2$ **d** $300\,\text{cm}^2$

   e $3\,\text{cm}^2$ **f** $75\,\text{cm}^2$ **g** $300\,\text{cm}^2$ **h** $7500\,\text{cm}^2$

3 **a** $12.6\,\text{cm}^2$ **b** $28.3\,\text{cm}^2$ **c** $78.5\,\text{cm}^2$ **d** $314.2\,\text{cm}^2$

   e $3.1\,\text{cm}^2$ **f** $78.5\,\text{cm}^2$ **g** $314.2\,\text{cm}^2$ **h** $7854.0\,\text{cm}^2$

Purposeful practice 2

1 $12.6\,\text{cm}^2$ (1 d.p.)

2 $38.5\,\text{cm}^2$ (1 d.p.)

3 $141.8\,\text{cm}^2$ (1 d.p.)

4 $47.5\,\text{m}^2$ (1 d.p.)

5 $26.73\,\text{m}^2$ (2 d.p.)

Purposeful practice 3

1 **a** 6 mm (nearest mm)

   b 1.8 cm (nearest mm)

   c 0.2 m (nearest 0.1 m)

2 **a** 16 mm (nearest mm)

   b 5.0 cm (nearest mm)

   c 0.5 m (nearest 0.1 m)

Problem-solving practice

1 9 boxes

2 $124.9\,\text{cm}^2$

3 **a** Jamie has squared the diameter instead of the radius before multiplying by π.

   b $38.5\,\text{cm}^2$

4 $50.3\,\text{cm}^2$

5 $13.7\,\text{cm}^2$

6 $15.5\,\text{cm}^2$

7 No, as the area of the whole circle $= \pi \times 14^2 = 615.75\,\text{cm}^2$ and the shaded area $= \pi \times 14^2 - \pi \times 7^2 = 461.81\,\text{cm}^2$.

   Half the area of the whole circle is $615.75 \div 2 = 307.875$, which is not the same as the shaded area ($461.81\,\text{cm}^2$).

8 25.0 m

7.3 Pythagoras' theorem

Purposeful practice 1

1 **a** 5 cm   **b** 19.5 cm   **c** 7.5 cm   **d** 17.5 cm

2 **a** 12.2 cm   **b** 33.3 cm   **c** 7.2 cm   **d** 12.6 cm

Purposeful practice 2

1 B

2 **a** 17 cm (nearest cm)   **b** 3.1 m (1 d.p.)

   c 130 mm (nearest mm)   **d** 3.75 m (2 d.p.)

Purposeful practice 3

1 7.8 m (1 d.p.)
2 76 cm (nearest cm)
3 524 mm (nearest mm)
4 10.51 m (2 d.p.)

Problem-solving practice

1 36.1 km
2 24.6 cm
3 26.2 kg
4 Yes, as $8^2 + 15^2 = 64 + 225 = 289 = 17^2$, which is Pythagoras' theorem.
5 8 cm or 11.7 cm
6 No. Length of missing side in metres: $10^2 + 5^2 = 125$, $\sqrt{125} = 11.2$; perimeter of garden = 12 m + 10 m + 17 m + 11.2 m = 50.2 m
7 58.5 cm

7.4 Prisms and cylinders

Purposeful practice 1

1 $1 \, cm^3 = 1000 \, mm^3$
2 $0.1 \, cm^3 = 100 \, mm^3$
3 $0.2 \, cm^3 = 200 \, mm^3$
4 $200 \, mm^3 = 0.2 \, cm^3$
5 $2100 \, mm^3 = 2.1 \, cm^3$
6 $210 \, mm^3 = 0.21 \, cm^3$
7 $1 \, m^3 = 1\,000\,000 \, cm^3$
8 $0.1 \, m^3 = 100\,000 \, cm^3$
9 $0.01 \, m^3 = 10\,000 \, cm^3$
10 $1 \, m^3 = 1000$ litres
11 $0.1 \, m^3 = 100$ litres
12 $0.01 \, m^3 = 10$ litres
13 $5 \, m^3 = 5000$ litres
14 $0.5 \, m^3 = 500$ litres
15 $0.05 \, m^3 = 50$ litres
16 $7\,000\,000 \, cm^3 = 7 \, m^3$
17 $7\,500\,000 \, cm^3 = 7.5 \, m^3$
18 $7500 \, cm^3 = 0.0075 \, m^3$

Purposeful practice 2

1 A (cube), B (cuboid), C (triangular prism) and G (trapezoid prism) are all right prisms.

Purposeful practice 3

1 a $108 \, cm^3$ **b** $150 \, cm^2$
2 a $54 \, cm^3$ **b** $120 \, cm^2$
3 a $108 \, cm^3$ **b** $168 \, cm^2$
4 a $162 \, cm^3$ **b** $198 \, cm^2$

Purposeful practice 4

Students' own choice of appropriate accuracy given in answers:
1 a $603\,186 \, mm^3$ (nearest mm^3) **b** $40\,212 \, mm^2$ (nearest mm^2)
2 a $325.2 \, cm^3$ (1 d.p.)   **b** $273.3 \, cm^2$ (1 d.p.)
3 a $42.4 \, cm^3$ (1 d.p.)   **b** $84.8 \, cm^2$ (1 d.p.)
4 a $1.59 \, m^3$ (2 d.p.)   **b** $8.69 \, m^2$ (2 d.p.)

Problem-solving practice

1 $1\,500\,000 \, cm^3$
2 a $1\,251\,360 \, cm^3$
   b £117.12 (or £125 if students assume the material has to be bought in full square metres)
3 17 cm
4 a 2 tins
   b 234.8 litres

7.5 Errors and bounds

Purposeful practice 1

1 a $150 \, g \leqslant m < 250 \, g$ **b** $195 \, g \leqslant m < 205 \, g$
   c $190 \, g \leqslant m < 210 \, g$ **d** $199.5 \, g \leqslant m < 200.5 \, g$
   e $197.5 \, g \leqslant m < 202.5 \, g$ **f** $199 \, g \leqslant m < 201 \, g$

2 a $25 \, m \leqslant l < 35 \, m$ **b** $29.5 \, m \leqslant l < 30.5 \, m$
   c $27.5 \, m \leqslant l < 32.5 \, m$ **d** $29 \, m \leqslant l < 31 \, m$
   e $29.995 \, m \leqslant l < 30.005 \, m$

Purposeful practice 2

1 $198 \, g \leqslant m < 202 \, g$
2 $196 \, g \leqslant m < 204 \, g$
3 $190 \, g \leqslant m < 210 \, g$
4 $195 \, g \leqslant m < 205 \, g$
5 $150 \, g \leqslant m < 250 \, g$

Purposeful practice 3

1 $33.25 \, cm^2 \leqslant A < 47.25 \, cm^2$
2 $38.48 \, cm^2 \leqslant A < 63.62 \, cm^2$
3 $70.88 \, cm^2 \leqslant A < 86.59 \, cm^2$
4 $16.625 \, cm^2 \leqslant A < 23.625 \, cm^2$

Problem-solving practice

1 Phil would be right if the height were measured to the nearest 2 cm; the interval should be $69.5 \, cm \leqslant h < 70.5 \, cm$.
2 $484.5 \, g \leqslant m < 535.5 \, g$
3 a 199.5 ml
   b Yes, as the upper bounds for the cordial and water are 24.5 ml and 175.5 ml, and 24.5 ml + 175.5 ml = 200 ml. The lower bound for the volume of the cup is 199.5 ml, which is less than the upper bound for the total volume of cordial and water.
4 $59.4 \, cm \leqslant P < 60.6 \, cm$
5 a 613.8
   b 666.6
6 $508.95 \, m \leqslant d < 547.35 \, m$
7 221.796 g
8 $100.75 \, cm^2 \leqslant A < 123.75 \, cm^2$
9 $284.625 \, cm^3 \leqslant V < 446.875 \, cm^3$
10 The lower bound of the length is 122.5 mm, so the lower bound for the volume is $122.5 \times 122.5 \times 122.5 = 1\,838\,265.625 \, mm^3$.

Mixed exercises B

Mixed problem-solving practice B

1 a, b

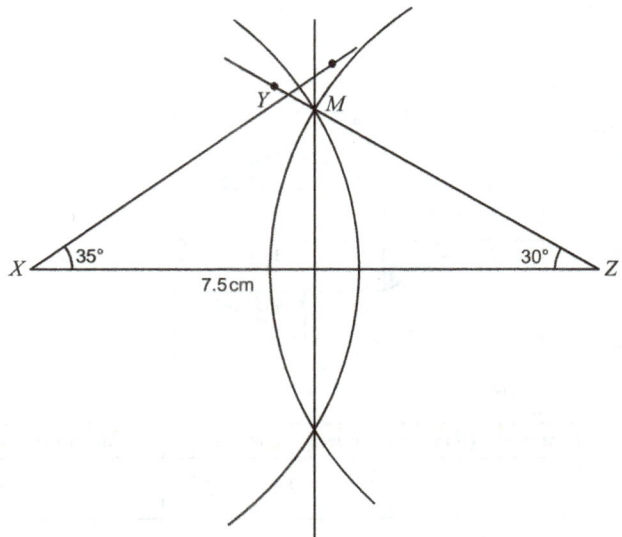

   c Approximately 43 m

2 a

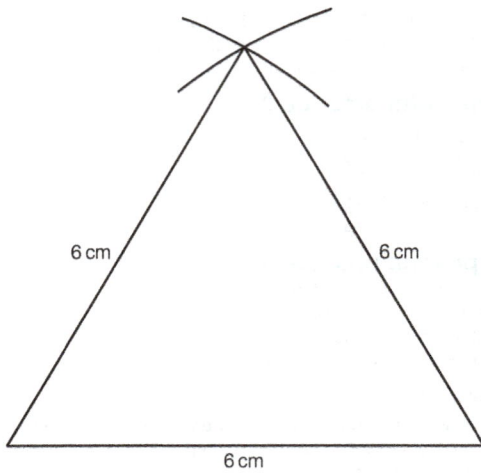

b 60°

c Equilateral triangle

d

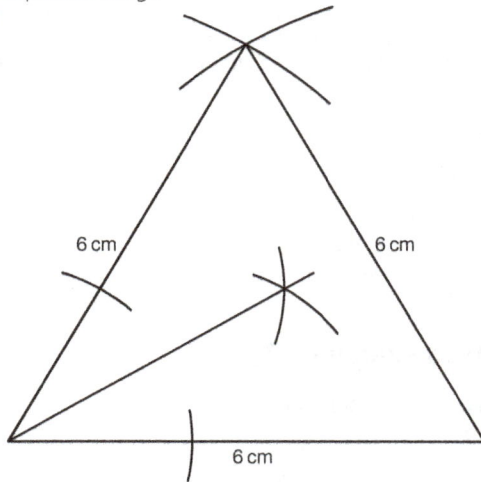

e 30°

3 Yes

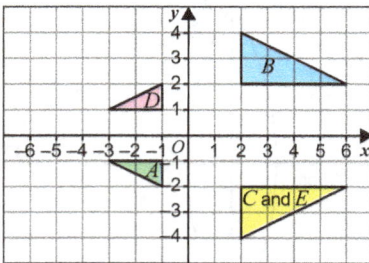

4 a 243

b

1st term	2nd term	3rd term	4th term	5th term
3	3×3 $= 3^2$	$3 \times 3 \times 3$ $= 3^3$	$3 \times 3 \times 3 \times 3$ $= 3^4$	$3 \times 3 \times 3 \times 3 \times 3$ $= 3^5$

c 59 049

d 3^n

5 Lower bound = 74.61 cm and upper bound = 75.98 cm

6 No, as when $\frac{5n-6}{2} = 30 - n$, 7n = 66 so n is not a whole number.

7 1111 ml

8 0.85 g/cm³

9 Lower bound = 144.29 miles and upper bound = 145.24 miles

10 50 005 × 380.5 ÷ 60 ÷ 60 = 5285 m or 5.285 km (to the nearest m)

11 38.3 cm

12 42.9 cm²

13 a $-9 \leqslant 4x - 1 < 19$

   b $-6 \leqslant 3x < 15$

14 a $-3 \leqslant x < 5$ has the lowest possible integer value of x, which is –3. The other two are –1 and –2.

   b $-4 < 2x \leqslant 14$ has the greatest possible integer value of x, which is 7. The other two are 5 and 6.

8 Graphs

8.1 Using $y = mx + c$

Purposeful practice 1

1

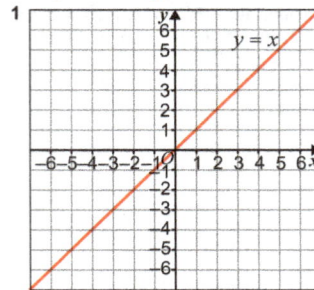

2

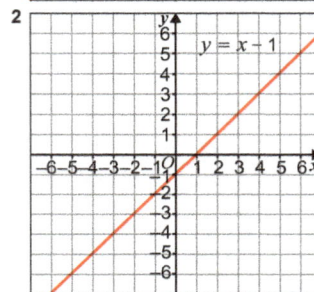

3

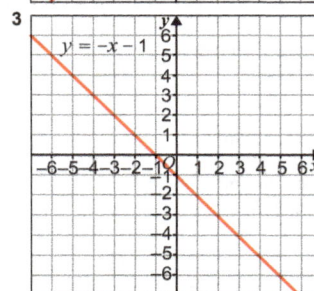

4

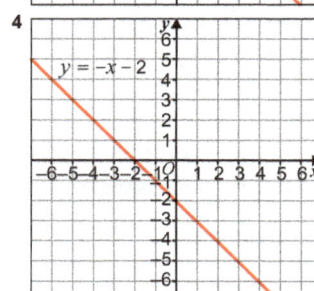

5

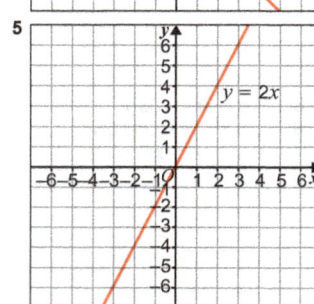

6

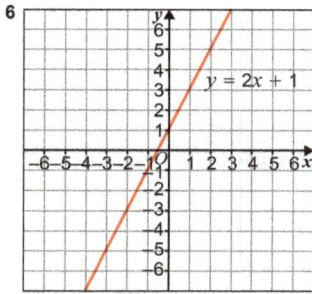
$y = 2x + 1$

7

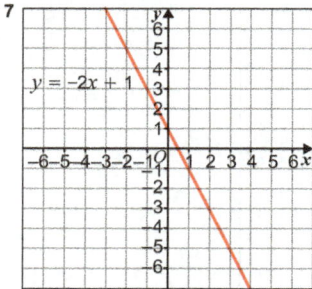
$y = -2x + 1$

8

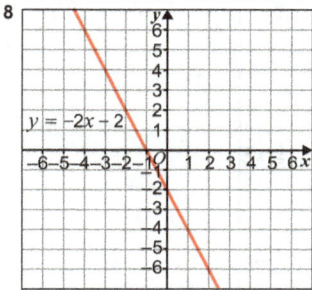
$y = -2x - 2$

Purposeful practice 2

1 a $y = x + 2$ **b** $y = x + 3$ **c** $y = x - 2$ **d** $y = x - 3$

2 a $y = 2x + 2$ **b** $y = 2x + 3$ **c** $y = 2x - 2$ **d** $y = 2x - 3$

Purposeful practice 3

1 a $(2, 3)$

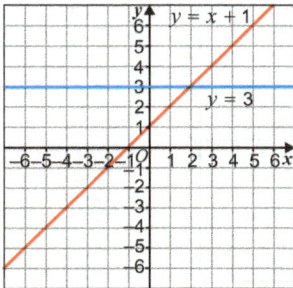
$y = x + 1$
$y = 3$

b $(-1, 1)$

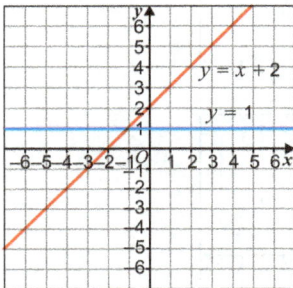
$y = x + 2$
$y = 1$

c $(1, 4)$

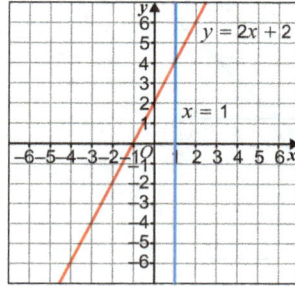
$y = 2x + 2$
$x = 1$

d $(-1, 1)$

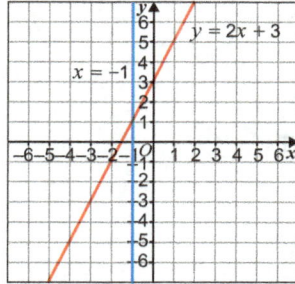
$y = 2x + 3$
$x = -1$

2 Students' own answers, using substitution to find the values of x and y given by the answers to **Q1**.

Problem-solving practice

1

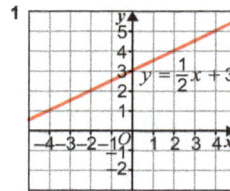
$y = \frac{1}{2}x + 3$

2 a

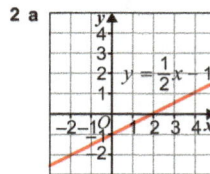
$y = \frac{1}{2}x - 1$

b $x = 3$

3 a, b i

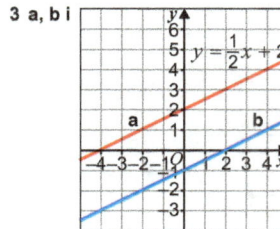
$y = \frac{1}{2}x + 2$
a   **b**

ii $y = \frac{1}{2}x - 1$

4 a

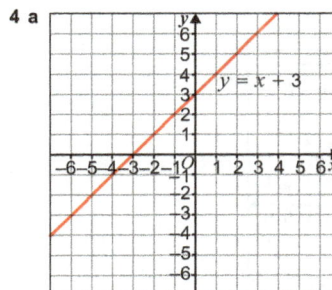
$y = x + 3$

b i

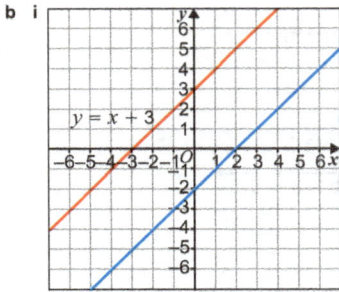

$y = x + 3$

ii $y = x - 2$

5 $y = 2x - 2$

6 a

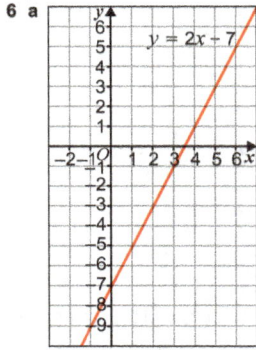

$y = 2x - 7$

b $y = 2x + 3$

7 $y = 3x - 1$

8 $(4, -1)$

9 a $(4, 10)$ **b** $(10, 10)$ **c** $y = 3x - 20$

10 a F   **b** C

8.2 More straight-line graphs

Purposeful practice 1

1 a

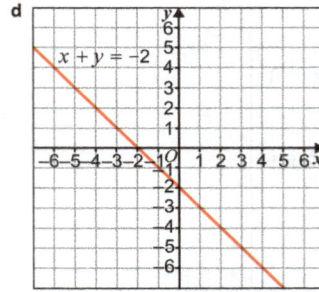

$x + y = 4$

b

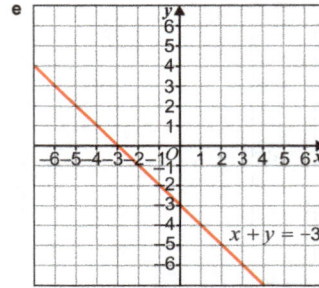

$x + y = 5$

c

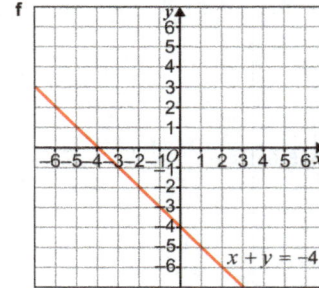

$x + y = 6$

d

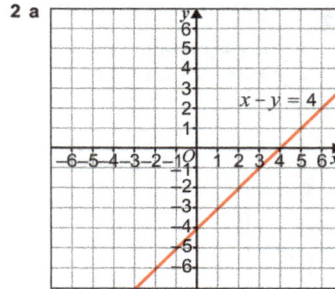

$x + y = -2$

e

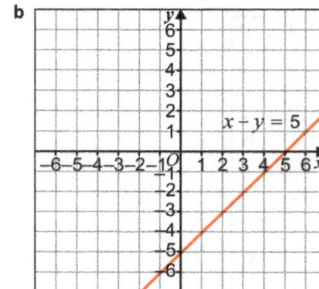

$x + y = -3$

f

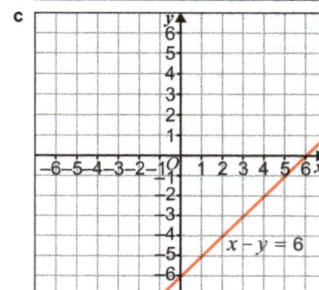

$x + y = -4$

2 a

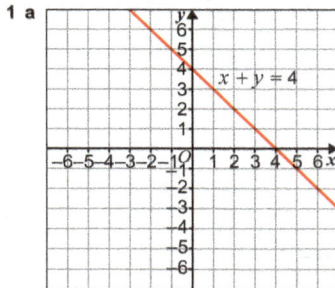

$x - y = 4$

b

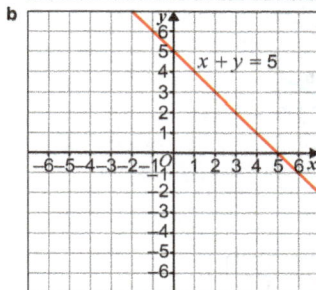

$x - y = 5$

c

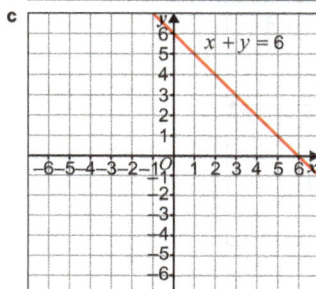

$x - y = 6$

d

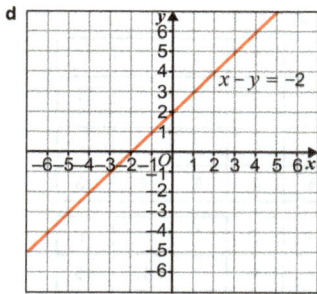

Graph showing line $x - y = -2$

e

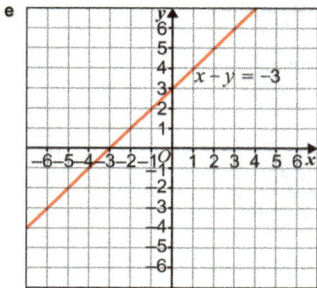

Graph showing line $x - y = -3$

f

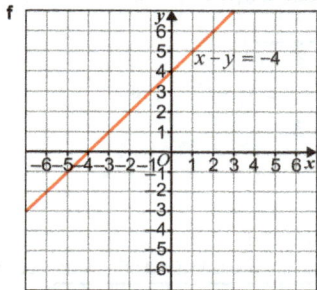

Graph showing line $x - y = -4$

Purposeful practice 2

Students' own working should be shown with each answer.

1 A, D
2 A, C
3 C
4 B
5 A and C
6 A and B

Problem-solving practice

1 a

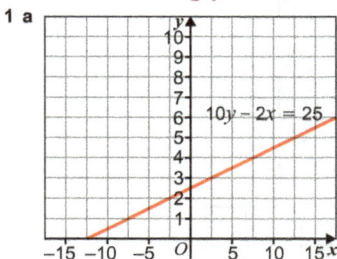

Graph showing line $10y - 2x = 25$

b i $y = 3.5$ **ii** $x = 12.5$

2 No, only line A has gradient 1; if the others are rearranged to the form $y = mx + c$, you can see that line B has gradient -1, line C has gradient $-\frac{1}{2}$ and line D has gradient $\frac{1}{2}$.

3 Lines D, C, B, A

4 Lines B, C, D, A

5 The gradient of line A is 4. Equation of line B: $2y = 8x + 1$, $y = 4x + \frac{1}{2}$ so the gradient is 4. The gradient of both lines is 4 so they are parallel.

6 Lines B and D

7 C ($2y - 6x = -4$) as it has gradient 3, but the others all have gradient 2.

8 E ($y - x = 1$) as its y-intercept is 1 but the others all have y-intercept -1.

9 $y = -3x + 3$

10 a Students' equations should have the coefficient of x in the second equation equal to double the first, but this must not be the case for the '+' value, for example, $y = 2x + 3$ and $2y = 4x + 5$.

b Students' equations should have a '+' value in the second equation that is double that in the first equation, for example, $y = 2x + 2$ and $2y = 3x + 4$.

8.3 Simultaneous equations

Purposeful practice 1

1 a $(-1, -4)$ **b** $x = -1, y = -4$
2 a $(3, 4)$ **b** $x = 3, y = 4$
3 a $(2, -3)$ **b** $x = 2, y = -3$
4 a $(-3, 2)$ **b** $x = -3, y = 2$

Purposeful practice 2

Students' graphs should give solutions:

1

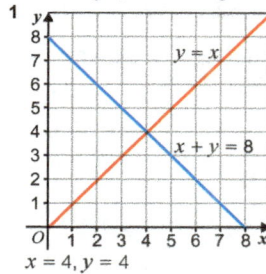

Graph showing lines $y = x$ and $x + y = 8$
$x = 4, y = 4$

2

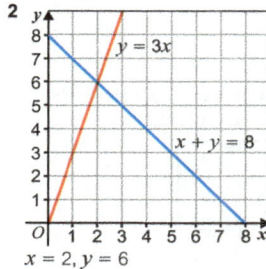

Graph showing lines $y = 3x$ and $x + y = 8$
$x = 2, y = 6$

3

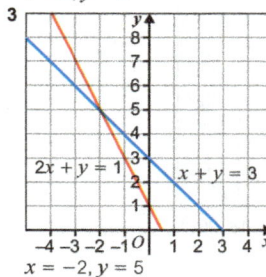

Graph showing lines $2x + y = 1$ and $x + y = 3$
$x = -2, y = 5$

4

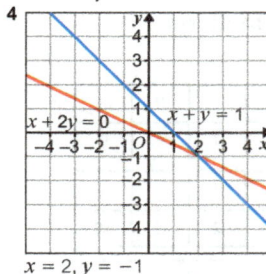

Graph showing lines $x + 2y = 0$ and $x + y = 1$
$x = 2, y = -1$

5

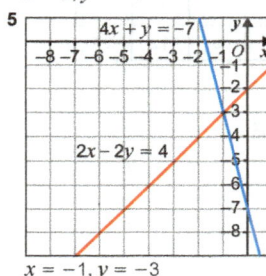

Graph showing lines $4x + y = -7$ and $2x - 2y = 4$
$x = -1, y = -3$

6

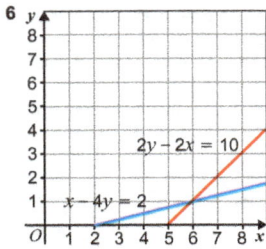

$x = 6, y = 1$

Problem-solving practice

1 a He has drawn the graph of $y = x + 2$ instead of $y = 2x$, and the graph of $x + y = 5$ instead of $x + y = 6$

b $x = 2, y = 4$

2 a $x = -3, y = -3$ **b** $x = 3, y = -5$

  c $x = 1, y = 5$ **d** $x = -3, y = -3$

3 (5, 7)

4 Students should draw the graphs of $y - 2x = 1$ and $y - 2x = -2$ to show they are parallel, therefore never intersect.

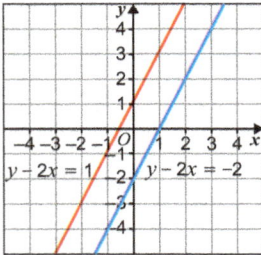

5 Students should draw a graph showing two straight lines that intersect at (2, 3) and write the equations of their lines.

6

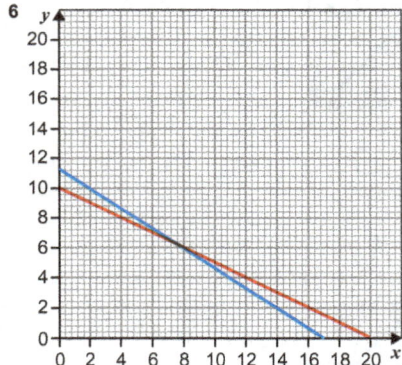

Adult ticket = £8, child ticket = £6

8.4 Graphs of quadratic functions

Purposeful practice 1

1 a

x	−3	−2	−1	0	1	2	3
y	9	4	1	0	1	4	9

b

x	−3	−2	−1	0	1	2	3
y	18	8	2	0	2	8	18

c

x	−3	−2	−1	0	1	2	3
y	27	12	3	0	3	12	27

2

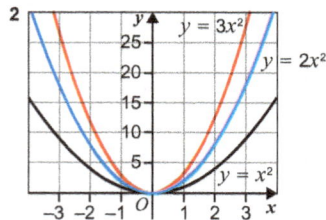

Purposeful practice 2

1 a

x	−3	−2	−1	0	1	2	3
y	11	6	3	2	3	6	11

b

x	−3	−2	−1	0	1	2	3
y	13	8	5	4	5	8	13

c

x	−3	−2	−1	0	1	2	3
y	15	10	7	6	7	10	15

2

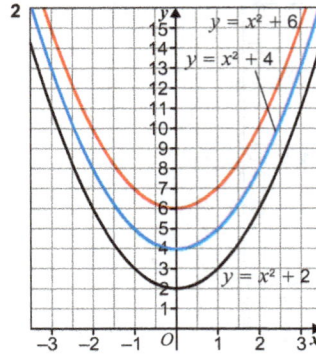

3 a Z   **b** W   **c** Y   **d** X

Purposeful practice 3

1 $x = 2, x = -2$

2 $x = 2.4, x = -2.4$

3 $x = 2.8, x = -2.8$

Problem-solving practice

1 Fleur has used a ruler to join the points instead of a smooth curve.

2 a

x	−3	−2	−1	0	1	2	3
y	6	1	−2	−3	−2	1	6

b

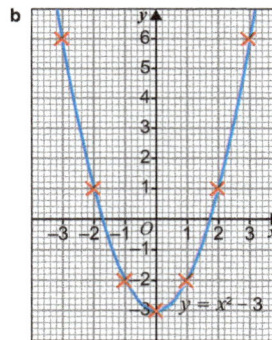

c $x = 1.7, x = -1.7$

3 a

x	−2	−1	0	1	2
y	5	2	1	2	5

b

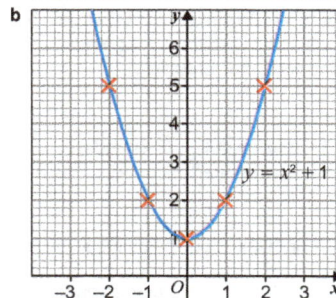

c $x = 1.4, x = -1.4$

4 a It is the wrong shape; it should be a curved parabola, or U-shape.

b Yasmin has forgotten that a negative number multiplied by a negative number gives a positive number. She has worked out the squares of negative numbers incorrectly so the first 3 values in the table for y are wrong: they are not -10, -5 or -2; they are 8, 3, 0.

c

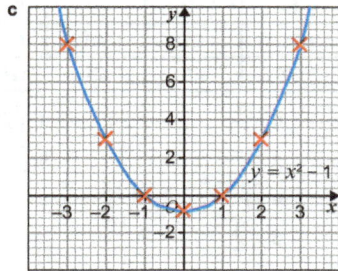

5 a $y = x^2 + 3$

b

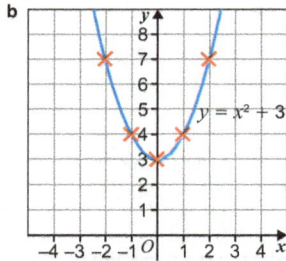

8.5 More non-linear graphs

Purposeful practice 1

1 a 6 people   **b** 4 people   **c** 3 people
2 2 hours
3 2.4 hours
4 $k = 24$
5 $x = \frac{24}{y}$

Purposeful practice 2

1 a £24   **b** £21   **c** £33   **d** £27
2 a £3   **b** £12 (i.e. £15 − £3)

Problem-solving practice

1 a 24 °C
  b About 14.5 minutes
  c About 21 minutes
  d No, 0 °C is freezing and assuming that the kettle is indoors, it wouldn't get this cold.
  e No, because when the time doubles, the temperature does not halve.
2 $y = \frac{60}{x}$
3 a 20%   **b** £50 000.01 − £150 000
  c £2300   **d** £11 500

9 Probability

9.1 Mutually exclusive events

Purposeful practice 1

1 a $\frac{1}{4}$ **b** $\frac{3}{4}$ **c** 1
2 a $\frac{2}{4} = \frac{1}{2}$ **b** $\frac{2}{4} = \frac{1}{2}$ **c** $\frac{3}{4}$
3 a $\frac{1}{5}$ **b** $\frac{4}{5}$ **c** $\frac{4}{5}$
4 a $\frac{3}{8}$ **b** $\frac{5}{8}$ **c** 1
5 a $\frac{26}{52} = \frac{1}{2}$ **b** $\frac{13}{52} = \frac{1}{4}$ **c** $\frac{39}{52} = \frac{3}{4}$
6 a $\frac{26}{52} = \frac{1}{2}$ **b** $\frac{4}{52} = \frac{1}{13}$ **c** $\frac{28}{52} = \frac{7}{13}$
7 1, 4, 5 are mutually exclusive. 2, 3, 6 are not mutually exclusive. Students' own explanations, for example, **Q2**: 3 is an odd number and a prime number so 'odd' and 'prime' are not mutually exclusive. **Q3**: letter O is a vowel and has line symmetry. **Q6**: there are two cards that are black and kings.

8 Q1: $P(A) + P(B) = 1$,
  Q4: $P(A) + P(B) = 1$,
  Q5: $P(A) + P(B) = \frac{3}{4}$; $P(A) + P(B) = P(A \text{ or } B)$
9 Q2: $P(A) + P(B) = 1$ and $P(A \text{ or } B) = \frac{3}{4}$; $P(A) + P(B) \neq P(A \text{ or } B)$
  Q3: $P(A) + P(B) = 1$ and $P(A \text{ or } B) = \frac{4}{5}$; $P(A) + P(B) \neq P(A \text{ or } B)$
  Q6: $P(A) + P(B) = \frac{30}{52}$ and $P(A \text{ or } B) = \frac{28}{52}$; $P(A) + P(B) \neq P(A \text{ or } B)$

Purposeful practice 2

1 a i $\frac{1}{3}$ **ii** $\frac{1}{3}$ **iii** $\frac{1}{3}$ **iv** 1
  b i $\frac{1}{3}$ **ii** $\frac{2}{3}$ **iii** 1
2 a i $\frac{1}{6}$ **ii** $\frac{5}{6}$ **iii** 1
  b i $\frac{1}{2}$ **ii** $\frac{1}{2}$ **iii** 1

Problem-solving practice

1 a A and C
  b i $\frac{5}{8}$ **ii** 1
2 a Yes   **b** 0.1
3 a Yes   **b** 0.15
4 a 15%   **b** 30%   **c** 20 times

9.2 Experimental and theoretical probability

Purposeful practice 1

1 a i $\frac{1}{4}$ **ii** $\frac{28}{100}$ **iii** Probably fair
  b i $\frac{1}{3}$ **ii** $\frac{31}{90}$ **iii** Probably fair
  c i $\frac{1}{5}$ **ii** $\frac{75}{250}$ **iii** Probably not fair
2 a i $\frac{3}{8} = 0.375$ **ii** $\frac{46}{100} = 0.46$ **iii** Probably not fair
  b i $\frac{1}{6} = 0.1\dot{6}$ **ii** $\frac{33}{200} = 0.165$ **iii** Probably fair
  c i $\frac{2}{9} = 0.222...$ **ii** $\frac{23}{103} = 0.2233...$ **iii** Probably fair

Purposeful practice 2

1 Theoretical expected $= \frac{1}{2} \times 126 = 63$; probably not fair
2 Theoretical expected $= \frac{2}{5} \times 800 = 320$; probably not fair
3 Theoretical expected $= \frac{1}{6} \times 2000 = 333.3$; probably fair

Problem-solving practice

1 Yes, as the probability of rolling each number on a fair 6-sided dice is $\frac{1}{6}$ and $\frac{1}{6}$ of 150 = 25 so 25 is the number of times you would expect to roll each number. 42 is much higher than 25 and 8 is much lower.
2 No, as the experiment suggests that $P(< 3) \approx \frac{199}{300}$ but $P(\geq 3) \approx \frac{101}{300}$
3 a Yes, because he would expect the spinner to land on each number a similar number of times.
  b This is the theoretical probability.
  c The approximate number of times, out of 200, that Hamid would expect to roll each number if the spinner is fair.
4 Dan is not correct because Amelia doesn't have an equal number of red and black cards.

9.3 Sample space diagrams

Purposeful practice

1 a

Spinner 2	**4**	1, 4	2, 4	3, 4	4, 4
	3	1, 3	2, 3	3, 3	4, 3
	1	1, 1	2, 1	3, 1	4, 1
		1	**2**	**3**	**4**
		Spinner 1			

b i $\frac{2}{12} = \frac{1}{6}$ **ii** $\frac{3}{12} = \frac{1}{4}$ **iii** $\frac{6}{12} = \frac{1}{2}$

2 a

Spinner 2			
6	2, 6	3, 6	4, 6
5	2, 5	3, 5	4, 5
3	2, 3	3, 3	4, 3
	2	3	4
	Spinner 1		

b i $\frac{2}{9}$ ii $\frac{3}{9} = \frac{1}{3}$ iii $\frac{5}{9}$

3 a

Spinner 2				
6	2, 6	3, 6	4, 6	5, 6
5	2, 5	3, 5	4, 5	5, 5
4	2, 4	3, 4	4, 4	5, 4
3	2, 3	3, 3	4, 3	5, 3
	2	3	4	5
	Spinner 1			

b i $\frac{4}{16} = \frac{1}{4}$ ii $\frac{4}{16} = \frac{1}{4}$ iii $\frac{7}{16}$

4 a

Spinner 2				
2	3	4	5	6
1	2	3	4	5
0	1	2	3	4
	1	2	3	4
	Spinner 1			

b i $\frac{6}{12} = \frac{1}{2}$ ii $\frac{9}{12} = \frac{3}{4}$ iii $\frac{4}{12} = \frac{1}{3}$

5 a

Spinner 2			
5	6	7	9
4	5	6	8
3	4	5	7
1	2	3	5
	1	2	4
	Spinner 1		

b i $\frac{5}{12}$ ii $\frac{3}{12} = \frac{1}{4}$ iii $\frac{2}{12} = \frac{1}{6}$

6 a

Spinner 2				
8	9	11	13	15
6	7	9	11	13
4	5	7	9	11
2	3	5	7	9
	1	3	5	7
	Spinner 1			

b i 0 ii $\frac{1}{16}$ iii $\frac{4}{16} = \frac{1}{4}$

Problem-solving practice

1 $\frac{6}{36} = \frac{1}{6}$

2 a

Dice 2						
6	7	8	9	10	11	12
5	6	7	8	9	10	11
4	5	6	7	8	9	10
3	4	5	6	7	8	9
2	3	4	5	6	7	8
1	2	3	4	5	6	7
	1	2	3	4	5	6
	Dice 1					

b No, P(6) = $\frac{5}{36}$ but P(7) = $\frac{6}{36} = \frac{1}{6}$

3 $\frac{1}{16}$

4 $\frac{12}{24} = \frac{1}{2}$

5 $\frac{4}{25}$

6 a $\frac{3}{20}$ **b** £96

9.4 Two-way tables

Purposeful practice

1 a

	Jan–Mar	Apr–Jun	Jul–Sep	Oct–Dec	Total
Year 8	13	16	18	11	**58**
Year 9	10	21	21	10	**62**
Total	**23**	**37**	**39**	**21**	**120**

b 120 **c** 23 **d** $\frac{23}{120}$ **e** 13 **f** $\frac{13}{120}$

g 58 **h** $\frac{13}{58}$ **i** 60 **j** 31 **k** $\frac{31}{60}$

2 a $\frac{23}{120}$ **b** $\frac{13}{120}$ **c** $\frac{13}{58}$ **d** $\frac{60}{120} = \frac{1}{2}$

e $\frac{31}{60}$ **f** $\frac{29}{60}$ **g** $\frac{29}{120}$ **h** $\frac{10}{62}$

i $\frac{58}{120} = \frac{29}{60}$ **j** $\frac{60}{120} = \frac{1}{2}$

Problem-solving practice

1 a $\frac{232}{395}$ **b** $\frac{163}{395}$ **c** $\frac{53}{395}$ **d** $\frac{34}{395}$

2 a i $\frac{89}{300}$ ii $\frac{76}{300} = \frac{19}{75}$

b i $\frac{40}{120} = \frac{1}{3}$ ii $\frac{43}{120}$

c B (choosing a customer who bought a cold drink on the Sunday), as P(tea on Saturday) = $\frac{55}{180} = \frac{11}{36}$ but P(cold drink on Sunday) = $\frac{40}{120} = \frac{1}{3} = \frac{12}{36}$.

3 a

	Male	Female	Total
Brown	**2**	30	32
White	1	**7**	8
Total	**3**	**37**	40

b $\frac{30}{40} = \frac{3}{4}$

c $\frac{1}{8}$

4

	Football	Hockey	Tennis	Total
Year 9	96	16	48	160
Year 10	50	50	50	150
Total	146	66	98	310

9.5 Venn diagrams

Purposeful practice 1

1 a 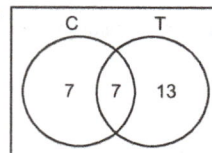 Venn diagram C, T: 7, 7, 13 **b** 27

2 a 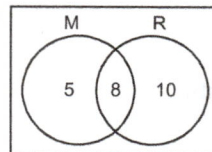 Venn diagram M, R: 5, 8, 10 **b** 10

3 a 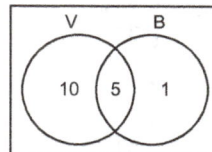 Venn diagram V, B: 10, 5, 1 **b** 10

4 a 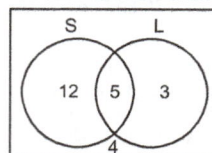 Venn diagram S, L: 12, 5, 3, 4 **b** 24

Purposeful practice 2

1 a $\frac{15}{22}$ **b** $\frac{11}{22} = \frac{1}{2}$ **c** $\frac{7}{22}$

2 a $\frac{19}{40}$ **b** $\frac{8}{40} = \frac{1}{5}$ **c** $\frac{21}{40}$ **d** $\frac{32}{40} = \frac{4}{5}$

3 a $\frac{12}{31}$ **b** $\frac{16}{31}$ **c** $\frac{7}{31}$ **d** $\frac{9}{31}$

Problem-solving practice

1 a

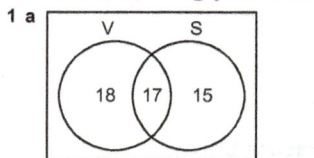

b i $\frac{17}{50}$ **ii** $\frac{18}{50} = \frac{9}{25}$ **iii** $\frac{15}{50} = \frac{3}{10}$

2 a

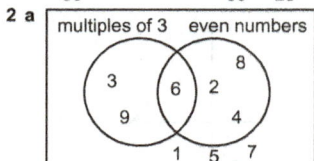

b i $\frac{3}{9} = \frac{1}{3}$ **ii** $\frac{4}{9}$ **iii** $\frac{1}{9}$

iv $\frac{6}{9} = \frac{2}{3}$ **v** $\frac{3}{9} = \frac{1}{3}$

3 a 100

b i $\frac{17}{100}$ **ii** $\frac{5}{100} = \frac{1}{20}$ **iii** $\frac{17}{100}$

iv $\frac{12}{100} = \frac{3}{25}$ **v** $\frac{34}{100} = \frac{17}{50}$ **vi** $\frac{30}{100} = \frac{3}{10}$

vii $\frac{10}{100} = \frac{1}{10}$ **viii** $\frac{64}{100} = \frac{16}{25}$

10 Comparing shapes

10.1 Congruent and similar shapes

Purposeful practice 1

1 A, C

2 A, B, C, D, G, H

3 E, F

Purposeful practice 2

1 a Congruent: ASA
  b Congruent: SSS
  c Not congruent; students could also write that the side lengths are not stated and therefore it is impossible to tell.
  d Congruent: AAS
  e Congruent: ASA
  f Not congruent

2 a 35° **b** 40° **c** 105°
  d 12.6 cm **e** 3.4 cm

Problem-solving practice

1 No, as 25° is the included angle in triangle B, but not in A.

2 B: SAS, C: SAS (or AAS)

3 a True: SSS
  b False – it depends where the sides are in relation to the right angle for each triangle
  c False – it depends where the sides are in relation to the 40° angle for each triangle
  d False – one could be an enlargement of the other

4 a Angle $ABC = 30°$ (angles in a triangle)
  Angle $BCD = 30°$ (alternate angles)
  Angle $ADC = 50°$ (alternate angles)
  Angle $CED = 100°$ (vertically opposite angles).
  b Angle ABC = angle $BCD = 30°$
  Angle BAD = angle $ADC = 50°$
  The included side is 6 cm in both triangles, so triangle ABE is congruent to triangle DCE – ASA.

5 Yes, $AD = BC$ and $BA = CD$ and the included angles BAD and DCB are both 90° – SAS. This can also be shown with SSS.

6 Yes, $QR = PS$ and $PQ = SR$ and the included angles PQR and RSP are both equal – SAS. This can also be shown with SSS.

10.2 Ratios in triangles

Purposeful practice 1

1 $l = 6$ cm
2 $l = 8$ cm
3 $l = 6$ cm
4 $l = 6$ cm
5 $l = 9$ cm
6 $l = 8$ cm

Purposeful practice 2

1 a Triangle ABE Triangle ACD
  angle A = angle A
  angle B = angle C (corresponding angles)
  angle E = angle D = 90°
  The triangles have the same size angles. Therefore, they are similar.
  b Triangle ABE Triangle ACD
  angle A = angle A
  angle B = angle C (corresponding angles)
  angle E = angle D (corresponding angles)
  The triangles have the same size angles. Therefore, they are similar.
  c Triangle ABE Triangle ACD
  angle A = angle A (vertically opposite angles)
  angle B = angle C (alternate angles)
  angle E = angle D (alternate angles)
  The triangles have the same size angles. Therefore, they are similar.

2 a i Triangle PQT Triangle PRS
  angle P = angle P
  angle Q = angle R = 90°
  angle T = angle S (corresponding angles)
  The triangles have the same size angles. Therefore, they are similar.
  ii $x = 6$ cm
  b i Triangle PQT Triangle PRS
  angle P = angle P
  angle Q = angle R (corresponding angles)
  angle T = angle S = 29° (given)
  The triangles have the same size angles. Therefore, they are similar.
  ii $x = 2$ cm
  c i Triangle PQT Triangle PRS
  angle P = angle P (vertically opposite angles)
  angle Q = angle R (alternate angles)
  angle T = angle S (alternate angles)
  The triangles have the same size angles. Therefore, they are similar.
  ii $x = 12$ cm

Problem-solving practice

1 $x = 10$ cm

2 $\frac{25}{10} = 2.5$, $\frac{20}{8} = 2.5$, $\frac{15}{6} = 2.5$

3 4.375 cm

4 No, as $\frac{GH}{AB} = \frac{25}{15} = 1.67$ but $\frac{FG}{BC} = \frac{20}{10} = 2$.

5 33 cm

6 3 cm or 17 cm

10.3 The tangent ratio

Purposeful practice 1

1 a i BC **ii** AC **iii** AB
  b i DE **ii** DF **iii** EF
  c i GI **ii** GH **iii** HI
  d i KL **ii** JK **iii** JL

2 a $\frac{7}{10}$ **b** $\frac{5}{9}$ **c** $\frac{9}{5}$

Purposeful practice 2

1 4.0 cm
2 9.5 cm
3 1.0 cm
4 8.0 cm
5 19.0 cm
6 2.0 cm

Purposeful practice 3

1 7.5 cm
2 4.5 m

3 5.7 cm
4 11.9 m

Problem-solving practice

1 6.9 cm
2 No, height of triangle $A = 6 \times \tan 35° = 4.2$ cm, but height of triangle $B = 10 \times \tan 25° = 4.66$ cm.
3 a 17.3 cm   **b** 173 cm^2
4 Katja is correct. Jamie has the first line of working correct but has then rearranged it incorrectly. Leo has the opposite and adjacent sides the wrong way around in his first line of working.
5 21.5 miles

10.4 The sine ratio

Purposeful practice 1

1 $\frac{3}{5}$

2 $\frac{5}{13}$

3 $\frac{8}{17}$

Purposeful practice 2

1 a 5.4 cm   **b** 17.1 mm   **c** 1.0 m
2 a 12.7 mm   **b** 8.8 cm   **c** 3.9 m
3 a 4.6 cm   **b** 1.4 m   **c** 119.0 mm

Problem-solving practice

1 2.96 cm
2 22.4 cm
3 4.39 m
4 14.1 cm
5 a 1.77 m
   b 2.04 m
6 54.4 cm^2
7 9.46 cm

10.5 The cosine ratio

Purposeful practice 1

1 $\frac{2}{4}$ or $\frac{1}{2}$

2 $\frac{3}{4}$

3 $\frac{1}{2}$

4 $\frac{6}{8}$ or $\frac{3}{4}$

Purposeful practice 2

1 a 8.2 m   **b** 6.7 cm   **c** 5.0 cm
2 a 17.00 m   **b** 5.0 cm   **c** 3.0 cm

Problem-solving practice

1 31.1 km
2 4 cm
3 2.285 m
4 86.2 cm^2
5 62.4 cm^2
6 39.5 cm
7 8 cm

10.6 Using trigonometry to find angles

Purposeful practice 1

1 a 19.3°   **b** 28.8°   **c** 43.5°
2 a 37.9°   **b** 39.8°   **c** 48.8°
3 a 20.5°   **b** 33.4°   **c** 71.8°
4 a 23.6°   **b** 22.0°   **c** 16.9°
5 a 69.5°   **b** 56.6°   **c** 18.2°
6 a 69.1°   **b** 41.4°   **c** 54.3°

Purposeful practice 2

1 60°
2 30°
3 45°

Problem-solving practice

1 54.9°

2 a Error 1 is using sin and not the inverse (sin^{-1}).
   Error 2 is using the inverse of cos and not the inverse of sin.
   Error 3 is that the opposite and hypotenuse (20 and 15) are the wrong way round.
   Error 4 is using the inverse of tan and not the inverse of sin.
   b 48.6°
3 No, as $\theta = \cos^{-1}\left(\frac{2}{5}\right) = 66.4°$
4 38°
5 130°
6 26.6°

Mixed exercises C

Mixed problem-solving practice C

1 a A and L, B and N, C and M, D and H, E and G, F and J
   b I and K:

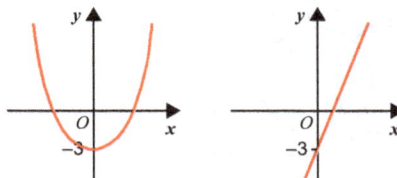

   c K and N
2 a $x = 0.08$ **b** $\frac{3}{36} = \frac{1}{12}$
3 £50
4 Yes; using Pythagoras' theorem on triangle ABC gives $AC = 72$ mm and using Pythagoras' theorem on triangle DEF gives $DE = 65$ mm, so triangles ABC and DEF are congruent (SSS).
5 180 cm^2
6 $\frac{25}{130} = \frac{5}{26}$
7 a $\frac{60}{100} = \frac{3}{5}$
   b $\frac{61}{100}$
8 7.96 cm
9 59.1°
10 a

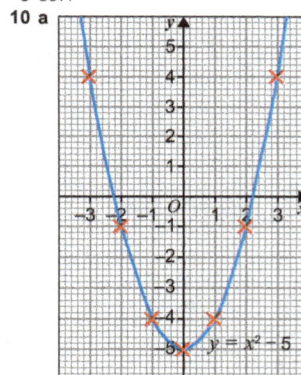

   b i $x = -2.2$, $x = 2.2$
   ii $x = -2.6$, $x = 2.6$
11 Students' own graph showing two straight lines, where the point of intersection gives the answer. Tea costs £2.00; coffee costs £2.50.

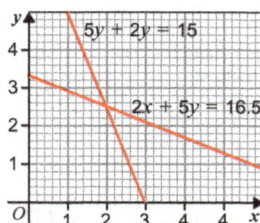

12 38.9°

Index